DEFENSIVE BRIDGE PLAY

Complete

Edwin B. Kantar

Melvin Powers
Wilshire Book Company

12015 Sherman Road, No. Hollywood, CA 91605

Library of Congress Catalog Card Number: 84311

ISBN 0-87980-287-1

Printed in the United States of America

FOREWORD

I am prepared to lay odds that more tricks are dropped on defense than on bidding and play combined!

The average player doesn't even realize how many tricks slip by through faulty signalling and discarding, "unlucky" leads, and failing to count. My experience has been that a good defensive player is <u>always</u> a winner over the long haul, and is a most desirable partner.

For some reason or another most of the literature of the game is devoted to bidding and declarer play, with defensive play all but forgotten.

So, after having made practically every error possible on defense over the years, I have decided to write a book devoted exclusively to defensive play. Because of the teacher in me, I have set it out in fifteen chapters, disgustingly complete, with a format that can be used for teacher and pupil alike.

If this book helps teach "your partner" how to avoid some of the mistakes he has been making, and teaches you both how "to think defensively" it will have served its purpose.

Edwin Kantar

TABLE OF CONTENTS

I. LEADS VS. SUIT CONTRACTS

The opening lead often determines the fate of a contract. The player on opening lead must always be aware of the bidding and, more important, of its significance.

Some points to consider are:

1. Is there going to be a long, strong side suit in the dummy?

   If the bidding indicates this to be a possibility, the opening leader must make an attacking lead, usually from a king, or perhaps from a king-jack combination. Trump leads and top of nothing leads are no-nos.

2. Have the opponents shied away from no trump?

   If the opponents have bid three suits and finally settled in a minor, the chances are strong that neither one of them has a stopper in the unbid suit. So you should usually lead that suit even if you have the ace-queen! Remember, if the king is to your right, no trump would have been bid.

3. Has your partner had a chance to overcall at the one level and failed to do so?

   Be careful about leading suits partner could have overcalled at the one level but did not. He is probably not too strong in those suit(s), particularly if the bidding has marked him with some high cards.

4. <u>Does ruffing power appear to be in the dummy?</u>

In other words, does dummy figure to have trump support and a short suit? This is usually the case when declarer bids two suits and dummy prefers the second. Dummy should be short in the first suit and, especially if the opening leader has strength in that suit, a trump lead often works out best.

5. <u>Is there any other time when a trump should be led?</u>

Yes, when it is right! (That's what expert Lew Mathe tells his partners.) However, there are two instances when a trump lead is mandatory. The first is when partner passes your takeout double at the one or two level. To justify the pass his trump holding is supposed to be super, and leading that suit usually has the effect of drawing declarer's trumps. The other situation that calls for a trump lead is when you and partner have most of the high card strength and the opponents are obviously sacrificing. Often their reason for sacrificing is that they have some side distribution, so a trump lead is usually effective.

6. <u>Has your partner bid?</u>

It is usually right to lead partner's suit (unless you have a strong sequence of your own). However, it is very important to lead the proper card so he will know what you have. The general rules for leading partner's suit are:

a. With any two cards, lead the higher.

b. Holding the ace, regardless of length, lead the ace.

c. With three to an honor (ten or higher) lead low.

d. With three or four small (nine or lower) lead the lowest if you have not supported the suit; lead the highest if you have supported the suit.

e. With two adjacent honors (with the exception of the ace-king) lead the higher honor, regardless of length.

f. With four or more cards headed by any honor other than the ace, lead fourth best.

g. Experts sometimes lead the king when holding Kxxx or Kxxxx in partner's suit and no other high card strength. The reason is that dummy may have a singleton in that suit and it may be important to hold the lead in order to play through dummy's strength in a side suit. However, this is done rarely and the rule of "LEADING THE HIGHEST CARD IN PARTNER'S SUIT" IS STRICTLY FOR LADIES' TEA PARTIES.

7. <u>What about short suit leads?</u>

Short suit leads can be very effective, particularly when holding a certain trump entry. Trump holdings

such as Ax, Axx, or Kxx make short suit leads
particularly attractive. The reason it is important
to have a high trump honor is that declarer will not
be able to run his good tricks without letting you in.
Hopefully, you will then be able to put your partner
on lead and get your ruff.

Another time it is right to lead a short suit is when
you have a very weak hand and have reason to believe
that the only way to defeat the contract is by ruffing
away some of the opponents' good tricks.

Sometimes you can detect from the bidding that partner
is short in a suit. For example, if both of your
opponents have bid diamonds and the eventual contract
is spades, and if you have four or five small diamonds,
you should suspect that your partner has a singleton
or void. A diamond lead might work very well in this
case -- especially if you have a trump entry which
will enable you to play a second round of diamonds.

8. <u>Can it be wrong to lead a short suit?</u>
    You better believe it. Particularly if the opponents
    have bid the suit and you have some outside strength
    but no trump control. Declarer may be able to draw
    trumps and run his side suit, discarding losers that
    you and your partner might have been able to cash had
    you led an unbid suit. It is also wrong to lead a

short suit with a particularly strong trump holding
such as J10xx, QJ10x, A10xx. With these holdings you
lose a natural trump trick even if you do get a ruff.
Besides, leading a short suit often finesses partner
out of a queen or jack, or both.

In fact, it is usually, but not always, wrong to lead
a short suit when holding four trumps (unless you have
reason to believe that declarer has seven or eight).
In most cases when holding four trumps, or believing
partner does, it pays to lead your LONGEST SUIT.

This has the effect of forcing declarer to ruff.
Eventually the player with the four trumps will have
as many or more trumps than the declarer and the hand
will explode for the poor fellow. (You know how _you_
feel when you play a hand and find that one defender
has as many or more trumps than you.)

9. <u>What are the best leads against suit contracts?</u>
Probably the best is the king from the ace-king. (Some
American and many European experts lead the <u>ace</u> from
ace-king to avoid confusing it with the lead of the
king from king-queen.) This lead gives you a chance
to look at dummy and to see partner's signal at the
same time.

The top card from honor sequences such as KQJ, QJ10,
or J109 is also a strong lead. Even slightly weaker

holdings such as KQx(x), QJx(x), J10x(x) provide
reasonable leads, again starting with the top card.
Note that if you are leading from a holding such as
J10xx(x) or QJxx(x) and the suit has been bid to your
right or left (although it is unlikely that you would
be leading such a suit bid to your right), you should
lead fourth best rather than the top honor; for there
is a great chance that either partner or declarer has
a singleton honor and your high card would merely be
wasted if led. Experts holding KQxxx would almost
always lead a low card rather than the more revealing
king if the suit has been bid to the left. (Declarer
probably has a singleton, and if dummy has the ace it
will surely be played, while you retain your high
honors.)

Leading from a king or queen, believe it or not, usually
works out better than leading from a jack or top of
nothing. When leading from a king or queen, you need
find your partner with only one honor to make your
lead effective; when leading from a jack or top of
nothing, you almost have to find your partner with two
honors to make the lead effective. (Naturally it is
assumed you are leading an unbid suit.)

When faced with a choice of leading from either of two
unbid suits it is usually right to lead from the suit
that DOES NOT HAVE THE ACE. You can possibly use your

ace later to capture a high honor in declarer's hand. If neither unbid suit has the ace, lead from the stronger.

10. <u>What about leading an ace or underleading an ace?</u>
Studies have been made about leading aces. Against slam contracts it usually works out best, particularly at tournament bridge where you might even lose your ace if you don't lead it. Also, if the opponents have bid three suits strongly you might consider leading an ace in the unbid suit.

Underleading aces is a dangerous practice and should be considered only when the strong hand is to your left and a very weak one to your right. (Perhaps dummy has opened one no trump and right hand opponent has shown marked weakness by signing off in two of a major.)

11. <u>Which is the correct card to lead from three small in an unbid suit?</u>
There is considerable difference of opinion about this. Consider the lead from 862 in an unbid suit. Some experts lead the eight, others the deuce, and still others the six! Leading the six is a convention called MUD (Middle, Up, Down). Whichever card you lead, confusion is apt to result. If you lead the eight partner may think you have a doubleton, but at least

he knows you do not have an honor. If you lead the
deuce, partner may think you have an honor but at least
he knows that you do not have a doubleton. If you lead
the six, God only knows what partner will think. The
tendency among most experts is to lead low from three
so that the lead of a higher spot card definitely
promises a short suit. Whichever you think is best,
be sure to discuss it with your partner beforehand.
Also, if you decide to lead the eight, be sure to
play the six the second time. If you play the deuce,
you are showing a doubleton.

12. <u>Are there any new ideas regarding which card to lead</u>
<u>once the suit has been selected</u>?
Very definitely. The one that has caught on (used
particularly vs. no trump contracts but easily
applicable against suit) is:

a. The lead of a jack denies a higher honor.

b. The lead of a ten shows either AJ10, KJ10, top
of a sequence, or shortness. (Against suit
contracts, leading away from AJ10 is, for
practical purposes, non-existent.)

c. The lead of a nine shows either A109, K109, Q109,
top of a sequence, or shortness. Usually very
easy to read.

d. The lead of a queen from AKQ is used:

(1) After having shown a strong suit.

(2) After having shown a strong hand, leading

    into a weak one. A good partner has no

    trouble reading this lead, particularly if

    the jack is visible, and he should give the

    count. Opening leader will then know exactly

    how many tricks he can take in the suit.

These ideas, particularly the lead of the 9, 10 or J
will be discussed more thoroughly in the chapter "LEADS
VS. NO TRUMP CONTRACTS". These leads are all recommended
and will be used throughout the book. (But not the
queen from AKQ - I don't want to risk losing any readers
after only one chapter.)

I. Neither side vul.
    Dealer North

North
S. KQ10
H. 432
D. 76
C. AQJ98

West
S. 32
H. A765
D. K1052
C. 764

East
S. 54
H. QJ98
D. Q983
C. K52

South
S. AJ9876
H. K10
D. AJ4
C. 103

North	East	South	West
1C	Pass	1S	Pass
2S	Pass	4S	All Pass

Opening lead: Deuce of diamonds

II. East-West vul.
     Dealer East

North
S. J108
H. 875
D. AK10
C. QJ98

West
S. A652
H. KJ932
D. 84
C. 72

East
S. 7
H. AQ10
D. 97632
C. 10654

South
S. KQ943
H. 64
D. QJ5
C. AK3

East	South	West	North
Pass	1S	Pass	2C
Pass	3C	Pass	3S
Pass	4S	All Pass	

Opening lead: Three of hearts

III. Neither side vul.
      Dealer South

                              North
                              S. 64
                              H. KJ54
                              D. 9632
                              C. AKJ

West   East
S. Q8   S. AKJ1072
H. Q87632   H. 9
D. 10   D. 75
C. 10854   C. 9632

                              South
                              S. 953
                              H. A10
                              D. AKQJ84
                              C. Q7

South   West   North   East
1D   Pass   1H   2S (Weak)
3D   Pass   4D   Pass
5D   All Pass

      Opening lead: Queen of spades

IV.   East-West vul.
      Dealer East

                              North
                              S. Q75
                              H. Q2
                              D. AKJ1098
                              C. 73

West   East
S. 864   S. AKJ109
H. 95   H. 6
D. 763   D. Q52
C. AJ865   C. Q942

                              South
                              S. 32
                              H. AKJ108743
                              D. 4
                              C. K10

East   South   West   North
1S   4H   All Pass

      Opening lead: Four of spades

KEY PLAYS

I. West leads a diamond because it is usually best to lead from the unbid suit that does not contain the ace. South wins, draws two trumps, and runs the ten of clubs to East's king. East returns the queen of hearts (if partner does not have the ace of hearts the hand cannot be defeated), and the defenders take four tricks: two hearts, a diamond and a club. Notice how poorly an opening club lead (leading through strength) works. Partner wins the king, and declarer is able to throw away diamond losers on the established clubs. In general, it is wrong to attack dummy's length unless either trying for a ruff or trying to give partner a ruff. Leading through strength refers to short suits such as AQx, KJx, or Kxx.

II. West leads a heart because he has four trumps and hopes to make declarer ruff. The defenders play three rounds of hearts, forcing South. When declarer tries to extract trumps, West must duck the first two rounds. If declarer persists with a third, West wins and again forces South with a heart. South must ruff with his last trump and the hand is defeated two tricks, for West remains with a long trump and a good heart. If south reverts to either minor suit after West ducks two trump leads, West ruffs the third round of either minor and the hand is defeated one

trick. Notice that if West leads a diamond originally,
the hand is made easily.

III.   West makes the normal lead of the queen of spades, which
East reads as either a singleton or a doubleton. (With
greater length West would lead low.) East overtakes
(mandatory in case the lead is a singleton) and plays a
second and third spade, allowing West to overtrump dummy.
(East knows that South has the odd spade from the lead.)
It is incorrect for East to shift to a singleton heart
at trick three. If West has the ace (unlikely for the
bidding), the hand will always be defeated. The better
chance, by far, is to hope that West can overtrump dummy.

IV.   East cashes two spades, noting that West plays first the
four (his lead) and then the six, indicating possession
of a third spade. The diamond suit is so menacing that
East switches to a club at trick three, before declarer's
clubs can be discarded on dummy's diamonds. This shift
defeats the contract one trick. Hand IV points out the
advantage of leading low from three small in partner's
suit when it has not been supported; it enables him to
know how many tricks he can cash in the suit.

LEADS VS. SUIT CONTRACTS   PROBLEMS

I. You are West and the bidding has proceeded:

South	North
1S	2C
2H	2S
3S	4S
Pass	

Which card do you lead from each of the following hands?

a. S. 1085   b. S. A65
    H. AJ96   H. Q87
    D. Q975   D. 1087653
    C. 64   C. 10

c. S. A764   d. S. Q43
    H. 108   H. J9
    D. K8754   D. K108
    C. 85   C. QJ1094

II. You are West, and you hold:

S. Q874   H. J65   D. 43   C. AQ86

The bidding has proceeded:

South	North
1D	1H
3D	3S
4D	5D
Pass	

What is your lead?

III. You are West, and you hold:

S. AQ108   H. J1032   D. K108   C. Q4

The bidding has proceeded:

South	North
1S	1NT
2H	Pass

What is your lead?

IV. You are West, and you hold:

S. A432   H. 65   D. Q10765   C. 97

The bidding has proceeded:

South	North
2C*	2D**
2S	2NT
3H	3S
4S	Pass

* Strong and artificial
** Negative response

What is your lead?

V. You are West, and you hold:

S. 8762   H. 64   D. J74   C. QJ103

The bidding has proceeded:

East	South	West	North
1S	2H	Pass	4H
All Pass			

What is your lead?

VI.   You are West, and you hold:

S. A5   H. QJ72   D. 8643   C. 1075

The bidding has proceeded:

North	South
1D	2S
2NT	3D
3S	4NT
5D	6S
Pass	

What is your lead?

VII. Your partner has bid hearts, and you have never supported the suit. Assume that each of the following combinations are hearts, and you have to select the proper card. Which card would you lead?

a. 85	e. K84	i. 8532
b. 864	f. J103	j. KQ6
c. J984	g. J1032	k. K106
d. A96	h. Q105	l. Q7

VIII. Would your lead vary with any of these combinations if you had supported the suit?

I. a. **The five of spades.**   Your hearts are strong and dummy figures to be short in hearts. An immediate trump lead should cut down dummy's ruffing power. A low diamond would be the second choice. (When leading trumps it is almost always right to lead low from three small because you may get the chance to over-trump either dummy or declarer with your higher trump.) Many experts lead the middle trump with three small and then play their lower one next, to conventionally show three. Leading a low trump and then playing a higher one shows either two or four when using this convention.

b. **The ten of clubs.**   Your best chance to defeat this contract is to try for club ruffs. You have the ace of trumps, which makes a short suit lead attractive.

c. The five of diamonds.   When holding four trumps the
                                lead from a long suit is
                                usually best.

d. The queen of clubs.   Even though the opponents have
                                bid the suit, your strong
                                sequence should be led.

II. The ace of clubs.   The opponents are screaming at
                                you that neither one has clubs
                                stopped. Certainly if South
                                had the king of clubs he would
                                have bid three no trump over
                                three spades.

III. The deuce of hearts.   Your strong spade holding plus
                                dummy's obvious spade shortness
                                calls for an immediate "heart
                                attack". A low trump from J10x
                                or J10xx is generally best
                                just in case partner has a
                                singleton honor.

IV. The six of diamonds.   With four trumps the normal
                                lead is the long suit.

V. The queen of clubs.   The sequence lead is more
                                attractive than four small in
                                partner's suit. One of the few

times you forego leading partner's suit. (Have apologies ready just in case.)

VI. A low diamond.

Partner figures to have a singleton diamond and you can envision giving him a ruff upon gaining the lead with the ace of trumps.

VII. a. The eight.

Top of a doubleton.

b. The four.

Low from three small when you have not supported.

c. The four.

Fourth best.

d. The ace.

The ace with any length against a suit contract.

e. The four.

Low from three to an honor.

f. The jack.

Top of two touching honors.

g. The jack.

Same as "f".

h. The five.

Low from two non-touching honors not including the ace.

i. The deuce.

Low from four small when you have not supported.

j. The king.   Same as "f".

k. The six.   Same as "h".

l. The queen.   Same as "a".

VIII. Yes.   With "b" lead the eight.

With "i" lead the eight.

All other leads remain the same.

II. LEADS VS. NO TRUMP CONTRACTS

When leading against a no trump declaration, there is more to know than "fourth highest from your longest and strongest". Sometimes the opponents have bid your best suit, sometimes you have two suits of relatively equal length and strength, and sometimes your partner's or your opponents' bidding will tip you off to the proper lead.

1. Tend to lead any suit partner has overcalled unless you have a strong suit of your own plus an outside entry.

2. Strong sequence leads from four card suits (KQJx, KQ10x, QJ10x) are to be preferred to weaker broken holdings in five card suits (Jxxxx, Qxxxx).

3. Faced with a choice of leading from an unbid major or an unbid minor, with relatively similar holdings in both suits, tend to lead the major. (Opponents seldom conceal major suit length during the bidding, but often conceal minor suit length.)

4. If dummy uses the Stayman Convention in response to either one or two no trump, he is assumed to have at least one four card major. It is frequently possible to determine which one. For example: If R.H.O. (right hand opponent) opens one no trump, L.H.O. bids

two clubs (Stayman), R.H.O. responds two spades, and L.H.O. signs off in three no trump, dummy must have four hearts, otherwise why did he bother with Stayman? Avoid leading hearts on this auction unless you have a strong sequence.

5. Sometimes your hand will be so abysmally weak that you will try to hit partner's long suit even though he hasn't bid. Keep in mind that if he had a chance to overcall at the one level and did not, your chances of hitting him in one of those suits is poor.

6. If the dummy is known to have a long strong suit, it is imperative to make an attacking lead. AKx, KQx or QJx are to be preferred over weaker longer suits.

7. It is imperative that your partner know whether or not you have honor strength in the suit you are leading, for a quick switch may be vital. The following is recommended:

a. The lead of a low card in an unbid suit promises an honor. With weaker holdings such as 8632, start with the eight. Sometimes the highest card may be too valuable to lead. For example, from 9732, you might try the seven. Hopefully you won't have to lead from suits like that very often; but if you lead low, partner may foolishly return the suit looking for your non-existent strength.

Both sides vul.
Dealer South

                          North
                          S. 863
                          H. 65
                          D. AJ106
                          C. AQ107

West   East
S. AQJ4   S. 10972
H. 10843   H. QJ9
D. 73   D. K52
C. 865   C. 942

                          South
                          S. K5
                          H. AK72
                          D. Q984
                          C. KJ3

South   West   North   East
1NT   Pass   3NT   All Pass

Opening lead: Eight of hearts.

Experience has shown that leading from four card suits such as AQ10x, AQJx, AJ10x, or AK10x frequently costs a trick. If declarer has the king in the first three cases and the queen in the next, there goes one trick down the drain. Furthermore, when leading from a four card suit, once you concede a trick you establish only three. This, along with partner's expected

(hoped for) entry, is still only four tricks,
hardly enough to defeat three no trump. Alter-
natively, if any of the above combinations are
attached to a five card suit, they are excellent
leads: Four tricks can be established after one
is surrendered.

With all this in mind, West does not lead a
spade. On the other hand, he passionately
wishes his partner to lead one if and when he
gets the lead. In order to insure a switch,
West leads the eight of hearts, purposely in-
ducing East to think that the lead is from top
of nothing.

As the play develops, South wins the first heart
and runs the nine of diamonds to East's king. To
defeat the contract, East must shift to a spade
rather than continue hearts. It is not at all
difficult for East to shift after the lead of
the eight of hearts; but had West led a low
heart, the shift would be next to impossible.

b. The lead of a jack denies a higher honor. This
is an invaluable convention which enables the
partner of the opening leader to immediately
assess the honor situation around the table and

determine whether or not there is any future in that suit. In "olden times", it was hard to tell whether the jack was from top of a sequence or from an interior sequence headed by KJ10 or AJ10.

c. The lead of a ten shows either two higher honors (AJ10 or KJ10), top of a sequence, or shortness. How does partner tell? If the jack is visible, the lead must be top of a sequence. If the nine is visible, the lead must be from strength. If neither is visible, assume the lead is from an interior sequence.

d. The lead of a nine shows either two higher honors (A109, K109, Q109) or is a top card. If the ten is visible, the nine must be a top card. If the ten is not visible, assume two higher honors. After all, the lead of a suit headed by the nine is rare at no trump.

Incidentally, these leads can be used throughout the hand or on opening lead only. If you are not used to them, try them on opening lead to see how you get along.

e. The lead of a queen shows either top of a sequence

(QJ10, QJ9) or a combination headed by the KQ109.
Partner is supposed to drop the jack (if he has
it) under the lead of a queen vs. no trump.

f. The lead of a king is either from a sequence
    (KQJ, KQ10) or is a short suit lead (AKx, KQx).
    Notice the queen is not led from KQ10 unless the
    leader has either the nine or a five or six
    card suit.

g. The lead of an ace shows a powerful holding and
    is rare. The most common holdings are suits
    headed by: AKQ, AKJ10, AKJ, and sometimes AQJ
    with an outside entry. This lead will be dis-
    cussed in detail in the chapter "SIGNALLING VS.
    NO TRUMP CONTRACTS".

8. With all other holdings, lead fourth highest if you
    do not have a sequence. A sequence for no trump
    purposes is a suit with three cards in a row, at the
    HEAD of the suit (QJ1054), or with the third card
    in the sequence missing by one spot (QJ954). If the
    third card dips by more than one spot (QJ854), lead
    fourth best. If the sequence is in the middle of
    the suit and is headed by a nine or lower (Q9874),
    disregard it and make your normal fourth best lead.

9. Every so often you will hold a five card suit headed
   by a perfect three card sequence such as KQJ54 or
   QJ1054. Naturally your normal lead is the top card.
   But, if the suit has been bid adversely, you are
   better off in the long run to lead fourth best to
   avoid blocking the suit. Partner may have a doubleton honor or an opponent or partner a singleton
   honor. This idea may seem wild, but it is theoret-
   ically sound.

I.   Neither side vul.
     Dealer South

                           North
                           S. 52
                           H. K76
                           D. QJ98
                           C. A652

     West   East
     S. K9743   S. A86
     H. 93   H. A854
     D. 4   D. 76532
     C. K9743   C. 10

                           South
                           S. QJ10
                           H. QJ102
                           D. AK10
                           C. QJ8

South	West	North	East
1NT	Pass	3NT	All Pass

     Opening lead: Four of spades

II. North-South vul.
     Dealer South

                           North
                           S. Q742
                           H. AQ105
                           D. Q4
                           C. J65

     West   East
     S. J65   S. 1083
     H. J432   H. K6
     D. J65   D. A972
     C. 832   C. KQ107

                           South
                           S. AK9
                           H. 987
                           D. K1083
                           C. A94

South	West	North	East
1D	Pass	1H	Pass
1NT	Pass	2NT	Pass
3NT	All Pass		

     Opening lead: Eight of clubs

III. East-West vul.
Dealer South

                          North
                          S. Q1085
                          H. J32
                          D. 85
                          C. AKJ6

West   East
S. KJ432   S. 96
H. 76   H. Q1098
D. KJ432   D. Q76
C. 2   C. 9874

                          South
                          S. A7
                          H. AK54
                          D. A109
                          C. Q1053

South	West	North	East
1NT	Pass	2C	Pass
2H	Pass	3NT	All Pass

Opening lead: Three of diamonds

IV. Both sides vul.
Dealer North

                          North
                          S. 54
                          H. Q8
                          D. 87
                          C. AQJ10982

West   East
S. KQ6   S. A9832
H. J10932   H. K65
D. J2   D. Q1095
C. 743   C. 5

                          South
                          S. J107
                          H. A74
                          D. AK643
                          C. K6

North	East	South	West
3C	Pass	3NT	All Pass

Opening lead: King of spades

KEY PLAYS

I. West leads a spade rather than a club on the well-tested
    theory that with all things equal, it is better to lead a
    major suit than a minor. East wins the ace and returns
    the eight. West allows South to win the second spade,
    and when East eventually gets in with the ace of hearts,
    he returns his last spade to defeat the hand one trick.

II. West leads a top club because he can tell from the
    opponents' bidding that East must have a fairly good
    hand; yet he didn't bid. Why? Probably because he had
    no suit to overcall at the one level (spades) and was
    afraid to overcall at the two level between two bidding
    opponents. Surely there is more reason to lead a club
    than a spade on this reasoning. With a club lead, declarer
    figures to go down at least one trick. With a spade
    lead, the hand is cold.

III. This time West leads a diamond because he knows dummy
    has four spades to justify his original Stayman response.
    The diamond lead proves to be the toughest and would
    surely cause most declarers to go down. If South wins
    the third diamond, he can no longer make the hand; but if
    he wins the second, cashes four clubs and two hearts and
    exits with a diamond, West will eventually be endplayed
    in spades. If South is good enough to make that play,

cut out of the game immediately -- you are over your head.

IV. The fact that dummy is known to have seven reasonably good clubs indicates to West that an attacking lead is called for. The more normal lead of the jack of hearts would be proper if neither opponent was known to have a long, strong suit. As luck would have it (I set up the hand, silly), the spade lead defeats the contract one trick.

LEADS VS. NO TRUMP CONTRACTS   PROBLEMS

I. Sitting West, you hear the following bidding:

South	North
1NT	2NT
3NT	Pass

What would you lead from each of the following hands?

a. S. Q1084   b. S. AJ1085   c. S. QJ108
    H. Q754   H. K5   H. Q9743
    D. Q4   D. 543   D. Q5
    C. J87   C. 1097   C. 103

d. S. J654   e. S. A765   f. S. KJ6
    H. A2   H. J1032   H. 1098
    D. Q1098   D. 876   D. AQ102
    C. J43   C. Q6   C. Q76

II. Again you are West, but this time the bidding has proceeded:

South	North
1C	1H
1NT	2NT
3NT	Pass

What would you lead from each of the following hands?

a. S. A5   b. S. A43   c. S. A543
    H. J10982   H. J8   H. 543
    D. J86   D. J76   D. Q1072
    C. Q76   C. QJ1032   C. K3

d. S. J76   e. S. 1097   f. S. J76
    H. Q432   H. KJ76   H. 543
    D. 1093   D. K65   D. AKJ10
    C. 543   C. AJ3   C. 765

III. Using the lead conventions discussed earlier, which card do you lead from each of the following combinations?

a. KJ1085   k. AKJ98

b. A10975   l. 8643

c. Q9874   m. 972

d. KQ753   n. Q10965

e. J107542   o. AK1093

f. K10975   p. AQ1093

g. QJ965   q. AK842

h. AKQ104 (you should be   r. KQ1094
   so lucky)

i. 1042   s. J9872

j. 842   t. A75

I. a. Four of spades.   Your spades are stronger than
                               your hearts.

    b. Ten of spades.   Shows zero or two higher honors.

    c. Queen of spades.   A solid four card sequence should
                               be led in preference to a ratty
                               five card suit.

    d. Nine of diamonds.   Your diamonds are so much better
                               than your spades that they should
                               be preferred, even though the
                               suit is a minor. Remember, the
                               nine shows zero or two higher
                               honors, one of which must be
                               the ten.

    e. Deuce of hearts.   Four to the jack-ten is more
                               attractive than four to the ace.
                               Suits that have two honor cards
                               are usually better leads than
                               suits that have only one.

    f. Ten of hearts.   One of the few times one makes
                               a passive lead against a no trump
                               declaration. You have most of
                               the strength, so sit back, relax,
                               and let declarer take all of his
                               losing finesses into you.

II. a. Jack of hearts.   Even though the suit has been
                                  bid, your sequence is strong
                                  enough to lead.

     b. Three of clubs.   The normal lead is the queen,
                                  but when the suit has been bid,
                                  it is better to lead low to
                                  avoid blocking, in case partner
                                  has 9x, Kx or Ax.

     c. Deuce of diamonds.   Again, a suit with two honor
                                  cards should be preferred to a
                                  suit with only one, particularly
                                  when that one honor is either
                                  the jack or the ace.

     d. Ten of diamonds.   Partner has an opening bid, but
                                  was silent. Surely he can't
                                  have spades, but he might have
                                  diamonds.

     e. Ten of spades.   Play the waiting game when you
                                  have most of the high card
                                  strength and no five card suit
                                  to lead.

     f. Ace of diamonds.   From holdings headed by AKJ10,
                                  the ace is the proper lead.

III. a. The ten.   Shows zero or two higher honors
                              (one of the two higher must be
                              the jack).

      b. The nine.   Shows zero or two higher honors.

      c. The seven.   Fourth highest - just like the
                              good old days.

      d. The five.   Same as "c".

      e. The five.   Same as "c".

      f. The nine.   Some as "b".

      g. The queen.   Top of a sequence.

      h. The ace.   Shows a very powerful holding.

      i. The deuce.   Low from three to an honor.
                              (The ten is considered an honor.)

      j. The eight.   Top of nothing vs. no trump to
                              show partner you are trying to
                              find his strength.

      k. The ace.   Same as "h".

      l. The eight.   Same as "j".

      m. The nine.   Same as "j".

      n. The nine.   Same as "b".

      o. The nine.   With no outside entry, the nine
                              is the proper lead. With a
                              certain outside entry, the ace
                              is. (Leading the nine from this
                              combination is an exceptional
                              case.)

p. The nine.   Although a good case can be made
                  for leading the ace when holding
                  a certain outside entry. If you
                  have reason to suspect the king is
                  in dummy, lead the queen. (The
                  lead of the nine from this
                  holding is another exceptional
                  case.)

q. The four.   Same as "c".

r. The queen.   Asks partner to throw the jack
                  if he has it. This eliminates
                  confusion when the king holds
                  and neither the jack nor the
                  ace is visible.

s. The seven.   Same as "c".

t. The five.   Same as "i".

III. LEAD DIRECTING DOUBLES

There are any number of opportunities to make "lead directing doubles". A lead directing double is a form of penalty double, but it is seldom passed by the original bidder or his partner because of the nature of the auction. Nevertheless, the partner of the doubler is alerted to the best lead, and a player who is familiar with lead directing doubles has an enormous advantage over one who is not.

I. ALL DOUBLES OF ARTIFICIAL BIDS (STAYMAN, JACOBY TRANSFER, BLACKWOOD AND GERBER RESPONSES, CUE BIDS, ARTIFICIAL TWO CLUB OPENINGS, ETC.) ARE LEAD DIRECTIVE - NEVER FOR TAKEOUT.

A. STAYMAN AND JACOBY TRANSFER

South	West	North	East
1NT	Pass	2C	Dbl.

East's double of North's artificial two club bid (Stayman) shows good clubs, typically a five or six card suit to three honors, and requests a club lead if South becomes the declarer. East should not double two clubs if he has length in the suit but no strength. If North-South are using the weak no trump (12-14), the double is better used to show general high card strength rather than clubs, but that is an exception.

If North-South are using Two-Way Stayman, then two

diamonds is also an artificial response and a double
of that bid shows good diamonds.

If North-South are using Jacoby Transfer Bids,
responses of two diamonds, two hearts, and two
spades are all artificial and doubles of any of
these bids are lead directing.

B. BLACKWOOD RESPONSES

South	West	North	East
1S	Pass	3S	Pass
4NT	Pass	5D	Dbl.

Doubles of Blackwood responses are lead directing
because the responses are artificial. East's double
of five diamonds asks West to lead a diamond against
an eventual spade contract. Again, East would not
double to show diamond length, but to show high card
strength. In this example, East could have as
little as KQx of diamonds for his bid.

East has another chance to make a lead directing
double if South bids five no trump, asking for kings.
East's failure to double a Blackwood response indicates he has little or no interest in that suit
being led.

South	West	North	East
1S	Pass	3S	Pass
4NT	Pass	5D	Pass
5NT	Pass	6H	Pass
6S	Pass		

West can infer that East is not interested in either red suit, so with no clear cut lead (a sequence) he should consider leading a club.

C. GERBER RESPONSES

Many players now use the Gerber Convention, whereby a jump to four clubs over a previous no trump bid asks for aces and a follow-up bid of five clubs asks for kings. Doubles of these responses are all lead directing.

South	West	North	East
1S	Pass	2NT	Pass
4C	Pass	4H	Dbl.

North's response shows one ace, and East doubles for a heart lead in case spades becomes the eventual contract. Negative inferences are available when partner does not double Gerber responses.

D. CUE BIDS

In the modern game, cue bids abound. Doubles of most cue bids, particularly those at the higher levels, are all lead directing.

South	West	North	East
1C	Pass	1D	Pass
1S	Pass	3S	Pass
4C	Pass	4H	Dbl.

After spades have been agreed, South tries for a slam by cue bidding a control in clubs and North cue bids a heart control. East's double asks for

a heart lead against an eventual spade contract.
East's failure to double four hearts would suggest
a lack of interest in that suit.

Some cue bids do not show controls, but, rather,
two suited hands. Doubles of those cue bids are
not lead directing.

South	West	North
1H	2H	Dbl.

Assume for the moment that East-West are using the
direct cue bid to show a two suited hand -- for the
sake of argument, spades and clubs (the "top and
bottom" cue bid). North's double simply shows a
good hand and is more easily compared to a redouble
than a request for any specific lead.

Be careful about doubling cue bids if you are the
one who is going to be on lead. Remember, you don't
have to remind yourself what to lead!

South	West	North	East
1D	Pass	1H	Pass
3H	Pass	4C	?

Assume that East has good clubs, perhaps KQJx; he
does not double because <u>he</u> is going to be on lead
against hearts. A double at this point is more
sacrifice-oriented than lead directing and occurs
rarely.

E. ARTIFICIAL OPENING BIDS

Today, many bridge systems feature an artificial opening bid of one club to show 17 or more high card points. What does a double of an artificial one club opening mean?

Most experts use the double of an artificial one club opening to show both major suits; the double, therefore, is not lead directing. Using this method, an overcall of one no trump is for the minors and all suit overcalls are natural.

In most standard systems, the "weak two" opening has supplanted the strong two bid. In these systems an opening bid of one club is natural, and the strong artificial and forcing opening bid is two clubs. Most experts play a double of a two club opening as lead directing, showing clubs, although there are some who use the double to show a two-suited hand.

The majority of systems use artificial responses to artificial club openings. For example:

South	West	North	East
1C	Pass	1D	Dbl.

The one diamond response shows a weak hand in response to an artificial club opening. East's double shows diamonds. The same is true in this very common sequence:

South	West	North	East
2C	Pass	2D	Dbl.

Again, East is showing good diamonds and is not, repeat not, doubling for takeout.

F. DOUBLES OF THE FOURTH SUIT

Here is a common bidding sequence:

South	West	North	East
1S	Pass	2D	Pass
2H	Pass	3C	Dbl.

East's double shows good clubs, and if South happens to bid three no trump, West will have been forewarned.

II. DOUBLES OF SLAMS

Slam doubles can easily be divided into two categories: no trump and suit. Doubles of no trump slams simply call for dummy's first bid suit.

Doubles of voluntarily bid suit slams (as opposed to sacrifices) are a bit more involved. Basically, it amounts to this: If the doubler has the contract defeated in his own hand, regardless of the lead, he doubles. But most of the time it takes a specific lead to defeat a slam contract; therefore, doubles of slams are lead directing, asking for the unusual or unexpected lead, and the opening leader must be aware of the rules. Here are the "Do nots":

1. Do not lead a trump.

2. Do not lead any suit that you or your partner has bid.

3. If there is only one unbid suit, do not lead it. That is the expected lead, and if partner wants that lead, he passes.

Here are the "Dos":

1. If the opponents have bid only one suit (excluding trump), lead that suit.

2. If partner has made a preemptive bid and then doubles a slam, it is usually because he has a void. A great player like you can work out which is the void suit by looking at your hand.

3. When in doubt, lead dummy's first bid suit.

4. Another reason for doubling, other than having a void, is having AKx in a side suit the opponents have mentioned. If your hand and the sound of the bidding make it unlikely that partner has a void, lead a bid suit and hope for the best.

III. DOUBLES OF NO TRUMP CONTRACTS

A. Doubles of one no trump -- two common cases:

1.
South	West	North	East
1H	Pass	1NT	Pass
Pass	Dbl.		

West has an opening one heart bid. The double is not for takeout, and a heart lead is expected but not mandatory.

2. | South | West | North | East |
    |-------|------|-------|------|
    | 1C | Pass | 1S | Pass |
    | 1NT | Pass | Pass | Dbl. |

East has an opening one spade bid, and if every-one passes, West should usually lead a spade.

B. Doubles of two no trump:

1. | South | West | North | East |
    |-------|------|-------|------|
    | 2NT | Pass | Pass | Dbl. |

East has a solid suit and West should lead his shortest suit, preferably a major, but definitely a suit that has no honor cards.

2. | South | West | North | East |
    |-------|------|-------|------|
    | 1C | Pass | 1H | Pass |
    | 2NT | Pass | Pass | Dbl. |

East is asking for a heart lead, dummy's first bid suit.

C. Doubles of three no trump:

1. When no suits have been bid.

South	West	North	East
1NT	Pass	3NT	Dbl.

East has a solid suit or perhaps a KQJ10x suit with an outside ace. West is supposed to figure out from his hand which suit East has. If West holds: S. Jxxx H. Qxx D. x C. Q10xxx, he leads a diamond, partner's most likely suit.

2. When two suits have been bid by the opponents.

South	West	North	East
1C	Pass	1H	Pass
1NT	Pass	2NT	Pass
3NT	Pass	Pass	Dbl.

East is asking for a heart lead, dummy's first bid suit.

3. When dummy has bid two suits.

South	West	North	East
1C	Pass	1H	Pass
2C	Pass	2D	Pass
2NT	Pass	3NT	Dbl.

West must decide from his hand which suit East wants, hearts or diamonds. (Some play that the double unequivocally calls for a heart lead, but that is rather restrictive.) One thing is certain, East does not want the "obvious" spade lead.

4. When the doubler has bid a suit.

South	West	North	East
1C	Pass	1H	2D
2NT	Pass	3NT	Dbl.

East is asking for a diamond lead.

5. When the doubler's partner has bid a suit.

South	West	North	East
1C	1H	1S	Pass
1NT	Pass	2NT	Pass
3NT	Pass	Pass	Dbl.

The double definitely shows strength in dummy's first bid suit, so the opening leader must have a strong sequence in his own suit to lead it in preference to dummy's.

6. When the doubler and his partner have each bid a suit.

South	West	North	East
1C	1H	1S	2D
2NT	Pass	3NT	Dbl.
All pass			

Here the opening leader is called upon to use his judgment. If:

a. His own suit has a sequence, he leads it.

b. He has a high honor in partner's suit and a weak suit of his own, he leads partner's suit.

c. His own suit is weakish and he has an indifferent holding in partner's suit, he leads dummy's suit -- for partner has promised strength in that suit.

The most common lead in this situation, however, is partner's suit.

If West holds.

1. S. 654   H. KQJ84   D. 2   C. K932,

   He leads the king of hearts.

2. S. 654   H. K5432   D. K5   C. A103,

   He leads the king of diamonds.

3. S. 942   H. K10432   D. 8   C. AQ92,

   He leads the nine of spades.

I.   Both sides vul.
     Dealer North

North
S. AJ103
H. 108
D. K2
C. AQJ109

West
S. 4
H. J7652
D. QJ107
C. 863

East
S. 62
H. KQ43
D. 9543
C. K42

South
S. KQ9875
H. A9
D. A86
C. 75

North	East	South	West
1C	Pass	1S	Pass
3S	Pass	4NT	Pass
5H	Dbl.	5NT	Pass
6D	Pass	6S	All Pass

Opening lead: Five of hearts

II. Neither side vul.
     Dealer North

North
S. Q3
H. K7632
D. AKQJ
C. 105

West
S. K9854
H. J
D. 10984
C. 742

East
S. 762
H. AQ1098
D. 32
C. A63

South
S. AJ10
H. 54
D. 765
C. KQJ98

North	East	South	West
1H	Pass	2C	Pass
2D	Pass	2NT	Pass
3NT	Dbl.	All Pass	

Opening lead: Jack of hearts

III. Neither side vul.
      Dealer South

North
S. 10
H. J973
D. 76
C. J108752

West
S. 63
H. 1086542
D. 84
C. KQ9

East
S. 752
H. none
D. AQJ10932
C. 643

South
S. AKQJ984
H. AKQ
D. K5
C. A

South	West	North	East
2C	Pass	2D	3D, 4D, or Dbl.
4NT	Pass	5C	Pass
6S	Pass	Pass	Dbl. (All pass)

Opening lead: Deuce of hearts

IV. East-West vul.
     Dealer South

North
S. AJ32
H. K65
D. QJ109
C. 54

West
S. 109876
H. J98
D. K4
C. 872

East
S. 4
H. Q1073
D. 852
C. AQJ93

South
S. KQ5
H. A42
D. A763
C. K106

South	West	North	East
1NT	Pass	2C	Dbl.
Pass	Pass	3NT	All Pass

Opening lead: Deuce of clubs

KEY PLAYS

I. West leads a heart instead of the queen of diamonds because of partner's lead directing double. South wins the ace of hearts, draws trumps, plays king, ace, and ruffs a diamond, and leads the ten of hearts from dummy. East must play low and allow West to win the jack or else East will be endplayed. If West does not have the jack of hearts, the hand cannot be defeated. Six spades is cold with any other lead.

II. East's double calls for one of dummy's suits. West reasons that East is long in hearts and leads the jack. Dummy plays low and East overtakes to continue the suit. Eventually East gets in with the ace of clubs and scores his remaining hearts to defeat the hand one trick. Without the double, West leads a spade and South takes ten tricks without working up a sweat.

III. East's double forbids West to lead a diamond, a suit he has bid. Since East is likely to have a void, West leads the DEUCE of hearts to show club strength. East ruffs and must score the ace of diamonds whether or not he cashes that card at trick two. With any other lead, six spades is cold. If South elects to run to six no trump, West leads the king of clubs.

IV. East's double asks for a club lead. South's pass indicates

a club stopper and no four card major. With no club
stopper and no four card major, South bids two diamonds.
With four or five good clubs, South redoubles. West
leads as if he were leading his partner's suit (low from
three or four; top of a doubleton). East plays the jack
to retain communication with his partner's hand. South
does best to duck the jack, but East counters by playing
any club other than the ace. South wins, but West remains
with a club, which he plays upon winning the king of
diamonds. Only a club lead defeats three no trump.

LEAD DIRECTING DOUBLES   PROBLEMS

I. Sitting West you hold:

S. KJ65   H. 54   D. J1076   C. Q43

What do you lead in each of the following bidding sequences?

a. | South | West | North | East |
    | --- | --- | --- | --- |
    | 1NT | Pass | 2NT | Pass |
    | 3NT | Pass | Pass | Dbl. |
    | All Pass | | | |

b. | South | West | North | East |
    | --- | --- | --- | --- |
    | 1C | Pass | 1H | Pass |
    | 1NT | Pass | 2NT | Pass |
    | 3NT | Pass | Pass | Dbl. |
    | All Pass | | | |

c. | North | East | South | West |
    | --- | --- | --- | --- |
    | 1H | Pass | 1NT | Pass |
    | Pass | Dbl. | All Pass | |

II. Again you are West, and you hold:

S. 5   H. J1094   D. J1096   C. 7652

The bidding proceeds:

North	East	South	West
1C	Pass	2S	Pass
3S	Pass	4NT	Pass
5D	Pass	5NT	Pass
6D	Pass	6S	All Pass

What do you lead?

III. The bidding proceeds:

South	West	North	East
1NT*	Pass	2C**	?

    * Strong no trump
    ** Stayman

What should East bid with each of the following hands?

a. S. A5   H. 765   D. Q8   C. Q87654

b. S. A5   H. 654   D. J5   C. KQ10943

c. S. 54   H. A43   D. none   C. KQJ108765

IV. The bidding proceeds:

South	West	North	East
2NT	Pass	3NT	Dbl.
All Pass			

What should West lead with each of the following hands?

a. S. 1098652   H. A76   D. 654   C. 3

b. S. 54   H. 54   D. QJ843   C. J876

V. Sitting East you hold:

S. 64   H. AKQJ864   D. J1098   C. none

The bidding proceeds:

South	West	North	East
2C	Pass	2D	4H
4NT	Pass	5D	Pass
6S	Pass	Pass	?

What is your call?

VI. Sitting West you hold:

S. 542   H. QJ109   D. J76   C. 6532

The bidding proceeds:

South	West	North	East
1S	Pass	2C	Pass
4C	Pass	4S	Pass
4NT	Pass	5C	Pass
6S	Pass	Pass	Dbl.
All Pass			

What do you lead?

VII. Sitting East you hold:

S. AKJ8   H. 6543   D. A2   C. 654

The bidding proceeds:

North	East	South	West
1H	1S	5D	Pass
6D	?		

What call do you make?

VIII. Here's a real life hand I once held in an important tournament. See if you can figure out what I should have led.

Sitting West I held:

S. J987642   H. 103   D. J65   C. 2

The bidding proceeded:

South	West	North	East
3C	Pass	4NT	5D
5H*	Pass	6C	Dbl.
All pass			

* Showing one ace.

What is your opening lead?

I. a. The five of hearts. Partner is supposed to have a
        solid suit, and from your hand it looks as though
        it is hearts.

    b. The five of hearts. Lead dummy's suit if neither
        you nor partner has bid.

    c. The five of hearts. Partner's double is announcing
        that _he_ holds an opening one heart bid. Give him a
        break and lead his suit.

II. The jack of hearts. Partner had two chances to double
     diamonds, but he didn't. He could have doubled six
     spades if he wanted a club lead (dummy's first suit),
     but he didn't. So by the process of elimination, we
     select a heart.

III. a. Pass. Your clubs are not strong enough.

      b. Double. You want a club lead against any eventual
          contract, particularly no trump.

      c. Four clubs. You could double, but when holding a
          strong seven or eight card suit, a preemptive jump
          is usually more effective. (See Lesson Hand III.)

IV. a. The three of clubs. Partner is supposed to have a
         solid suit or a one-loser suit, and from your hand
         it looks as though clubs is it.

b. It helps to be religious on this one. Partner is loaded in either hearts or spades, and you have to guess which. Good luck.

V. Double. Your double bars partner from leading a heart or a trump. Hopefully, he will work out your club void.

VI. A club. When the opponents have bid only one side suit, partner's double calls for that suit. He is almost certainly void, with an outside ace.

VII. PASS! A double by you would forbid a spade lead, the lead you want. So you'll beat the hand (maybe) without doubling. Remember, you only get an extra 50 points for beating a non-vulnerable doubled contract one trick, so the double is more worthwhile to direct the lead. You want your own suit led, so pass.

VIII. Did you lead a spade in order to give your partner a ruff? You did? So did I, but this was the entire deal:

```
                        North
                        S. AK3
                        H. KJ987
                        D. A
                        C. Q983
      West                                    East
      S. J987642                              S. Q5
      H. 103                                  H. AQ42
      D. J65                                  D. KQ10974
      C. 2                                    C. 4
                        South
                        S. 10
                        H. 65
                        D. 832
                        C. AKJ10765
```

As you can see, we spade leaders were not so clever.
Partner knew the king of hearts must be in dummy and wanted
to warn me off the diamond lead. Notice the hand can be
made with a diamond lead, but I wasn't smart enough to
figure out to lead a heart. I told my partner afterward
that the next time he wants a heart lead, he should beat
on his chest rather than make a lead directing double.
I'll catch on faster.

IV. SIGNALLING VS. SUIT CONTRACTS

Ask the average player what he knows about signalling and he
usually tells you that he high-lows with a doubleton, a deuce
asks for a club shift, anything above a six is a signal, anything below a seven is not, and a smile from partner is the
equivalent of an encouraging signal. No wonder we have so many
traffic accidents - nobody knows how to signal!

I. The HIGH-LOW with a doubleton.

Probably the most common signal is the high-low to show

a doubleton. The most easily recognized is the following:

A.

	North	
	S. Q86	
West		East (You)
S. AK953		S. 102
	South	
	S. J74	

West leads the king against a suit contract, and you

begin a high-low by playing the ten. When you follow

with the deuce under the ace, your partner knows you are

now void and can trump the third round. In this case,

the high-low was obvious because of the size of the

first card, the ten. However, a high-low can be a three

followed by a deuce.

Is it ever right not to high-low with a doubleton? Yes.

There are a couple of pat situations in which a high-low

would be incorrect.

B.   North
                                S. A109

West   East (You)
S. KQ765   S. J4

                    South
                    S. 832

Again your partner leads the king and dummy wins the ace.
If you were to play your jack to start a high-low, you
would be giving declarer a second trick with his ten-nine.
The only time you might purposely do something like this
is with the ace of trumps or a quick trump entry, in
which case you know that you will be able to return your
smaller one and trump dummy's established ten.

CONCLUSION: WHEN PARTNER LEADS THE KING, IT IS FAR

              SAFER TO HIGH-LOW WITH JX WHEN THE QUEEN

              IS IN DUMMY THAN WHEN THE ACE IS IN DUMMY.

Another situation in which the high-low is not given is
the following:

C.   North
                                S. 974

West   East (You)
S. AK83   S. Q6

                    South
                    S. J1052

Partner leads the king and you have the doubleton queen.
As we will soon see, dropping the queen under the king

GUARANTEES THE JACK. Therefore, unless the jack is
visible in the dummy, you simply cannot high-low with
a doubleton queen. Partner will often lead low to your
assumed jack, which will be disastrous.

In this situation, you are allowed to drop the queen:

D.   North
                            S. J74

West   East (You)
S. AK932   S. Q5

                            South
                            S. 1086

In this case, the JACK IS VISIBLE in the dummy so partner
cannot misread your intentions. You must have either
a singleton or a doubleton queen.

The high-low is given after partner has bid a suit,
leads the ace, and the king appears in dummy.

E.   North
                            S. KQ102

West   East (You)
S. AJ8763   S. 94

                            South
                            S. 5

West leads the ace and you play the nine. West must now
decide who has the missing card. If you play the four
and declarer the five, West figures you for the singleton
because you failed to start a high-low.

II. <u>Dropping the Queen under the King to show the Jack.</u>

A few examples will illustrate the importance of this
signal.

East-West vul.
Dealer West

                        North
                        S. AJ102
                        H. A876
                        D. 76
                        C. J108

    West   East
    S. 876   S. Q94
    H. 93   H. J102
    D. AK104   D. QJ532
    C. AQ65   C. 93

                        South
                        S. K53
                        H. KQ54
                        D. 98
                        C. K742

    West   North   East   South
    1D   Pass   2D   Pass
    Pass   Dbl.   Pass   2H
    Pass   Pass   Pass

Opening lead: King of diamonds

Under the king of diamonds, East drops the queen,
GUARANTEEING THE JACK. West can now safely lead a low
diamond to East who returns the nine of clubs. West
takes two clubs and returns a third which East ruffs.
East exits with a trump, and South must locate the
queen of spades in order to make the contract.

Here's another:

```
East-West vul.          North
Dealer North            S. A2
                        H. AQ109
                        D. AQJ107
                        C. 53

        West                                    East
        S. KJ1084                               S. 976
        H. 32                                   H. 54
        D. 64                                   D. K983
        C. AK74                                 C. QJ62

                        South
                        S. Q53
                        H. KJ876
                        D. 52
                        C. 1098

        North           East            South           West
        1D              Pass            1H              1S
        4H              Pass            Pass            Pass
```

Opening lead: King of clubs

East plays the queen of clubs at trick one, promising
the jack. West can see two club tricks and realizes
that in order to beat the game, the defense must get
one spade trick and partner must have one red king.
Leading spades can be dangerous if South has the queen,
so West leads a low club to East's jack and East's spade
return comes through the queen.

Declarer is helpless against this defense. After trumps
are drawn, the diamond finesse is attempted; but when it
fails, the defense cashes a spade trick. No other defense defeats the contract.

Notice how futile it would be for West to shift to a diamond at trick two. Even if South finesses, the diamonds are now established for spade discards and the defense takes only three tricks. For this reason good defenders seldom lead through dummy's long suit early in the hand. By doing so defenders establish dummy's suit and more often than not lose their tricks in the other suits -- the suits that they should be attacking before dummy's long suit can be established by the DECLARER.

Occasionally, the shorter suits that should be attacked must be led by one particular defender, as in the last two examples. The queen from the queen-jack signal gives the defenders the opportunity to decide from which side to attack any particular side suit. Notice that playing the queen under the king is not a command for the opening leader to underlead to partner's jack. Rather, it gives him the option to do so if he wishes.

III. The Equal Honor Signal

Another common signal is the equal honor signal, which is occasionally confused with the high-low doubleton signal.

As the name suggests, the signal is used when partner leads an honor card and you have an honor of equal value.

A.   North
                                S. QJ109

West   East (You)
S. A2   S. K843

                                South
                                S. 765

West leads the ace, and you have an equal honor, the king.
Apparently partner is short-suited (the ace is not often
led against game or part score contracts unless the
opening leader is short-suited or has reason to believe
from his own extensive length that partner is), so East
signals with the eight, asking partner to continue the
suit.

The most common application of the equal honor signal
arises when partner leads the king.

B.   North
                                S. J73

West   East (You)
S. AK94   S. Q62

                                South
                                S. 1085

West leads the king, and you begin a high-low with the
six to show an equal honor. If partner continues with
the ace, you play the deuce, completing the echo. Unless
you have supported the suit or the bidding is very
revealing, West cannot always be sure whether you are
signalling with a queen or a doubleton; but he is
usually safe in playing the suit a third time, for you

will either trump or furnish the queen.

A word of caution. East must be careful about using the equal honor signal when there is a danger of establishing a trick in dummy or if he wants another suit led. (See "The Common Sense Signal".)

C.

                              North
                              S. J1094

West   East (You)
S. AK73   S. Q82

                              South
                              S. 65

When partner leads the king, play the deuce. If you play the eight partner will continue with the ace, and when you follow with the deuce he will assume you have a doubleton. When West plays the third round, declarer ruffs your queen and dummy's jack is established. (If you had supported the suit, you could safely play the eight to show an equal honor.)

WHEN DUMMY HAS CONSIDERABLE LENGTH, THE HIGH-LOW IS GENERALLY RESERVED FOR A DOUBLETON TO AVOID SETTING UP DUMMY'S LONG SUIT.

Naturally this is not a blanket rule, for you may have the same number of cards as dummy and yours may be better.

D.   North
                          S. J754

West   East (You)
S. AK2   S. Q1083

                          South
                          S. 96

West leads the king and you can afford to signal with
the eight because your spots are better than dummy's.
Furthermore, by continuing the suit partner will not
set up a long card in dummy. West, on the other hand,
must trust your signal when there are four cards in the
dummy. He knows you would not start an equal honor
signal unless you had dummy's spot cards well covered
and had either the same or greater length than dummy to
prevent long suit establishment.

Another sticky situation arises when partner leads the
king and dummy has the ace.

E.   North
                          S. A32

West   East (You)
S. KQ98   S. J74

                          South
                          S. 1065

If a LOW card is played from dummy, East signals with the
seven to show an equal honor. In this situation (dummy
playing low), it is usually incorrect for East to high-low
with a doubleton. A signal to show the jack is more
important to West, who needs to know whether it is safe

to continue the suit if he himself does not hold the jack.

But, if the ace is played from dummy, East signals with
a doubleton. (The assumption is that if the ace is
played, declarer does not have the jack or else he would
have played low from dummy originally.)

It goes without saying that some of these situations are
much clearer when there has been a little bidding. For
example, if East had ever supported spades, there could
be no confusion as to the meaning of the signal.

When the king is led and you have the ace, an equal honor
signal is usually made unless the ace is doubleton:

F.   North
                             S. 1086

    West   East
    S. KQ73   S. A92

                             South
                             S. J54

West leads the king and East plays the nine to indicate
an equal honor.

G.   North
                             S. 1086

    West   East
    S. KQ732   S. A4

                             South
                             S. J95

In this case, East overtakes the king and returns the
four. West wins and returns a third round for East to

trump. In this way the defenders realize three tricks
from the suit. If East plays low originally, the suit
is blocked and declarer may be able to rid himself of
his third spade. On the other hand, if East holds good
trumps (QJ10), he does not overtake, for trumping the
third round would cost his natural trump trick.

When the queen is led, the king is considered an equal
honor.

H.   North
                        S. 1043

West   East
S. QJ92   S. K75

                        South
                        S. A86

West leads the queen and East signals with the seven to
show an equal honor. Assuming South wins the ace, West
knows that East has the king and South has the eight!

How does West know all of this? First, East would not
signal with a doubleton when partner leads the queen
unless both the ace and king are in dummy or unless it
will soon be obvious that the declaring side holds both
top honors. Otherwise, the opening leader would not be
able to distinguish whether the signal was from a
doubleton or an equal honor. In ambiguous cases, when
the queen is led, the equal honor signal prevails.

Second, when signalling, the highest equal spot card is
played. Therefore, East's play of the seven denies the
eight (but says nothing about the six).

I.   North
                            S. A54

West   East
S. K2   S. Q10983

                            South
                            S. J76

West leads the king; dummy plays the ace, and East signals
with the ten. The signal of the ten indicates an interest
in the suit (equal honor), but denies the jack. Therefore,
West knows that East has the queen, but not the jack.
(If East had QJ109, he would play the queen, the highest
equal.)

Back to the lead of the queen.

J.   North
                            S. A92

West   East
S. QJ1063   S. 85

                            South
                            S. K74

In this case, if the deuce is played from dummy, East
can safely signal with the eight because East knows that
South is going to take the trick and partner will not be
misled by the signal.

On the other hand, if the ace is played from dummy, East

usually plays the five because the eight would indicate an equal honor.

With a doubleton king or ace, the honor is played on the queen unless it will cost a trick.

K.
                        North
                        S. 863

West   East
S. QJ1052   S. K4

                        South
                        S. A97

West leads the queen and East unblocks with the king. This frees West to take the next two tricks with the jack-ten. However, if the ten is in dummy, East cannot afford the luxury of overtaking.

L.
                        North
                        S. 1063

West   East
S. QJ975   S. K4

                        South
                        S. A82

East must play low under the queen. If East overtakes with the king, dummy's ten becomes a third round trick. The same principle of signalling with an equal honor applies when a jack is led. A signal shows the queen unless it is impossible for you to hold the queen, in which case the signal shows a doubleton.

M.
                       North
                       S. AK3

West   East
S. J1092   S. Q754

                       South
                       S. 86

West leads the jack, and when dummy takes the trick
East signals with the seven, showing the queen.

N.
                       North
                       S. KQ5

West   East
S. J10982   S. 74

                       South
                       S. A63

Once again West leads the jack, and dummy plays low.
East can safely signal with the seven to show a doubleton because the equal honor, the queen, is in dummy and
partner cannot be confused. Even if dummy plays the
queen East can signal with the seven, because if East
had the ace he would normally win the trick. So the
signal must once again denote a doubleton.

But when the jack is led and the queen is in dummy, the
king and the ace are considered equal honors and signalling
is reserved to show one or the other.

O.
                       North
                       S. Q63

West   East
S. J1092   S. K74

                       South
                       S. A85

West leads the jack, and if dummy plays low, East signals
with the seven to show either the king or the ace. But
if East held 74 doubleton and dummy played low, East
would also play low to deny an honor. However:

P.   North
                            S. Q63

    West   East
    S. J1092   S. 74

                            South
                            S. AK85

If dummy plays the QUEEN, East signals with the seven
to show a doubleton because he cannot have the ace or
king and not cover.

Notice that in all these cases you signal partner to
show either an equal honor or a doubleton, with the
equal honor prevailing in doubtful cases.

Finally, the truly impossible situation:

Q.   North
                            S. 8642

    West   East
    S. KQ103   S. 95

                            South
                            S. AJ7

West leads the king and East signals with the nine
showing West either a doubleton or an equal honor. This
is one of the few times that the opening leader cannot
be sure which signal is being given. If South keeps

his head and plays low, West will usually continue, enabling South to win a cheap trick with the jack. There is really no solution for this dilemma because East does not know whether West is leading from ace-king or king-queen, and West does not know whether East is showing a doubleton or the ace. (It goes without saying that if East had supported spades during the bidding, the nine would indicate an equal honor.)

Because of situations like this, many players, especially Europeans, lead the ace from ace-king and the king from king-queen to eliminate the confusion.

However, even that solution is not a cure-all. When one leads the ace from ace-king, it is difficult for partner to read the lead of the ace if the opening leader does not have the king to back it up.

IV. Suit Preference Signals

This, the simplest and most elegant of all the suit signals, is the one that has created the most havoc among the average player because he insists on using it when it doesn't apply!

An example of this signal in action will help:

East-West vul.
Dealer South

                              North
                              S. Q75
                              H. K107
                              D. AKQ102
                              C. 42

        West   East
        S. AKJ62   S. 104
        H. 532   H. 64
        D. none   D. J9753
        C. QJ1087   C. 9653

                              South
                              S. 983
                              H. AQJ98
                              D. 864
                              C. AK

        South   West   North   East
        1H   1S   2D   Pass
        2H   3C   4H   Pass
        Pass   Pass

Opening lead: King of spades

West leads the king of spades and East plays the ten,
an obvious doubleton (or singleton), because the only
equal honor, the queen, is in dummy. West continues
with the ace and then a third spade for East to trump.
But which spade?

WHEN GIVING PARTNER A RUFF, A SUIT PREFERENCE SIGNAL
IS USED.

A LOW card asks partner to return the LOWER ranking of
the two remaining side suits (excluding trumps, naturally).
An UNUSUALLY HIGH card asks partner for a return of the

HIGHER ranking of the two remaining side suits.

In this case West wants a diamond return after East ruffs the third spade, so West leads the JACK OF SPADES, asking partner for the higher ranking of the two remaining side suits (diamonds and clubs).

Had West wished a club return, he would have returned his smallest spade for partner to ruff.

The confusion that results from this signal is this:

Many players think that whenever their partners play a deuce, they are asking for the lower ranking suit, usually clubs, and whenever their partners give them a high card, they are asking for a switch to the highest ranking suit.

THE ABOVE STATEMENT IS TRUE WHEN A CARD IS BEING LED FOR PARTNER TO TRUMP, NOT IN THE GENERAL COURSE OF PLAY.

North
S. QJ7

West
S. AK103

East
S. 8642

South
S. 95

West leads the king of spades against a heart contract, and East plays the deuce. HE IS NOT ASKING FOR A CLUB SHIFT. He is simply announcing a lack of interest in a spade continuation and probably has some honors outside of spades, but NOT NECESSARILY IN CLUBS. East's honor strength can just as easily be in diamonds. As a general rule, a low card played under partner's ace or king simply asks for a shift, but does not say to which suit.

Neither side vul.
Dealer North

```
                        North
                        S. 104
                        H. KJ2
                        D. KQJ97
                        C. KQ9

West                                         East
S. J982                                      S. Q7653
H. 43                                        H. A76
D. A1083                                     D. 2
C. A82                                       C. 10765

                        South
                        S. AK
                        H. Q10985
                        D. 654
                        C. J43
```

North	East	South	West
1D	Pass	1H	Pass
2H	Pass	3H	Pass
4H	All pass		

Opening lead: Two of spades

South wins the first trick with the ace, East playing the queen. A trump is led to the jack and ace, and East shifts to his singleton diamond. West wins the ace and must be careful to return the three of diamonds for East to ruff. The return of the three asks East to return the lower ranking of the two remaining side suits (clubs and spades). East ruffs, returns a club, and subsequently ruffs another diamond to defeat the contract two tricks.

Before leaving this deal, assume for the moment that West originally led from the king of spades and does not have the ace of clubs. In that case, West returns the TEN OF DIAMONDS asking East to return the higher ranking of the two remaining side suits after ruffing the diamond. A spade to the king and another diamond ruff once again defeats the contract two tricks.

Perhaps you are wondering what to return when giving partner a ruff and you have no great desire for partner to return either of the two remaining side suits. In that case, give partner a middle card to ruff and watch him sweat trying to work out whether it is high or low. When he finally comes to the conclusion that he cannot tell, he will use his own judgment. When using this signal, you must trust partner.

Finally, if declarer or dummy leads a side suit which is ruffed on the first round by second hand, fourth hand gives a suit preference return signal --- just as he would if he, himself, were giving the ruff.

Both sides vul.
Dealer South

```
                        North
                        S. KQJ
                        H. KQ76
                        D. QJ103
                        C. 76

      West                                        East
      S. 2                                         S. A10963
      H. 842                                       H. 5
      D. K7642                                     D. A98
      C. J1093                                     C. Q542

                        South
                        S. 8754
                        H. AJ1093
                        D. 5
                        C. AK8
```

South	West	North	East
1H	Pass	3H	Pass
4H	Pass	Pass	Pass

Opening lead: Two of spades

East reads the opening lead as a singleton, but must be careful about his return. In this case, East returns the TEN OF SPADES for West to ruff, requesting West to return a diamond, THE HIGHER RANKING of the two remaining side suits.

After West ruffs, he must trust East and lead a diamond from his king even though he sees the QJ10 in dummy. It is not for West to reason why, it is for West to do or die! The diamond return followed by another spade ruff defeats the contract one trick.

NOTE: From this point to the quizzes, the discussion on
      signalling will apply mainly to advanced players
      (you, but probably not your partner).

Before leaving the suit preference signal, it might be
worthwhile mentioning three other situations in which
the suit preference play can be used, but these are rare
and must be completely OBVIOUS TO BOTH PLAYERS.

Neither side vul.
Dealer West
                          North
                          S. J76
                          H. KQ8
                          D. 765
                          C. 8732

West   East
S. Q   S. 54
H. A97653   H. J102
D. KJ3   D. A1092
C. Q105   C. J964

                          South
                          S. AK109832
                          H. 4
                          D. Q84
                          C. AK

West   North   East   South
1H   Pass   2H   4S
Pass   Pass   Pass

Opening lead: Ace of hearts

On this hand, it is apparent as soon as the ace of hearts
is led that it is logically impossible for East to want
a heart continuation. THEREFORE, WHEN IT IS IMPOSSIBLE

FOR THE PARTNER OF THE OPENING LEADER TO WANT A CONTINU-
ATION IN THE SUIT LED, AND THE BIDDING HAS MADE IT CLEAR
THAT HE HAS THREE OR MORE CARDS IN THAT SUIT, THE SIZE
OF THE CARD HE PLAYS CAN BE CONSTRUED AS A SUIT PREFERENCE
SIGNAL.

If East is on his toes, he will play the jack of hearts,
asking for a diamond switch. West leads a low diamond
at trick two, East wins and returns a diamond and the
contract is defeated one trick.

Remember, you are playing with fire if you construe every
high card partner plays as a request for the higher
ranking side suit or every low card as a request for the
lower ranking side suit. It would be better if you had
never heard of the signal.

Ninety-five times out of a hundred a high card asks for
a continuation and a low card requests a shift, BUT IT
DOES NOT TELL THE OPENING LEADER TO WHICH SUIT TO SHIFT.
It is only when the appearance of the dummy, plus the
bidding, make it obvious that a shift must be made that
the suit preference signal applies.

For example, in the above hand if East has not supported
hearts, it is dangerous for him to play the jack at trick
one for fear that partner will read it as a singleton.

It is wiser to simply play low and hope partner finds the right shift.

However, after supporting hearts it is safe to play the jack, for partner knows you have length and cannot logically want a continuation.

A great deal of confusion exists when dummy has a singleton and the partner of the opening leader gives him a violent signal. Is he signalling for a continuation or is it a suit preference signal, asking for the higher ranking of the two remaining side suits?

East-West vul.
Dealer North

```
                        North
                        S.  AKQ
                        H.  3
                        D.  AQJ42
                        C.  KQ62

West                                            East
S.  7                                           S.  J95
H.  AKJ87                                        H.  10652
D.  1097                                         D.  865
C.  J874                                         C.  1093

                        South
                        S.  1086432
                        H.  Q94
                        D.  K3
                        C.  A5
```

North	East	South	West
1D	Pass	1S	Pass
3C	Pass	3S	Pass
4NT	Pass	5D	Pass
6S	Pass	Pass	Pass

Opening lead: King of hearts

At trick one, East plays the ten. What does it all mean? The normal meaning of a high card under the king or ace is a request for a continuation. West must be on sure ground before he reads it as anything else.

In this case, East is literally dying for a heart continuation in order to force dummy to trump and promote his jack of spades for the setting trick. West should play the ace of hearts at trick two.

FOR A HIGH SPOT CARD NOT TO BE A COME-ON SIGNAL, THERE MUST BE ABSOLUTELY NO CHANCE FOR TRUMP PROMOTION.

In other words, when dummy has a singleton partner may still want the suit continued in order to promote a trump trick for himself. However, if the bidding and the looks of the dummy make this completely impossible, then and only then should a violent signal be construed as suit preference.

Another suit preference situation arises when a player has shown a six card suit or longer and his partner leads a high honor in that suit.

Since a player with six or more cards in a suit has a great choice of plays, a medium-to-high spot card asks for a continuation. A very low card asks for a shift to the lower ranking side suit, and a very high card (usually an honor) asks for a shift to the higher ranking suit.

It must be repeated that this signal applies only when a player has shown at least a six card suit during the bidding.

East-West vul.
Dealer North

```
                        North
                        S. AQ7
                        H. 7
                        D. AK85
                        C. A9743

West                                          East
S. 652                                        S. 3
H. A86                                        H. QJ109432
D. 76432                                      D. none
C. 65                                         C. KQJ108

                        South
                        S. KJ10984
                        H. K5
                        D. QJ109
                        C. 2
```

North	East	South	West
1C	4H	4S	Pass
4NT	Pass	5C	Pass
6S	Pass	Pass	Pass

Assume West leads the ace of hearts and East drops the queen. What does that mean? In this case, East has shown at least six hearts (probably seven or eight) so the queen must be a suit preference signal, asking for the higher ranking of the two remaining suits. The diamond switch at trick two defeats the contract.

East could have avoided much of this aggravation had he

doubled six spades asking for an unusual lead. (See lead directing doubles of suit slams.)

Conclusion: Other than the obvious instances of giving partner a ruff, the suit preference play MIGHT appear in three other situations:

1. The opening leader has inadvertently established a number of discards for declarer on opening lead. Partner's unusually high or low signal in that suit can be construed as a request to shift to the higher or lower of the two remaining side suits. (But partner must be marked with three or more cards in the suit or else a high card merely shows a singleton or doubleton.)

2. There is a singleton in the dummy and declarer's trump holding is obviously solid. In this case (usually vs. a slam), an unusually high or low card can be construed as a suit preference signal.

3. A player has shown a six card suit or longer during the bidding, and his partner leads a high honor in that suit. A middle spot card asks for a continuation, a low spot card asks for a shift to the lower ranking side suit, and an unusually high spot card (almost always an honor) asks for a shift to the higher ranking side suit.

IN ALL OTHER CASES, a high card asks for a continuation and a low card requests a shift, but does not dictate which suit.

V. The Common Sense Signal

By far the most important and most widely used signal is the common sense signal. It occasionally conflicts with the equal honor signal, but takes precedence over it!

Neither side vul.
Dealer North

```
                        North
                        S. 965
                        H. J92
                        D. Kl05
                        C. AQ103

West                                            East
S. J42                                          S. 87
H. KQ8                                          H. A7543
D. 972                                          D. AQJ3
C. K865                                         C. 72

                        South
                        S. AKQ103
                        H. 106
                        D. 864
                        C. J94
```

North	East	South	West
Pass	1H	1S	2H
2S	Pass	Pass	Pass

Opening lead: King of hearts

West leads the king of hearts and East has an equal honor, the ace. Although one usually signals to show an equal honor, the reason for signalling is NOT TO SHOW THE EQUAL HONOR AS MUCH AS IT IS TO REQUEST A CONTINUATION IN THAT SUIT.

If for any reason the partner of the opening leader wishes
a switch to a different suit, he plays LOW. (Except for
the three rare suit preference exceptions mentioned earlier.)

The opening leader must then judge which suit partner wants
and plays accordingly. In this case, East plays the three
of hearts because he wants a shift. West figures by looking
at the dummy and his own hand that diamonds is the most
logical suit. So he shifts to the nine of diamonds. The
ten is played and East wins the jack and leads a low heart
to West's queen for a second diamond play. After cashing
two more diamonds East plays his last diamond, establishing
West's jack of spades for the setting trick.

Notice clearly that the low heart East plays at trick one
is not a request for clubs. It simply asks partner to
figure out which other suit to play. Naturally, if East
wants a heart continuation he signals with the seven.

Another example that might hit home:

```
Neither side vul.            North
Dealer North                 S. 103
                             H. 84
                             D. QJ10
                             C. AKJ987

West                                              East
S. Q4                                             S. 2
H. J5                                             H. AKQ10732
D. K98643                                         D. A75
C. 1052                                           C. 64

                             South
                             S. AKJ98765
                             H. 96
                             D. 2
                             C. Q3


North          East           South          West
1C             4H             4S             Pass
Pass           Pass
```

Opening lead: Jack of hearts

East overtakes the opening lead and cashes a second heart.
At trick three, East plays the ace of diamonds. Which
diamond does West play and why? West plays his lowest
diamond! West does not want a diamond play, he wants
another heart to insure making his queen of spades. Once
again the common sense signal takes precedence over the
equal honor signal.

If West has only small spades, he signals with the nine
of diamonds because, in that case, he wants a diamond
continuation.

The whole trick to this signalling with an equal honor business is simply to ask yourself one question: DO I WANT THE SUIT THAT MY PARTNER HAS LED CONTINUED? If the answer is yes, play a big one. If the answer is no, play a small one.

Because a low card under the lead of an ace or king usually indicates possession of strength in another suit, one must occasionally give false encouragement in the suit led to prevent partner from making a disastrous shift.

East-West vul.
Dealer North

```
                        North
                        S. QJ10
                        H. 953
                        D. AQJ10
                        C. AQ

West                                          East
S. AK54                                       S. 972
H. A2                                         H. K
D. 765                                        D. 9432
C. J872                                       C. 96543

                        South
                        S. 86
                        H. QJ108764
                        D. K8
                        C. K10
```

North	East	South	West
1NT	Pass	4H	All Pass

Opening lead: King of spades

East can immediately see that no minor suit winners are available, and rather than encourage partner to make a

disastrous shift to one minor or the other, East starts
a false signal by playing the seven. This encourages
West to lay down his ace -- and with the two trump tricks,
the hand is defeated. If East thoughtlessly plays low on
the first spade, West might well shift to a minor suit,
for East PROMISES a high honor in one of the minors when
he asks for a shift. An immediate shift would result in
the loss of a spade trick as declarer discards it on the
third round of diamonds.

The idea of a false signal when the partner of the opening
leader cannot stand a shift to any other suit was rammed
home to me quite forcefully a few years ago when this
deal cost my partner and me a National Championship:

```
Neither side vul.        North
Dealer South             S. J85
                         H. AQJ109
                         D. Q54
                         C. K3

     West                                    East
     S. A2                                   S. K43
     H. 876                                  H. 542
     D. AK10                                 D. J8732
     C. 98642                                C. 75

                         South
                         S. Q10976
                         H. K3
                         D. 96
                         C. AQJ10

     South        West         North         East
     1S           Pass         2H            Pass
     2S           Pass         4S            All pass
```

Opening lead: King of diamonds

Sitting East, I nonchalantly played the deuce at trick one.
My partner reasoned correctly that I must have a high honor
in another suit to make this play. The most logical high
card on the bidding was the king of hearts, so he shifted
to a heart rather than establish dummy's queen of diamonds
for a possible heart discard.

What happened next is too gory to discuss. Declarer
proceeded to play three rounds of hearts, discarding his
losing diamond, and conceded two spade tricks to make
his game.

To the uninformed, it looks as if my partner blew the
hand by not cashing the ace of diamonds. However, any
expert will tell you that it was my fault for not giving
my partner false encouragement in diamonds to prevent
him from making a disastrous shift. Interchange the
major suit kings, and the heart shift at trick two is
vital. I wish my partner would stop trusting my signals
so much.

VI. The Trump Echo Signal

The trump echo signal is a high-low in the trump suit used
when either ruffing or desiring a ruff. It indicates
possession of a third trump. This signal is used typically
in four situations:

1. Some players use the trump echo signal when leading a trump -- to give partner (and declarer) a count on the trump suit; they lead the middle card when holding three and low when holding two or four. For example, many experts lead the five of trumps when holding 654, and then play the four, to show a three card holding.

2. These same experts also play the five and then the four when declarer is drawing trumps, in order to show partner a three card holding; the high-low here does not indicate a desire to ruff anything, it is simply given for count purposes.

3. A second group uses the high-low in the trump suit exclusively to alert partner that they are short suited and desire a ruff.

4. Finally, both groups use the trump echo when actually ruffing, in order to show a holding of exactly three trumps. This is the main purpose of the convention, as the following hand indicates.

Both Sides vul.
Dealer North

```
                        North
                        S. KQ109
                        H. 8
                        D. KJ1096
                        C. Q76

        West                                East
        S. J                                S. A6432
        H. 432                              H. A7
        D. AQ84                             D. 7532
        C. 108532                           C. 94

                        South
                        S. 875
                        H. KQJ10965
                        D. none
                        C. AKJ
```

North	East	South	West
Pass	Pass	4H	Pass
Pass	Pass		

Opening lead: Jack of spades

East wins the ace and returns a middle spade (no desire
for any particular return) as West ruffs with the THREE.
West exits with a club to South's ace. South plays the
king of hearts, West playing the DEUCE. East wins the
ace of hearts and plays a third spade, secure in the
knowledge that West has another trump. If West ruffs
first with the deuce and then plays the three, he is
announcing no more trumps, and East is better advised
to return a diamond upon winning the ace of hearts for
fear that declarer might discard a possible diamond
loser on the spade.

After all, from East's point of view declarer might have:

S. xxx   H. KQJ10xxxx   D. x   C. A

in which case a third spade is disastrous.

VII. <u>The Count Signal</u>

The count signal will be discussed at length in at least
three chapters of this book. The most common use of the
count signal arises when declarer attacks a side suit
and the defenders tell each other how many cards they each
have in the suit. This is done by playing high-low with
a doubleton, low from three or five cards, and second
high followed by third high with four. (If the second
highest card is going to be valuable, play the third
highest followed by the fourth highest.) Although the
count signal can help the defenders count the declarer's
hand, the signal works as a two-edged sword. Declarer
gets an easy count on the defenders' hands as well. For
example, playing against religious count signal givers
this situation becomes clear:

<u>North</u> (Dummy)
S. Q1054

<u>West</u>
S. J963

<u>East</u>
S. 82

<u>South</u>
S. AK7

If South is playing against countomaniacs, he plays the
king-ace of spades and notices that East and West are

high-lowing each other to show an even number. When
South leads the seven, he can safely finesse the ten.

Good players know when to give the count signal and when
not to. One time when it is mandatory is when declarer
leads up to a strong suit in the dummy, usually missing
the ace. If the dummy has no apparent side entries,
it behooves the player with the ace to take the trick at
a time when he can cut declarer from dummy, to wit:

East-West vul.
Dealer South

```
                      North
                      S. J64
                      H. KQJ
                      D. 42
                      C. 86432

West                                        East
S. 8                                        S. Q109
H. 10853                                    H. A972
D. QJ10987                                  D. 653
C. K10                                      C. QJ9

                      South
                      S. AK7532
                      H. 64
                      D. AK
                      C. A75
```

South	West	North	East
1S	Pass	2S	Pass
4S	All pass		

Opening lead: Queen of diamonds

South wins the lead, cashes two top spades and leads a
heart. East must know to win the second heart. How will

he know? West plays the eight of hearts the first time
the suit is led. East works out that if West has two
hearts South has four, and it makes no difference which
heart he takes. But if West has four hearts then South
has two, in which case it is right to win the second lead
of the suit. Declarer goes down one against this defense.

If West carelessly plays the three of hearts the first
time the suit is led, East reasons thus: If West has
three hearts then South also has three and it doesn't
matter which heart is taken. But if West has five hearts
then South has one, so it must be right to win the first
heart.

The count signal is also given when partner leads the
king, dummy has the queen, and: (1) The contract is at
the five level or higher or (2) Third hand has supported
the suit.

North
S. Q65

West
S. AKJ10

East
S. 9732

South
S. 84

If South is playing a contract at the five level or
higher and West leads the king of spades, East plays
the seven. West must work out whether this is from
two or four cards, using the previous bidding to guide

him. Obviously, against a slam contract, it is vital for West to know whether or not the second spade will cash.

Also, if East has supported spades he should play the seven, alerting West that he has four card support. If East has not supported spades and West leads the king against a <u>lower</u> level contract, East usually plays the DEUCE unless he can tell from his own hand and the dummy that any shift partner makes will be costly. In this rare instance he gives partner a false signal and plays the seven, making partner think he has a doubleton. (See the final hand Part V.)

Another use of the count signal, discussed earlier in the chapter, arises when partner bids a suit, leads the ace, and the king appears in dummy. (See Part I-E.)

Finally, the count signal should be given any time partner shows out and your holding is known to declarer. Let partner in on the secret too.

North
D. KJ104

West		East
D. none		D. 9862

South
D. AQ753

South leads a low diamond to dummy's king (suit or no trump), and West shows out. East should play the eight (second high with four) to make sure West knows what is going on in the suit. If East plays the deuce, West will assume that East started with an odd number of diamonds.

SIGNALLING VS. SUIT CONTRACTS   LESSON HANDS

I. East-West vul.   North
    Dealer West   S. KJ9
                                H. 1063
                                D. KJ2
                                C. J1098

West   East
S. 86   S. 543
H. AK87   H. Q92
D. 765   D. AQ108
C. 7654   C. Q32

                                South
                                S. AQ1072
                                H. J54
                                D. 943
                                C. AK

West   North   East   South
Pass   Pass   Pass   1S
Pass   2S   All pass

Opening lead: King of hearts

II. North-South vul.   North
    Dealer South   S. QJ104
                                H. 7
                                D. KQJ98
                                C. K52

West   East
S. 3   S. A98762
H. Q95   H. 42
D. 7643   D. A105
C. J8764   C. Q9

                                South
                                S. K5
                                H. AKJ10863
                                D. 2
                                C. A103

South   West   North   East
1H   Pass   2D   2S
4H   All pass

Opening lead: Three of spades

III. East-West vul.
Dealer South

North
S. 987
H. J976
D. AQJ10
C. 65

West
S. AKJ
H. 103
D. 6543
C. Q983

East
S. 10543
H. 52
D. 987
C. A1042

South
S. Q62
H. AKQ84
D. K2
C. KJ7

South	West	North	East
1H	Pass	2H	Pass
2NT	Pass	4H	All pass

Opening lead: King of spades

IV. Both sides vul.
Dealer North

North
S. K985
H. AQ985
D. 87
C. 43

West
S. 76
H. 432
D. AK2
C. AQJ109

East
S. 4
H. J106
D. QJ6543
C. 876

South
S. AQJ1032
H. K7
D. 109
C. K52

North	East	South	West
Pass	Pass	1S	2C
3S	Pass	4S	All pass

Opening lead: King of diamonds

KEY PLAYS

I.   East plays the deuce of hearts hoping for a diamond shift.
     (Notice the deuce does NOT, REPEAT NOT, mean clubs.) West
     shifts to a diamond (the logical suit from his hand) and
     East wins. East returns a heart to West who plays a
     second diamond, and the defenders take the first six tricks.

II. East wins the first trick, South falsecarding with the
     king, and returns the NINE of spades. West ruffs and
     returns a diamond to East's ace. A third spade now
     promotes West's queen of hearts to the setting trick.

III. East plays the three of spades, South falsecarding with
     the six, and West decides South must have the queen of
     spades on the bidding. He shifts to a club because
     dummy's diamonds are too strong. If East has the king
     of diamonds, he will always get the lead to play a spade.
     East wins the club ace and returns a spade to defeat the
     contract one trick.

IV. East plays the queen of diamonds, promising the jack, and
     West plays the deuce of diamonds at trick two to that jack.
     East wins and returns a club to defeat the hand one trick.
     Notice how seldom good defenders attack dummy's long suit.
     It is a very dangerous play and done only as a last
     resort, when, perhaps, a ruff is being contemplated, or
     when there is a certainty that partner has great strength
     in the suit.

I. Assume for the purpose of this quiz that you are East.
Partner's lead will be given and you are to decide from
the lead and from the card that is played from dummy
which card you should play.

Partner leads the king. Which card do you play?

A.
<pre>
                        North (Dummy)
                        S. 764

    West   East (You)
    S. K   a. S. 102
                                            b. S. QJ103
                                            c. S. Q5
                                            d. S. A983
                                            e. S. AJ3
</pre>

B.
<pre>
                        North (Dummy)
                        S. J72

    West   East (You)
    S. K   a. S. Q103
                                            b. S. Q3
                                            c. S. A5
                                            d. S. A43
                                            e. S. 9864
</pre>

C.
<pre>
                        North (Dummy)
                        S. J983

    West   East (You)
    S. K   a. S. Q642
                                            b. S. Q1075
                                            c. S. Q72
                                            d. S. 72
                                            e. S. Q5
</pre>

II. This is a two part problem. Assuming dummy plays the ace, which card do you play in the East seat; and if dummy plays low, which card do you play?

A.
                   North (Dummy)
                   S. A65

West
S. Q

East (You)
a. S. K92
b. S. 83
c. S. 942
d. S. K3
e. S. K982

Another two part problem. Which card do you play if dummy plays the king, and which card do you play if dummy plays low?

B.
                   North (Dummy)
                   S. K64

West
S. J

East (You)
a. S. Q93
b. S. 73
c. S. A73
d. S. 9732
e. S. AQ98

III. Neither side vul.   North (Dummy)
     Dealer South   S. 76
                      H. KQ7
                      D. AKQ1042
                      C. 82

West (You)
S. AK98
H. 53
D. 975
C. AQJ3

South	West	North	East
3H	Dbl.	4H	All pass

Opening lead: King of spades

-102-

Partner plays the queen, declarer the deuce. What is

your next play?

IV. North-South vul.   North (Dummy)
     Dealer West   S. KQJ97
                                   H. AK109
                                   D. 76
                                   C. 82

         West (You)
         S. 1052
         H. 432
         D. AJ9
         C. AKJ5

         West   North   East   South
         1C   Dbl.   3C   4H
         All pass

Opening lead: King of clubs

Partner plays the ten and declarer the six. What is your

next play?

V. North-South vul.   North (Dummy)
    Dealer South   S. QJ
                                   H. AQ6
                                   D. K109832
                                   C. Q2

         West (You)
         S. A10
         H. KJ1098754
         D. 5
         C. 96

         South   West   North   East
         1D   4H   5D   All pass

Opening lead: Ace of spades

Partner plays the deuce and declarer the six. What is your

next play?

VI. East-West vul.   North (Dummy)
     Dealer South   S. Q5
                                 H. 7
                                 D. AQJ84
                                 C. AQ1032

          West (You)
          S. none
          H. AK1043
          D. 7652
          C. J987

          South   West   North   East
          1S   Pass   2D   Pass
          3S   Pass   4NT   Pass
          5D   Pass   6S   All pass

Opening lead: King of hearts

Partner plays the nine and declarer the queen. What is

your next play?

VII. Both sides vul.   North (Dummy)
     Dealer East   S. KQJ
                                 H. A1082
                                 D. Q532
                                 C. Q4

          West (You)
          S. 2
          H. 64
          D. 9864
          C. 1098765

          East   South   West   North
          1S   2H   Pass   4H
          All pass

Opening lead: Deuce of spades

Partner wins the ace and returns the nine, declarer playing

the five and seven. You ruff; what do you return?

I. A. a. The ten.   To show a doubleton. It is conceivable that partner will play you for the ace if he has led from KQ, but that can't be helped.

b. The queen.   Promising the jack and allowing partner to underlead if he wishes.

c. The five.   The queen would promise the jack.

d. The nine.   Signal with the higher of equal spot cards once you decide to signal. If for any reason, however, you want a switch more than you want a spade continuation, play the three.

e. The ace!   The jack would look too much like Jx and partner might not continue. Of course, if you overtake and later find out partner was leading from Kx, you might as well forget you were ever born!

B. a. The ten.   Beginning an equal honor signal.

b. The queen.   With the jack in the dummy you can afford to play the queen from Qx without fooling partner.

c. The ace.   To unblock the suit and trump the third round.

d. The four. The biggest card you can afford, to start your equal honor signal.

e. The four. With three or more small cards one usually avoids any kind of signal.

C. a. The two. Your spots aren't good enough to signal and you don't want to set up dummy's jack. Had you supported the suit you could play the six and partner would know that it was an equal honor signal. Without support he will assume that the six is from a doubleton and may continue the suit.

b. The seven. Notice that this time you have the spots over the dummy and declarer will not be able to establish a trick in the suit even if partner continues with the ace.

c. The two. Same reason as in "a".

d. The seven. To show a doubleton.

e. The five usually. You could, however, play the queen to show a doubleton if you thought that declarer had as many as three cards in the suit, in which case you could trump the third round. If, however, declarer has a singleton or doubleton your play of the queen won't win any medals.

II. A. a. In either case the nine should be played.

b. If the ace is played, play low to deny the king. If a low one is played you signal with the eight because you know that declarer is going to take the king and partner will not misread your signal.

c. In either case the deuce.

d. If the ace is played the king should be unblocked, otherwise play low. Partner knows you have the king when the queen holds.

e. The nine in either case. One signals with the higher of equal spot cards to show an equal honor. (However, if you want partner to switch to another suit, play low.)

B. a. The nine in either case.

b. The three in either case. Partner will assume you have the queen if you signal.

c. Naturally you win the ace if the king is played, and you play the seven if it is not.

d. The deuce in either case.

e. Win the ace if the king is played and play the nine if it is not.

III.

```
                              North
                              S. 76
                              H. KQ7
                              D. AKQ1042
                              C. 82

        West                                        East
        S. AK98                                     S. QJ43
        H. 53                                       H. 6
        D. 975                                      D. 863
        C. AQJ3                                     C. 109654

                              South
                              S. 1052
                              H. AJ109842
                              D. J
                              C. K7
```

A small spade. Partner has promised the jack and you

want a club lead through declarer's likely king.

IV.

```
                              North
                              S. KQJ97
                              H. AK109
                              D. 76
                              C. 82

        West                                        East
        S. 1052                                     S. 843
        H. 432                                      H. 6
        D. AJ9                                      D. Q532
        C. AKJ5                                     C. Q10943

                              South
                              S. A6
                              H. QJ875
                              D. K1084
                              C. 76
```

A small club. Partner's ten promises an equal honor,

which must be the queen. (It obviously isn't a double-

ton; and if you thought this meant shift to a spade,

reread the entire chapter - slowly.) You want a diamond lead through declarer's possible king before he discards diamonds on spades.

V.

                              North
                              S. QJ
                              H. AQ6
                              D. K109832
                              C. Q2

        West   East
        S. A10   S. K85432
        H. KJ1098754   H. none
        D. 5   D. 76
        C. 96   C. K8543

                              South
                              S. 976
                              H. 32
                              D. AQJ4
                              C. AJ107

Partner has either a heart void or the ace-king of clubs from his signal. Since the ace-king of clubs is unlikely (what would South have for an opening bid?), the heart shift at trick two figures to be right. Notice that partner does not encourage with the eight of spades to ask you to continue spades; instead he says, "I would like a shift, let's see if you can figure out what I have in mind".

VI.

North
S. Q5
H. 7
D. AQJ84
C. AQ1032

West
S. none
H. AK1043
D. 7652
C. J987

East
S. J842
H. J9862
D. K109
C. 5

South
S. AK109763
H. Q5
D. 3
C. K64

With your spade void you should interpret partner's
high heart as asking for a continuation. The continuation is right if partner has either Kxx or Jxxx
of spades. If partner had wanted a shift he would
have played a low heart and given you an option.
Notice that the primary meaning of a high card in
response to the lead of the king or ace is a request
for a continuation, even though dummy has a singleton!

VII.

                    North
                    S. KQJ
                    H. A1082
                    D. Q532
                    C. Q4

West   East
S. 2   S. A98643
H. 64   H. 53
D. 9864   D. AJ7
C. 1098765   C. K2

                    South
                    S. 1075
                    H. KQJ97
                    D. K10
                    C. AJ3

Partner has returned a high spade for you to ruff,

so it is not for you to reason why, it is for you

to do or die. Return the nine of diamonds (to deny

an honor) and let nature take its course. In this

case partner wins and gives you another spade ruff.

V. SIGNALLING VS. NO TRUMP CONTRACTS

As with suit contracts, the most important defensive signalling vs. no trump comes at trick one. Third hand must be prepared to signal properly to give partner the maximum amount of useful information.

I. THE LEAD OF THE ACE.

Unless there has been a preemptive bid or a clear-cut indication that either dummy or declarer has a long running suit, the lead of an ace shows great strength.

An ace is most commonly led against a no trump contract when the opening leader holds a four card suit (or longer), which is lacking one high honor; e.g., AKQ10, AQJ10, AKJ10, AKJxx. (In the case of AQJ10 the queen is often led when the opening leader has no outside entry.)

Therefore, the opening leader is interested in two things:
1. Does partner have the missing high honor?
2. If not, how many small cards does partner have?

In response to the lead of an ace, third hand: throws any high honor (jack or better) he may hold; or, barring possession of a high honor, gives a distributional count. The count is given by playing the top card from a doubleton, low from three, and second highest from four.

                         North
                         S.76

West   East
S. AKQ102   S. 94

                         South
                         S. J853

West leads the ace and East signals with the nine.
West knows that East does NOT have the jack because
he did not play it at trick one. Therefore, the nine
must be the start of a high-low from a doubleton.
South must have four to the jack and West is usually
best advised to shift and wait for partner to lead
through declarer's guarded jack.

Change one card:

                         North
                         S. 76

West   East
S. AKQ102   S. 943

                         South
                         S. J85

West leads the ace and East plays the three. West
knows that South has the jack and that East has exactly
three spades because East did not start a high-low.
West KNOWS he can take five spade tricks.

Some bridge textbooks still tell you that third hand
must throw its highest card under the lead of an ace.
Those books are outdated. Burn them.

```
Neither side vul.
Dealer South              North
                          S. 987
                          H. K84
                          D. AQ3
                          C. J432

        West                              East
        S. AKJ54                          S. 1032
        H. 76                             H. J10952
        D. J109                           D. 7652
        C. 975                            C. K

                          South
                          S. Q6
                          H. AQ3
                          D. K84
                          C. AQ1086


        South        West         North        East
        1NT          Pass         3NT          All pass
```

Opening lead: Ace of spades

East plays the deuce at trick one (low from three when partner leads the ace) and West reasons that either East has a singleton, in which case it is unlikely the hand will be defeated, or East has three small and declarer's queen will drop under the king. The king is played at trick two and West races off five spade tricks.

Those players who drop the ten at trick one to show their highest card leave partner with an impossible guess at trick two: If the ten is from 10x West must shift, but if it is from 10xx the king must be played. Bridge is a tough enough game without giving partner additional migraines.

II. THE LEAD OF THE KING.

Although the lead of the king is occasionally made from
short suit holdings such as AKx or KQx, more often than
not the opening leader will have led from combinations
headed by KQJ or KQ10. (With KQ9x(x) or less, fourth
highest is led.)

If the opening leader has led from a KQJ combination,
even if partner plays low and the king is allowed to
hold, it is almost always right to continue with a
second high honor. But even here trouble can arise.
Take this extremely common situation:

```
                      North  (Dummy)
                      S. 32

West                                    East
S. KQJ98                                S. 65

                      South
                      S. A1074
```

West leads the king and queen, both allowed to hold,
partner following with the five and then the six. Now
how does West know whether or not East has the ten?
(As we will soon see, East should play the five and six
from 1065 as well as from 65 doubleton.) The answer is
available but not many players are familiar with it.

If West wants his partner to play his highest remaining
card he plays the jack after the king is allowed to hold.
If he does not he plays the queen.

In the above example West can afford for his partner to play the ten so he continues with the jack. When East does not play the ten, West knows that South remains with the ace-ten.

In other words, if East's original spade holding is 1065 he plays the five under the king and the ten under the jack. But if West instead continues with the queen after the king is allowed to hold, East follows with the six.

This little convention can be invaluable in the following common but equally frustrating position:

```
                    North (Dummy)
                    S. 32

West                                    East
S. QJ1087                               S. 954

                    South
                    S. AK6
```

West leads the queen of spades, East plays the four, and South wins the king. Later West gets in and plays a spade honor which is allowed to hold the trick, East playing the five. West must now guess whether South remains with the bare ace or the A9. Some Wests must guess, that is, but not you. If you hold the West cards your second play is the ten, asking partner to play his highest remaining spot card. East plays the nine and West knows what is going on.

Notice that to continue with the lower honor of an original three card sequence you must be prepared for partner to

play his highest remaining spot card. If you cannot
afford for partner to make this play, lead the immediately touching honor.

North (Dummy)
S. 32

West   East
S. KQJ6   S. 1054

South
S. A987

West leads the king, which holds, East playing the four.
West continues with the queen, telling partner not to unblock with his highest remaining spot card. When East
plays the five the second time it is true that West cannot
be sure of the position, but at least no tricks have van-
ished.

When the opening leader has led from a KQ10 combination
and the king holds, things are not always so clear.*

North (Dummy)
S. 62

West   East
S. KQ1074   S. 983

South
S. AJ5

The number of tricks that have been lost by the defense
in this common situation would require 100 abacuses
working 24 hours a day to compute.

*Many experts lead the queen from KQ10 and partner is ex-
  pected to play the jack if he has it.

West leads the king and it is allowed to hold. All too
often West will continue the suit, giving declarer an un-
deserved trick with the jack. Much of the time the fault
can be placed with East who has mistakenly played "second
high" under his partner's lead of the king.

WHEN PARTNER LEADS A KING HE WANTS TO KNOW WHETHER YOU HAVE
A HIGH HONOR - THE JACK, QUEEN OR ACE. IF YOU DO, SIGNAL
BY PLAYING YOUR NEXT HIGHEST CARD; IF YOU DO NOT, PLAY LOW.

In the example given, East plays the three, denying a high
honor, and West shifts. Those misguided souls who play
the eight at trick one are courting disaster.

An important exception arises in the case of a doubleton
jack. In this case the jack is generally thrown under the
king if dummy has two or three small cards. If dummy has
10xx or 9xxx, third hand simply plays low.

With a doubleton ace, third hand usually overtakes, and
with a doubleton queen he plays low; if the opening leader
wants to see the queen he leads the ace.

Neither side vul.
Dealer North

                        North
                        S. 43
                        H. 1065
                        D. AKJ98
                        C. 764

West   East
S. KQ1062   S. 987
H. J3   H. Q9872
D. 1072   D. Q53
C. KJ9   C. 108

                        South
                        S. AJ5
                        H. AK4
                        D. 64
                        C. AQ532

North	East	South	West
Pass	Pass	1C	1S
2D	Pass	3NT	All pass

Opening lead: King of Spades

West leads the king of spades; East plays the seven and
South the five. West can definitely read East's seven
as a non-signal because it must be East's lowest spade.
West can see the deuce, three, four, five and six of
spades between his own hand and dummy, and the play to
the first trick.

Remember, it is the relative size, not the absolute size,
of a card that determines whether or not it is a signal.
Thus, the number of lower cards which are not visible
determine whether or not partner's card is a signal.

Stop and think about it for a moment. If you can see every card lower than the one that your partner has played you know for a certainty that he cannot be signalling.*

If you notice only one card missing beneath the card partner has played, he may or may not be signalling. However, if there are two or more lower cards missing it is a very good bet that he is signalling.

*But when either dummy or declarer is marked for length in a suit you must accept the fact that partner cannot always signal encouragement (a high spot card) for fear of establishing a trick for declarer.

North (dummy)
S. Q1082

West
S. K4

East
S. AJ93

South
S. 765

Suppose that during the course of the hand West makes the inspired shift to the king of spades. Even though East loves the lead all he can do is play the three, his lowest card, because any higher card helps establish a later trick for South. Therefore, when four or five cards appear in dummy or are marked in declarer's hand, you must allow partner a certain amount of leeway in his signalling.

Maybe now you can see why a three might be a signal if the deuce is missing and why a seven or eight cannot be a signal if all the lower cards are visible.

Back to the hand. West shifts to the jack of hearts and East signals with the nine, declarer winning the king. A diamond is led to the jack and queen, East returning the nine of spades.

The only way declarer can make this hand is to win the ace, run the diamonds, come back to the ace of hearts and throw West in with the jack of spades, forcing him to lead away from his king of clubs. Not an easy play. However, if West continues a spade at trick two, even Aunt Emmy brings this one home.

III. THE LEAD OF THE QUEEN.

The queen lead can be easily mastered. It will either be from QJ10 or QJ9, with or without extended length.** (Many times it is right to lead fourth best from holdings such as QJ10x(x) and QJ9x(x), particularly when the suit has been bid by the opponents. You are hoping partner has the ten, king or ace and you will be better off to lead low if he does.)

**Or from KQ10 with length if you and your partner use that convention.

All partner wants to know when he leads the queen is
whether or not you have a high honor. In this case the
significant honors are the ace, king and TEN. The general rule, therefore, is to signal if you have one of
these cards and play low if you don't. With a doubleton
ten, king or ace, the honor is usually played at once.

<u>North</u> (Dummy)
S. 752

<u>West</u>
S. Q

<u>East</u>
S. 1083, 103
S. K83, K3
S. A83, A3

With each of the three card holdings above, East plays the
eight. With the doubleton holdings he plays his honor.
HOWEVER, IF EAST HAS ONLY SMALL CARDS HE PLAYS LOW TO DENY
AN HONOR.

IV.   THE LEAD OF THE JACK.

This lead was discussed in the chapter "Leads vs. No Trump
Contracts". The lead of the jack denies a higher honor,
and third hand plays accordingly. Typically, third hand
would signal with honor holdings such as Q83, K74 by playing the eight in the first case and the seven in the second.
Holding the ace, third hand must judge how to defend and
whether or not to win the first trick. His decision will
be based upon the appearance of dummy and the number of
ready tricks available to the declarer.

```
East-West vul.              North
Dealer South                S. 73
                            H. 53
                            D. AQJ986
                            C. A103

     West                                          East
     S. J10942                                     S. A86
     H. AQJ2                                        H. 10974
     D. 42                                          D. 107
     C. 64                                          C. QJ87

                            South
                            S. KQ5
                            H. K86
                            D. K53
                            C. K952

     South        West          North         East
     1C           Pass          1D            Pass
     1NT          Pass          3NT           All pass
```

Opening lead: Jack of spades

East knows at once that South has the king-queen of spades,
for two tricks, along with six diamonds and at least one
club. Therefore, the defense's only chance rests in the
heart suit. East wins the ace of spades and shifts to the
ten of hearts. Four heart tricks later the defenders are
quite pleased with themselves. However, with no lead convention to guide him, East might well return a spade at
trick two, and then it would be North-South who would be
quite pleased.

V.   THE LEAD OF THE TEN.

This shows either AJ10, KJ10, or top of a sequence. If
the jack is visible it is obviously top of a sequence.
If the nine is visible it is obviously from AJ10 or KJ10.

Confusion is minimal if the above is remembered. When in
doubt assume the stronger holdings.

                        North (Dummy)
                        S. 543

West   East
S. KJ1072   S. A6

                        South
                        S. Q98

West leads the ten, and even though East cannot see the
jack or nine to clarify the suit, he optimistically assumes
his partner has the strong holding, in this case KJ10.
Accordingly, East wins the ace and returns the suit. If
the jack, for example, falls from South under East's ace,
East must revise his conception of the position, knowing
that West has led from top of a sequence and that declarer
began life with KQJ.

VI.   THE LEAD OF THE NINE.

      The nine is led from holdings headed by A109, K109, Q109,
      or top of a sequence. If the ten is visible, then, obvi-
      ously, the lead is from top of a sequence. If the ten is
      not visible, the stronger holdings are assumed.

                        North (Dummy)
                        S.654

West   East
S. Q10982   S. A7

                        South
                        S. KJ3

West leads the nine, and even though East cannot see the
ten he assumes that West has led from interior strength.

If dummy has the ten East knows that South has the KQJ.

VII. SIGNALLING WHEN PARTNER LEADS A SPOT CARD.

The lead of a low spot card is usually fourth best. Normally the problem will not be one of signalling, because third hand simply protects partner by playing third hand high. However, when the DUMMY wins the trick, third hand can make an intelligent signal.

There are two possibilities when the dummy takes the trick:

1) The trick will be taken with an ace or a king.

2) The trick will be taken with a lower card.

In the first case, signal only if you have a high honor (queen or king).

<pre>
                        North (Dummy)
                        S. A7

West   East
S. J10432   S. Q96

                        South
                        S. K85
</pre>

West leads the three of spades. If dummy plays the ace, East plays the nine to indicate the possession of either the king or queen (most likely the queen because declarer normally ducks the opening lead if he has the queen).

IF DUMMY WINS THE TRICK WITH A CARD LOWER THAN THE KING, THIRD HAND GIVES THE COUNT SIGNAL.

West	North (Dummy)	East
S. K8743	S. QJ10	S. 962

South
S. A5

West leads the four of spades and dummy plays the ten.
East, who cannot beat the ten, gives the count signal.
He does this by playing high-low with a doubleton, low
from three or five, and second high from four (just as
if partner had led the ace or if _declarer_ had attacked
dummy's long suit).

The moment West sees the deuce he knows East has three
spades (unless the deuce happens to be a singleton),
and if West gets the lead early he can safely return a
small spade to drive out the ace.

One exception:
If the bidding has already marked the distribution of the suit,
third hand can signal the possession of the jack if the queen
if played from dummy.

North
S. Q4

West		East
S. K1093		S. J82

South
S. A765

Assume the bidding has marked South with exactly four spades
and West leads the three against either a suit or more likely
a no trump contract. When dummy's queen is played, East plays
the eight to show the jack.

Neither side vul.
Dealer South

                         North
                         S. J109
                         H. J109
                         D. K84
                         C. A1084

        West   East
        S. AQ843   S. 75
        H. K76   H. 854
        D. 1093   D. J765
        C. 96   C. K752

                         South
                         S. K62
                         H. AQ32
                         D. AQ2
                         C. QJ3

        South   West   North   East
        1NT   Pass   3NT *   All pass

* Don't be a slave to the point count. With nine points
  and two or three tens raise to 3NT. Besides, you don't
  have to play the hand, partner does.

Opening lead: Four of spades

Dummy wins the nine and East, who cannot beat dummy's card,
gives a count signal with the seven, showing a doubleton.
The jack of hearts is finessed into West who now knows
South's spade king is guarded. West shifts to the ten of
diamonds and declarer cannot come to nine tricks without
the club finesse. When this loses and a spade is returned
declarer is defeated.

The previous hand may look easy to defend, but change it
slightly to this:

```
                        North
                        S. J109
                        H. J109
                        D. K83
                        C. A1084

        West                            East
        S. AQ843                        S. 752
        H. K76                          H. 854
        D. 1092                         D. 764
        C. 96                           C. KQ72

                        South
                        S. K6
                        H. AQ32
                        D. AQJ5
                        C. J53
```

Now if West doesn't lay down his ace of spades upon gaining the lead with the king of hearts, declarer runs off
with nine tricks. But West knows to lay down the ace of
spades because at trick one East plays the deuce to show
three spades. Now West knows declarer's king will nestle
gently under his ace.

We are now left with a signal that occurs with relative
frequency against no trump contracts in the middle game.
It is our old friend, the count signal.

VIII. THE COUNT SIGNAL.

This signal has a great similarity to the signal we have
just been discussing, namely signalling when dummy wins
the first trick with a card lower than the king. It comes
up time and time again when dummy has a long suit.

```
                    North (Dummy)
                    S. KQJ104


West                                        East
S. 732                                      S. A98


                    South
                    S. 65
```

South leads a spade and WEST must give East a distributional count; then East will know how many spades South
had originally and which spade he must win in order to
shut South out of dummy.

When giving the distributional count signal (almost always given by the defender who is weaker in dummy's long
suit), play high-low with a doubleton, the lowest card
from three or five cards, and second highest from four.
(In some cases second highest will be too valuable a
card to waste, for it could conceivably take a trick.
In that case play third highest.)

In the example given, West plays the deuce, which East
counts as a three card holding (it couldn't be from five
because then declarer would be void) and wins the second
spade trick.

```
                    North (Dummy)
                    S. QJ109

West                                    East
S. 8765                                 S. A32


                    South
                    S. K4
```

South leads the king of spades and West plays the
seven (second highest from four). East reasons that
either the seven is top of a doubleton, in which case
South has four spades, or the seven is second highest
from four, in which case declarer has a doubleton.
Ninety-nine times out of a hundred the bidding will
be sufficiently illuminating to determine which is
which, but in this case East assumes that declarer
has two spades and wins the second round. (If declarer has four spades it is immaterial which spade
East takes.)

Both sides vul.
Dealer South

                              North
                              S. 74
                              H. Q32
                              D. 65
                              C. AQJ842

        West   East
        S. J1096   S. Q85
        H. 108   H. K9764
        D. J987   D. Q102
        C. 973   C. K6

                              South
                              S. AK32
                              H. AJ5
                              D. AK43
                              C. 105

        South   West   North   East
        1D   Pass   2C   Pass
        3NT   All pass

Opening lead: Jack of spades

East signals with the eight and declarer wins the king.
At trick two declarer plays the ten of clubs and West
gives count, playing the three. Dummy plays low and
East, who is a student of higher mathematics, counts
declarer for a doubleton and nonchalantly plays low.
(East knows that the spade suit cannot be run because
the lead of the jack denies a higher honor, remember?).
Declarer repeats the club finesse; East wins, and returns
the queen of spades.

With subsequent best defense declarer cannot make three
no trump. But try to beat this hand if East wins the first
club.

And please don't say that South might have played the ace
of clubs the second time. Any South who makes that type
of play is either so bad that you shouldn't be wasting
your time in the same game with him or his eyesight is so
good that you also shouldn't be playing in the same game
with him.

Briefly, the count signal is given in three common situations when defending against no trump:

1. When partner leads an ace and third hand has
    no honor card (jack or higher) to unblock.

2. When partner leads a suit and dummy takes
    the trick with the queen or a lower card.

3. When declarer leads up to a long suit in
    the dummy or, conceivably, when declarer
    is trying to establish a long suit in his
    own hand.

The signal is invariable: With two cards play high-low,
with three or five play your lowest and with four play
second high unless it will cost a trick (usually occurs
in "3"), in which case you play third highest.

Incidentally, "2" and "3" apply against suit contracts as
well.

CAPSULE SUMMARY OF OPENING LEADS
AND THE PROPER SIGNAL TO THEM BY THIRD HAND

LEAD OF THE ACE: Unblock any high honor (jack or better) or, lacking a high honor, give the count signal.

LEAD OF THE KING: Signal with the highest spot card you can afford if you hold the ace, queen, or jack; overtake with the ace doubleton, unblock with jack doubleton; play low with all other holdings.

LEAD OF THE QUEEN: Signal with the highest spot card you can afford if you hold the ace, king, or ten; overtake with the doubleton ace or king, unblock with the doubleton ten; play low with all other holdings. *

* If you and your partner lead the queen from KQ10 combinations then it is mandatory for third hand to drop the jack, regardless of length, under the lead of the queen.

LEAD OF THE JACK: Denies a higher honor. Signal if you hold the queen or king and use your judgment with the ace. Play low with all other holdings.

LEAD OF THE TEN: Shows either AJ10, KJ10, or top of a
                    sequence. If dummy has only small cards,
                    overtake with the ace or king. If either
                    dummy or third hand has the jack the lead
                    is known to be from top of a sequence.
                    Third hand must then use his judgment
                    when holding the ace. With the jack visi-
                    ble in dummy third hand should not play
                    the king unless dummy's jack is played,
                    for declarer is marked with the ace-queen.
                    If the nine is visible the opening leader
                    is marked with the AJ10 or KJ10 combina-
                    tion and third hand should play accord-
                    ingly. (Play the ace, king, or queen on
                    the ten.)

LEAD OF THE NINE: Shows either two higher honors (A109,
                    K109, or Q109) or top of a sequence. If
                    dummy or third hand has the ten the lead
                    must be a top card. If the ten is not
                    visible the lead is assumed to be from an
                    interior sequence. If dummy has no honor
                    card, third hand plays high on the lead
                    of the nine. (See the chapter on "Third
                    Hand Play".)

LEAD OF A LOWER SPOT CARD: These leads are all assumed to be
                             fourth best, but care must be taken
                             to make sure. If a high spot is led
                             partner may have something like 9732
                             or 8752 and may have chosen to play
                             a high spot rather than his fourth
                             best.

I. Both sides vul.   North
    Dealer South   S. QJ9
                                 H. K72
                                 D. 987
                                 C. A976

         West   East
         S. K10654   S. 832
         H. 10985   H. Q43
         D. AQ   D. 6542
         C. 53   C. QJ10

                                 South
                                 S. A7
                                 H. AJ6
                                 D. KJ103
                                 C. K842

         South   West   North   East
         1NT   Pass   3NT   All pass

    Opening lead: Five of spades

II. East-West vul.   North
    Dealer West   S. K5
                                 H. 83
                                 D. 63
                                 C. KQJ10987

         West   East
         S. QJ964   S. 32
         H. AKJ94   H. 652
         D. 108   D. AQ972
         C. 2   C. 654

                                 South
                                 S. A1087
                                 H. Q107
                                 D. KJ54
                                 C. A3

         West   North   East   South
         1S   3C*   Pass   3NT
         All pass

    * Weak jump overcall

    Opening lead: Ace of hearts

III. East-West vul.
Dealer South

North
S. K74
H. 832
D. 432
C. QJ103

West
S. 3
H. J1097
D. J987
C. 9842

East
S. A109652
H. 64
D. Q10
C. A76

South
S. QJ8
H. AKQ5
D. AK65
C. K5

South	West	North	East
2NT	Pass	3NT	All pass

Opening lead: Jack of hearts

IV. Both sides vul.
Dealer North

North
S. A2
H. AK2
D. KQJ1064
C. Q4

West
S. J10965
H. 98
D. 92
C. KJ95

East
S. 843
H. J6543
D. A7
C. A83

South
S. KQ7
H. Q107
D. 853
C. 10762

North	East	South	West
1D	Pass	1NT	Pass
3NT	All pass		

Opening lead: Jack of spades

KEY PLAYS

I.   When dummy wins the first trick with an honor, East plays
     the deuce to show three spades. When West wins the queen
     of diamonds at trick two he can safely continue with a low
     spade, knowing South's ace will fall.

II. When East plays the deuce of hearts at trick one, he denies
     the queen and shows an odd number of small hearts (the
     count signal). West must assume declarer has the ace of
     clubs, otherwise East will always get in to lead a heart,
     and he shifts to a diamond. The three no trump bid has
     located the spade ace, and there is too great a chance
     that declarer has nine black tricks with a spade shift.
     East wins the ace of diamonds and returns a heart to
     defeat the contract two tricks.

III. South wins the first heart and plays the king of clubs.
     West plays the eight (second highest to show four), and
     East wins the second club, cutting South off from dummy's
     suit. Later East manages his spades so that South cannot
     use the king for an entry, and the hand is defeated one
     trick.

IV. Dummy wins the spade ace and plays the king of diamonds
     to East's ace. East can count declarer for three spade
     tricks (jack denies a higher honor), five diamonds, and
     at least two hearts, for ten. Obviously, East must shift
     to a club, a low one. West wins the king, returns a low
     club to East's ace, and the subsequent club return from
     East buries another contract.

SIGNALLING VS. NO TRUMP CONTRACTS   PROBLEMS

Assume that you are defending three no trump in the East position
(the bidding has gone 1NT - 3NT). In each case you are given your
partner's opening lead and you are to answer which card you should
normally play.

I. A.   North (Dummy)
                                S. 73

        West   East (You)
        S. A   a.   S. Q82
                                                    b.   S. 1073
                                                    c.   S. 9752
                                                    d.   S. 86
                                                    e.   S. J96
                                                    f.   S. K95

                                South
                                ???

    B.   North (Dummy)
                                S. 73

        West   East (You)
        S. K   a.   S. J82
                                                    b.   S. A8
                                                    c.   S. J6
                                                    d.   S. Q62
                                                    e.   S. 952
                                                    f.   S. 82

                                South
                                ???

    C.   North (Dummy)
                                S. 73

        West   East (You)
        S. Q   a.   S. K5
                                                    b.   S. K862
                                                    c.   S. A4
                                                    d.   S. 102
                                                    e.   S. 854
                                                    f.   S. A82

                                South
                                ???

D.   North (Dummy)
                            S. 73

West   East (You)
S. 10   a. S. KJ5
                                                        b. S. KQ5
                                                        c. S. A82
                                                        d. S. K6
                                                        e. S. Q865
                                                        f. S. AQJ82

                            South
                            ???

Now a more practical test of your newly acquired skills. On the
following four rubber bridge problems you will be given all the
necessary information to come up with the killing defense. Let's
see if you're up to it!

II. A.   North (Dummy)
                            S. 1043
                            H. AQ5
                            D. 75
                            C. KQJ104

        West (You)   East
        S. 65   D. 9
        H. 732
        D. AKJ632
        C. 73

                            South
                            D. 10

        South   West   North   East
        1NT   Pass   3NT   All Pass

You lead the ace of diamonds, partner plays the nine
and declarer the ten. What do you lead at trick two?

B.
                        North (Dummy)
                        S. Q109
                        H. K2
                        D. J1094
                        C. A876

West (You)   East
S. AJ765   S. 2
H. J103
D. K5
C. 932

                        South
                        S. 4

South   West   North   East
1NT   Pass   3NT   All pass

You lead the six of spades and dummy's nine wins the

trick, partner playing the deuce and declarer the four.

The jack of diamonds is led at trick two, partner plays

the deuce and you win the king. Now what?

C.
                        North (Dummy)
                        S. 74
                        H. A3
                        D. 763
                        C. AKJ973

West   East (You)
S. J   S. A82
                                        H. QJ106
                                        D. 1085
                                        C. 1052

                        South
                        S. 5

South   West   North   East
Pass   Pass   1C   Pass
2NT   Pass   3NT   All pass

West leads the jack of spades. Plan your defense.

D.
       North (Dummy)
       S. Q6
       H. 863
       D. KJ1093
       C. 853

West   East (You)
H. J   S. K1098
               H. 42
               D. A72
               C. J1097

       South
       H. K

South	West	North	East
2NT	Pass	3NT	All pass

Your partner leads the jack of hearts, you play the
deuce and declarer wins the king. Declarer plays the
queen of diamonds, partner the four and dummy the
king. Do you take this trick? Which diamond do you
plan to take if the suit is continued? What do you
return after winning your ace of diamonds?

I. A. a. The queen.   Partner is asking you to throw your
                          honor if you have one, so do it!

        b. The three.   Low from three small when partner
                          leads the ace. You are giving your
                          partner a count.

        c. The seven.   Second best from four small when
                          partner leads the ace. Again you
                          are simply giving count. (Your
                          second play is usually the next
                          one down the line, in this case
                          the five.)

        d. The eight.   Top of a doubleton when the ace is
                          led.

        e. The jack.   The jack or better is considered an
                          honor when partner leads the ace
                          against no trump.

        f. The king.   It's not for you to reason why, it's
                          for you to do or die. If you play
                          the nine, even if you do it with a
                          smile, your partner will play you
                          for a doubleton.

B. a. The eight.   Showing an honor...either the jack, queen or ace.

     b. The ace.   Unblocking so your partner can run his suit.

     c. The jack.   With a doubleton jack an unblock is usually correct.

     d. The six.   Showing an honor.

     e. The deuce.   Denying an honor.

     f. The deuce.   Denying an honor. Remember, you give count when your partner leads an ace, but not when he leads any other honor.

C. a. The king.   To unblock the suit for partner.

     b. The eight.   A signal here shows either the ace, king or ten.

     c. The ace.   To unblock.

     d. The ten.   Partner must have at least the QJ9 to lead the queen, so the ten should not cost a trick. If East had three or more cards headed by the ten he would simply signal with his second highest card (10752).

e. The four.   Denying an honor.

f. The eight.   Usually better than the ace since
                     declarer may be reluctant to hold
                     up if third hand does not go up
                     with the ace.

D. a. The king.   To start an unblock. Declarer has
                     the ace-queen, but we have to start
                     unblocking for partner who probably
                     has something like 1098xx.

    b. The queen.   Either declarer has the AJ or partner
                     has it. We shall soon see.

    c. The ace.   Partner is very likely to hold KJ10;
                     otherwise declarer holds the KQJ and,
                     if he has another card in the suit, is
                     very likely to have bid it.

    d. The king.   In case partner has the AJ10. If the
                     king loses to the ace you know declarer
                     has AQJ. (Ugh)

    e. The queen.   If partner has KJ10 it won't cost, and
                     if partner has AJ10 you will have clari-
                     fied the position.

        f. The eight.   Partner has made an unusually good

                            lead (for a change) and you should

                            let him know. In fact, if the nine

                            happens to turn up in dummy you can

                            afford to play the jack.

II. A.   North
                                 S. 1043
                                 H. AQ5
                                 D. 75
                                 C. KQJ104

        West   East
        S. 65   S. A9872
        H. 732   H. 984
        D. AKJ632   D. 94
        C. 73   C. 652

                                 South
                                 S. KQJ
                                 H. KJ106
                                 D. Q108
                                 C. A98

Partner's play of the nine of diamonds at trick one has at
once denied possession of the queen and shown a doubleton.
Clearly it would not be in your best interest to cash the
king and set up declarer's queen. Instead try to find
partner with an entry so he can lead through declarer's
guarded queen of diamonds.

Judging by the looks of the dummy the best chance is to
find partner with the ace of spades (if he has the ace of
clubs he is bound to get the lead early whether you lead
the suit or not) before declarer runs off a fistful of

tricks in hearts and clubs. The proper shift at trick two
is to the six of spades. Partner wins the ace and returns
a diamond to defeat the contract three tricks.

B.
```
                        North
                        S. Q109
                        H. K2
                        D. J1094
                        C. A876

    West                                East
    S. AJ765                            S. 832
    H. J103                             H. Q9876
    D. K5                               D. 832
    C. 932                              C. K5

                        South
                        S. K4
                        H. A54
                        D. AQ76
                        C. QJ104
```

Partner's play of the deuce of spades at trick one has in-
dicated three small cards. Therefore, the best chance to
defeat the contract is to hope partner has a club trick and
return a second small spade, retaining one spade in partner's
hand to lead in case he does have an entry.

With the actual lie of the cards declarer will be forced to
take the club finesse and the subsequent spade return will
defeat the contract one trick.

Notice how important it is to know HOW MANY spades partner
has. If partner plays a higher spade at trick one, showing
a doubleton, you have to reverse tactics and try to defeat
the contract in the heart suit, for your spade suit is dead
if partner holds a doubleton.

C.   North
                                S. 74
                                H. A3
                                D. 763
                                C. AKJ973

       West   East
       S. J10963   S. A82
       H. 987   H. QJ106
       D. AQJ4   D. 1085
       C. Q   C. 1052
                                South
                                S. KQ5
                                H. K542
                                D. K92
                                C. 864

From partner's lead of the jack you know declarer has both
the king and queen of spades (jack denies higher); you also
know that declarer has six club tricks staring you in the
face, as well as the ace of hearts.

In other words, outside of the diamond suit declarer has at
least nine tricks that you can SEE. Therefore, the only
hope is to take four tricks in diamonds before declarer gets
the lead.

In order to take four diamond tricks partner needs either
the AKJx or the AQJx. In either case it is safe to lead the
ten, and in the actual hand it is mandatory. If any other
diamond is led declarer simply ducks the nine into partner's
hand and he will be unable to run the suit. Notice how important it was to know what partner had in spades. Playing
the old way, East has to guess whether to return a spade or
a diamond. Even great players like you sometimes make bad
guesses when you don't know what partner has!

D.

```
                         North
                         S.  Q6
                         H.  863
                         D.  KJ1093
                         C.  853
        West                                     East
        S.  732                                  S.  K1098
        H.  J1097                                H.  42
        D.  864                                  D.  A72
        C.  Q62                                  C.  J1097
                         South
                         S.  AJ54
                         H.  AKQ5
                         D.  Q5
                         C.  AK4
```

Partner's play of the four of diamonds (his lowest) has shown exactly three cards; therefore, declarer has two diamonds. Plan to win the SECOND ROUND OF DIAMONDS.

At that point shift to the jack of clubs (a heart also works). You know the heart suit has no future, for declarer must have AKQ (jack denies higher). Declarer is in big trouble and cannot make the hand at this point if the defense plays correctly. His best bet the way the cards lie is to win the ace of clubs and play the jack of spades, hoping to establish the queen as an entry to the diamond suit. However, if you are smart enough to be playing jack denies higher, and to be using the count signal when declarer attacks dummy's long suit, you are surely smart enough to prevent declarer from getting to dummy to use his established diamonds. Once the jack of spades is ducked, declarer is out of business. Notice how easy the hand is if you either take the first diamond or allow declarer to steal two diamond tricks. In the first case he has 11 tricks, in the second, 9.

VI. DISCARDS

Literally millions of points have been thrown away by defenders who make faulty discards. We all know how tough it is to discard on the run of a long suit, but on most hands there are clues which help you know what to slough.

I. Try to keep length parity with the dummy for as long as possible.

```
North-South vul.        North
Dealer South            S. AQ93
                        H. 764
                        D. 54
                        C. KQJ10

        West                            East (You)
        S. J8                           S. 10752
        H. KQJ1052                      H. 93
        D. A82                          D. J1097
        C. 84                           C. 765

                        South
                        S. K64
                        H. A8
                        D. KQ63
                        C. A932
```

South	West	North	East
1NT	2H	3H*	Pass
3NT	All pass		

* Stayman

Opening lead: King of hearts

South wins the second heart and peels off three rounds of clubs. On the third club West discards the eight of diamonds -- a high spot card announcing strength. Now, when the fourth club is played East can throw away a diamond with no discomfort.

But what does East discard on the fourth club if West
follows to the first three? East reasons thus: "A
diamond discard is costly when declarer has AKQx or
AKQxx; however, in that case declarer has nine tricks
anyway. But a spade discard will cost every time declarer has Kx or Kxx and partner has the ace of diamonds,
for then declarer has only eight tricks if he cannot take
four spades. So a diamond discard is still correct."

If all this reasoning seems too sophisticated for you at
this point, relax. Just try to remember that if you see
a four card suit in the dummy and you also have four, be
very reluctant to part with one unless (1) all of dummy's
cards are higher than yours, (2) you have reason to believe
that partner also has four cards in the suit or (3) you
simply have to hang on to something else even more valuable (unlikely).

The same reasoning applies when you have cause to believe
(perhaps from the bidding or lead) that the closed hand
has a four card suit in which you also hold four. Again,
hang on if you can.

II. When faced with a choice of discarding a high card in a
suit you want led, or a low card in a suit you do not
want led, it is almost always right (particularly at no
trump) to make the negative discard so that you maintain
the original length of your strong suit.

This should not be confused with the preceding example in which the strong suit was already established; West then signalled with a high diamond to show East his entry, at the same time informing East that he could safely discard diamonds.

```
Both sides vul.         North
Dealer South            S. Q107
                        H. 765
                        D. 74
                        C. J10954

    West                                    East
    S. 98                                   S. 65432
    H. K93                                  H. AQ84
    D. J8632                                D. 105
    C. A32                                  C. 86

                        South
                        S. AKJ
                        H. J102
                        D. AKQ9
                        C. KQ7

    South       West        North       East
    2C          Pass        2D          Pass
    2NT         Pass        3NT         All pass
```

Opening lead: Three of diamonds

South wins the opening lead with the king (but West knows that South has AKQ9 from partner's play of the 10) and plays the king of clubs, which West ducks. East starts a count signal by playing the eight. West wins the third club and East must make a discard. He can discard a low spade to discourage that suit or a high heart to encourage that suit. The low spade is best - by far.

If East discards the eight of hearts (which is only the setting trick) and West dutifully returns a heart, the defenders will cash three tricks in the suit, but the declarer will take the rest. If East discards a low spade (which is equivalent to discarding a high heart), he retains his heart length and the defenders are able to take four hearts and a club to defeat the contract.

III. When discarding from a complete honor sequence (J1098, QJ109, KQJ10, AKQJ), a discard of the HIGHEST honor guarantees possession of the lower honors. Often this graphic description of your holding alleviates partner's discarding problems.

```
                        North
                        S.  K76
                        H.  K4
                        D.  KQJ106
                        C.  732

West                                          East
S.  J1094                                     S.  532
H.  10932                                     H.  J76
D.  875                                       D.  32
C.  K4                                        C.  QJ1098

                        South
                        S.  AQ8
                        H.  AQ85
                        D.  A94
                        C.  A65
```

South plays seven no trump (bad bidding will not be put into this book) and West leads the jack of spades, which declarer wins with the ace.

Next comes five rounds of diamonds. West could be in trouble on the discards. (Keep in mind that from his point of view declarer might hold AQxx of spades, which would make it necessary for West to clutch each and every one of his spades ever so tightly.) But East saves the day! His first discard is the <u>queen</u> of clubs, announcing possession of the lower club honors and making it possible for West to discard both of his clubs if he so chooses. He so chooses.

For his remaining two discards East discards spades, giving West a count on that suit. If West is alive at the table he hangs on to his four hearts -- the difference between defeating the grand slam and letting it make.

No more of these age old cries, "but partner, how could I tell?"

IV. When discarding from a suit that you obviously don't want led, give the count signal.

```
East-West vul.              North
Dealer North                S. 104
                            H. 83
                            D. KQJ965
                            C. 932
           West·                                  East
           S. 8532                                S. J7
           H. 952           South                 H. QJ764
           D. A3            S. AKQ96              D. 10872
           C. QJ84          H. AK10               C. K10
                            D. 4
                            C. A765
```

```
North         East          South         West
2D*           Pass          2S            Pass
3D            Pass          3NT           All Pass
*Weak Two Bid (Very Weak!)
```

West leads a club against South's three no trump. East wins the king and returns the ten. South ducks and West overtakes. When West returns the queen of clubs East must find a discard. East knows that his diamonds are worthless if South holds Ax or if West holds the singleton ace. The only critical case occurs when WEST holds Ax and will not know whether to win the first or the second round diamond trick. Therefore, East obligingly discards the EIGHT of diamonds to give partner the count.

West reads the discard as being from a four card suit (if it is from a doubleton a hold-up play is worthless as declarer has three diamonds) and wins the first diamond lead. South must then lose five tricks.

-155-

Now, when South leads a diamond at trick four West assumes that South has a singleton and rises with the ace. If East's discard of the eight was from a doubleton, then South has three and a hold-up would do no good. Besides, the bidding makes it impossible for South to have three diamonds. (See chapter on "Counting Declarer's Distribution".)

West cashes his club and exits with a major card, and South must lose a heart. (If West exits with a spade East must be careful not to permit the ten to become an entry if dummy plays low.)

V. When you are dying for your partner to lead a particular suit, a suit you cannot discard (perhaps you are void and want a ruff), discard negatively in the suit your partner is most apt to lead.

```
Both sides vul.          North
Dealer East              S. 985
                         H. 986
                         D. AQ104
                         C. Q108

      West                                          East
      S. J42                                        S. 3
      H. 102                                        H. AKQJ7
      D. 953                                        D. J762
      C. K7642                                      C. J95

                         South
                         S. AKQ10076
                         H. 543
                         D. K8
                         C. A3

      East          South          West          North
      1H            Dbl.           Pass          2D
      Pass          2S             Pass          3S
      Pass          4S             All pass
```

Opening lead: Ten of hearts

East overtakes and cashes three hearts. What should West discard on the third heart? West wants his partner to continue the suit in order to promote his jack of spades. How can he get his message across?

Well, he asks himself what suit partner is most likely to return looking at that dummy. Probably a club; so West discards the deuce of clubs to discourage the "obvious" shift. (An expert West discards the king of clubs, denying the ace and screaming bloody murder for a fourth heart. However, the deuce of clubs also shouts for a heart and won't scare poor partner out of his wits.)

VI. The defenders can often use the Rule of Eleven to help them make informative discards.

```
Both sides vul.            North
Dealer South               S. AQ4
                           H. 532
                           D. 85
                           C. K8765

        West                                       East
        S. 86                                       S. 97532
        H. J109                                     H. K876
        D. AK974                                    D. J103
        C. Q109                                     C. 4

                           South
                           S. KJ10
                           H. AQ4
                           D. Q62
                           C. AJ32

        South         West          North          East
        1NT           Pass          3NT            All pass
```

Opening lead: Seven of diamonds

East uses the Rule of Eleven and discovers that South has only one card higher than the seven. When his ten loses to the declarer's queen, East knows that his partner has led from an AK9 combination and that all of West's remaining diamonds are good. (West, however, does not know that all his diamonds are good. From his point of view South could have started with QJxx.)

When South leads a club to the king and a club back towards his hand, East has a chance to make an informative discard: the jack of diamonds. This clarifies the position for West and makes the defense simple.

-158-

If East did happen to start life with 10x or 10xx of diamonds plus the ace of hearts he would discard a high heart to tell partner how to put him in for a diamond lead through declarer.

VII. When discarding from a suit that partner has led, discard the same card you would have returned.

$$\begin{array}{c} \text{North} \\ \overline{\text{S. 74}} \end{array}$$

$$\begin{array}{c} \text{West} \\ \overline{\text{S. A10853}} \end{array} \qquad\qquad \begin{array}{c} \text{East} \\ \overline{\text{S. Q962}} \end{array}$$

$$\begin{array}{c} \text{South} \\ \overline{\text{S. KJ}} \end{array}$$

Assume South is playing a no trump contract and West leads the five of spades to the queen and king. West knows that South remains with the jack but he does not know that it will fall.

If East has a chance to make an early discard, he discards the deuce of spades to show an original holding of two or four cards. But since a good player rarely throws away his only remaining card in partner's suit, West can safely assume that East started with four.

If West is fortunate enough to obtain the lead later in the hand, he can confidently bang down the ace of spades knowing the jack will fall.

North
S. 74

West   East
S. A10853   S. Q92

South
S. KJ6

Again West leads the five against a no trump contract
and East's queen loses to South's king. If East gets
the lead early in the hand he returns the nine of spades,
the higher of his two remaining cards. If, instead, East
has to make a discard during the course of the hand, he
throws the nine of spades -- the same card he would have
returned had he obtained the lead, to show a three card
holding.

If East happens to have five cards in the suit partner
has led he discards his original fourth best, the same
card he would return. To wit:

North
S. 105

West   East
S. Q983   S. KJ762

South
S. A4

Assume South is playing a heart contract and West leads
the three of spades to the king and ace. If East later
gets the lead his proper return is the six, his original
fourth best. If instead East gets a chance to discard a
spade he discards the six. If he gets a second chance

to discard he plays the deuce, showing an original holding of three or five cards. (Remember, the bidding usually furnishes the necessary clues to partner's and declarer's distribution.)

VIII. Entry Creating Discards.

Nothing is more frustrating to a defender than to have good tricks established and no way to use them. In the chapter on "Third Hand Play" you will see how defenders maintain communication between their hands by using a ducking technique.

Yet another technique to insure suit establishment is the <u>unblocking discard</u>, which at times can be spectacular.

```
Neither side vul.        North
Dealer South             S.  KQ9
                         H.  743
                         D.  AQ6
                         C.  9543

    West                                      East
    S.  J32                                   S.  10876
    H.  KQJ109                                H.  52
    D.  1092                                  D.  J8754
    C.  Q6                                    C.  K2

                         South
                         S.  A54
                         H.  A86
                         D.  K3
                         C.  AJ1087

    South        West        North        East
    1NT          Pass        3NT          All pass
```

Opening lead: King of hearts

South wins the third heart and East must find a discard.
East should think in terms of creating an entry in partner's hand. Counting points tells him that West cannot
have an ace, but at most a king or a queen and a jack.

If West's high card is the king of diamonds that will
not help much, but if West has the queen of clubs ...
the discard of the king will promote an entry in West's
hand!

Notice that the discard cannot cost. If South has the
ace-queen of clubs the finesse is working anyway. On
the actual deal declarer is helpless once East discards
the king of clubs. If East woodenly throws a diamond
on a spade, declarer enters dummy with a spade and
leads a low club. If East plays the king he is allowed
to hold the trick, and if East plays low, South wins
the ace and plays a second club. In either case West
does not get the lead.

DO'S AND DONT'S ON DISCARDING

DO

1. Make your discards clear. A high-low indicates that (1) you have strength in the suit you have discarded or (2) you intend to keep that suit and partner should keep another while declarer is running off his long suit.

2. Keep the same length as dummy when discarding; particularly when dummy has four cards you should normally try to also keep four.

3. Discard the top card from an honor sequence; e.g., holding QJ109 discard the queen for complete clarity.

4. Give the count signal when discarding if it is _obvious_ to your partner that you have no interest in the suit and are only trying to help him. (Usually when dummy has a long, strong suit and the weaker hand is discarding from small cards in that suit.)

5. Discard from suits that declarer knows you hold. For example, if you have a long suit and partner has shown out during the play, declarer knows your exact length, so it is to your advantage to discard from that suit rather than give declarer any more information about your hand.

6. Discard the same card you would have returned if partner had led the suit. For example, if you hold Q94 and have already played the queen, discard the nine, the same card you would have returned. Similarly, with Q942 discard the deuce if you have already played the queen.

DON'T

1. Don't discard your last card in any suit partner has led unless you have absolutely no way of ever getting the lead later in the hand.

2. Against a no trump contract, as a rule, don't discard from any suit you want partner to lead. It is much more advantageous to discard from a suit or suits that you do not want partner to lead, thus saving your good cards in the suit you do want. A variation of this occurs when you discard from a suit you have led -- one which partner is likely to return. Generally, if you discard from your own suit it means you want partner to shift to another.

3. Don't waste high spot cards or honor cards to signal partner if you cannot afford to. This is a common error made by inexperienced players.

4. Don't discard down to a singleton or void unless defending a suit contract and there is a chance for a ruff. Once you show out of a suit declarer knows your partner's exact holding. (Another error that inexperienced players make.)

5. Don't worry about telling your partner every key card you own if you are the player that has the strong hand. Partner will not be involved too much in the defense and you will simply be helping declarer. On the other hand, if you have the weaker of the partnership holdings, you should go out of your way to give clear signals.

DISCARDS   LESSON HANDS

I.   Both sides vul.   North
     Dealer South   S. J1032
                             H. Q65
                             D. KJ8
                             C. KJ10

     West   East
     S. A9854   S. none
     H. 84   H. AKJ10
     D. 765   D. 109432
     C. 854   C. 7632

                             South
                             S. KQ76
                             H. 9732
                             D. AQ
                             C. AQ9

     South   West   North   East
     1NT   Pass   3NT   All pass

     Opening lead: Five of spades

II. Both sides vul.   North
     Dealer East   S. 1054
                             H. K9
                             D. J
                             C. KJ86432

     West   East
     S. 8   S. AKQ962
     H. J105   H. 3
     D. 10986542   D. 73
     C. AQ   C. 10975

                             South
                             S. J73
                             H. AQ87642
                             D. AKQ
                             C. none

     East   South   West   North
     2S *   4H   All pass

     * Weak Two Bid

     Opening lead: Eight of spades

III. Neither side vul.   North
      Dealer North   S. Q98
                              H. KJ
                              D. J743
                              C. J1073

      West   East
      S. 32   S. 7654
      H. Q987   H. 10654
      D. AKQ5   D. 108
      C. K65   C. A92

                              South
                              S. AKJ10
                              H. A32
                              D. 962
                              C. Q84

      North   East   South   West
      Pass   Pass   1S   Dbl.
      2S   All pass

      Opening lead: King of diamonds

IV. East-West vul.   North
     Dealer West   S. 98
                             H. KQ6
                             D. Q543
                             C. K843

      West   East
      S. A10764   S. QJ3
      H. 843   H. 9752
      D. 62   D. KJ1097
      C. Q72   C. 6

                              South
                              S. K52
                              H. AJ10
                              D. A8
                              C. AJ1095

      West   North   East   South
      Pass   Pass   Pass   1NT
      Pass   3NT   All pass

      Opening lead: Six of spades

KEY PLAYS

I. East discards the deuce of diamonds and then the deuce of clubs to show negative interest in those suits. If West is alive to what is going on he will shift to a heart upon winning the ace of spades.

II. East cashes his three top spades and West discards the queen and ace of clubs! This insures a set as a club return from East must promote a trump trick for West. If West keeps his clubs he must hope South has one; but discarding both clubs does not leave anything to chance.

III. East discards the nine of clubs on the third diamond, after being careful to start a high-low. West shifts to a low club; East wins the ace and returns the suit, getting a club ruff to defeat the contract.

IV. South wins the spade lead and tries the jack of clubs. West ducks (if he is smart); dummy wins the king and returns a club. East discards the queen of spades. He can tell from the Rule of Eleven that South has no more high spades; but without this revealing discard West could not possibly know who had the queen from the play to the first trick. When West gets in with the queen of clubs he runs his spades, defeating the contract.

I. Assume you are East and your partner has led the five

of spades against a no trump contract.

<u>North</u> (Dummy)
S. 76

<u>West</u>   <u>East</u> (You)
S. 5   a. S. Q83
                                                     b. S. Q832
                                                     c. S. 1042
                                                     d. S. K9432

In each case you play your highest spade which loses to

South's ace. Later in the hand you feel you must dis-

card a spade. Which spade do you discard to give part-

ner a count on the suit?

II. Neither side vul.   <u>North</u> (Dummy)
     Dealer East   S. 985
                              H. 752
                              D. AKQ10
                              C. 865

        <u>West</u> (You)
        S. 1043
        H. 93
        D. 864
        C. 109742

        <u>East</u>   <u>South</u>   <u>West</u>   <u>North</u>
        1H   Dbl.   Pass   2D
        Pass   2S   Pass   3S
        Pass   4S   All pass

Opening lead: Nine of hearts

East wins the queen, king, and ace of hearts, declarer

playing the jack on the third round. What do you dis-

card?

III.   North-South vul.   **North** (Dummy)
      Dealer South   S. J876
                            H. 764
                            D. Q765
                            C. 102

West (You)
S. Q10
H. 93
D. KJ1098
C. J876

South	West	North	East
2C *	Pass	2D	2H
2S	Pass	2NT	Pass
3C	Pass	4S	All pass

* Strong and artificial

Opening lead: Nine of hearts

Partner plays the three top hearts and declarer discards the deuce of diamonds on the third round. What do you discard?

IV.   Both sides vul.   **North** (Dummy)
      Dealer South   S. KJ
                            H. K43
                            D. J1094
                            C. AJ32

East (You)
S. AQ109
H. 9852
D. 875
C. 64

South	West	North	East
1NT	Pass	3NT	All pass

Opening lead: Ten of clubs

Declarer wins the queen and king of clubs and plays a club to the jack and then the ace. What do you discard on the third and fourth clubs?

DISCARDS   SOLUTIONS

I. a. The eight.

    b. The deuce.

    c. The four.

    d. The three.

In each case you are discarding the same card you

would have returned.

II.
                              North
                              S. 985
                              H. 752
                              D. AKQ10
                              C. 865

        West   East
        S. 1043   S. J
        H. 93   H. AKQ84
        D. 864   D. J932
        C. 109742   C. QJ3

                              South
                              S. AKQ762
                              H. J106
                              D. 95
                              C. AK

The deuce of clubs, the suit your partner is most

likely to lead. You prefer a heart play and your

discard of a low club strongly suggests that. If

partner leads a fourth heart, declarer must lose

a spade trick.

III.

                          North
                          S. J876
                          H. 754
                          D. Q765
                          C. 102

West   East
S. Q10   S. 95
H. 93   H. AKQ1082
D. KJ1098   D. 43
C. J876   C. 543

                          South
                          S. AK432
                          H. J6
                          D. A2
                          C. AKQ9

This time you want a heart play desperately (to
promote your queen of spades) so discard the king
of diamonds! This spectacular discard denies the
ace and alerts partner that something strange is
in the air. A good partner will play a fourth
heart. A bad one will return a diamond. (But a
bad one would have returned a diamond no matter
what you discarded.)

IV.

North
S. KJ
H. K43
D. J1094
C. AJ32

West
S. 876
H. J107
D. K62
C. 10987

East
S. AQ109
H. 9852
D. 875
C. 64

South
S. 5432
H. AQ6
D. AQ3
C. KQ5

Discard a low heart and a low diamond in that order.
When partner wins the king of diamonds he should return a spade if he watches your plays. Of course,
declarer played the hand like a ninny. He should
win the club lead in dummy with the ace and finesse
diamonds immediately without giving you a chance to
make your magnificent negative discards.

VII. SECOND HAND PLAY

I. WHEN AN HONOR IS LED, TO COVER OR NOT TO COVER?

Second hand is constantly being harassed by mean old declarers who are forever leading honor cards from dummy or from the closed hand, forcing second hand to decide whether or not to cover. Unfortunately, there is no single rule to cover this dilemma, but a little understanding will go a long way.

A. WHEN DUMMY IS TO THE LEFT

When the dummy is to your left you will be able to see the hand that is third to play.

Basically, the reason for covering an honor with an honor is to PROMOTE SOME SECONDARY CARD OR CARDS FOR EITHER YOU OR YOUR PARTNER. If it is impossible to do this DON'T COVER! (In the example diagrams we will assume that the suit being discussed is clubs, an arbitrarily chosen side suit, which seldom gets a chance to show off.)

North (Dummy)
C. AK109

West (You)
C. Q32

South
C. J

When South leads the jack of clubs from the closed hand (suit or no trump) there is no reason for West

to cover. Obviously he cannot promote anything for
himself, and dummy's spot cards are so imposing that
he cannot possibly promote anything for his partner.
But change one card:

                    North (Dummy)
                    C. AK108

West (You)
C. Q32

                    South
                    C. J

Now West covers because there is a chance for promotion. Partner could have 9xxx. If declarer has the
nine West was not going to take a trick with the
queen in any event. (However, if the bidding has
marked declarer with at least four clubs there is
no point in covering.)

                    North (Dummy)
                    C. AK1087

West (You)
C. Q432

                    South
                    C. J

Should West cover? Only if he is a masochist. Even
though partner may well have the nine, he cannot possibly have enough length to have the nine stand up.
(He cannot have more than three clubs.)

As we will see repeatedly, when trying to promote
secondary cards for partner his length in the suit
is critical. (This is doubly true in the trump suit.)

Sometimes your own length precludes covering.

North (Dummy)
C. A54

West (You)
C. K762

South
C. Q

Assume South has bid clubs and leads the queen. West should not cover. He can see the ace will fall in three rounds and that his king will be a fourth round trick. If he covers he is apt to get nothing.

However, if South were marked with no more than two clubs it could not hurt for West to cover. (Notice again the length factor entering into the picture.)

It should go without saying that if dummy has Ax it is even crazier for West to cover when holding the king with length.

However, if West has a doubleton king and dummy a doubleton ace he usually covers.

North (Dummy)
C. A5

West (You)
C. K6

South
C. Q

West should cover the queen to prevent his king
from being forced out by a small card on the second
round. South may have something like QJ10xx, in
which case an immediate cover produces a trick for
partner's 98xx. (Exception: If declarer has no
sure hand entry West should fiendishly duck to block
the suit.)

The next is typical:

                North (Dummy)
                C. A108

West (You)
C. Q74

                South
                C. J

Should West cover? Again the length factor is critical. If South has five or six clubs (from the bidding)
partner has either a singleton or a doubleton and no
good can come from covering. On the other hand, if
South is not marked with any particular club length
partner may have K9x(x)(x); then covering promotes an
additional trick for partner. But if South cannot reenter his hand to repeat the club finesse West should
definitely play low. And you thought bridge was a fun
game!

In most of the preceding examples, declarer has led an
honor and dummy has had the honor directly beneath the

one that was led. If dummy does not have the touch-
ing honor, second hand MUST ASSUME THAT WHEN DECLARER
LEADS A JACK HE HAS THE TEN TO BACK IT UP, AND WHEN
HE LEADS A QUEEN HE HAS THE JACK.

a.   North (Dummy)
            C. A32

West (You)
C. K54

            South
            C. Q

b.   North (Dummy)
            C. A32

West (You)
C. Q54

            South
            C. J

Should West cover? By recent count 4,875,432 tricks
were lost last year when West covered in these situations. In each case West should assume that South
has at least the honor directly beneath the one he
is leading and should follow the general rule of
COVERING THE SECOND EQUAL HONOR THAT COMES OUT OF
THE DECLARER'S HAND OR THE LAST EQUAL HONOR THAT IS
BEING LED FROM DUMMY.

```
Neither side vul.          North
Dealer South               S. 742
                           H. QJ92
                           D. A53
                           C. K76

        West                                    East
        S. AKQJ                                 S. 86
        H. 1087                                 H. K65
        D. J987                                 D. 1042
        C. 32                                   C. 109854

                           South
                           S. 10953
                           H. A43
                           D. KQ6
                           C. AQJ

        South        West          North           East
        1NT          Pass          3NT             All pass
```

Opening lead: Ace of spades

West cashes the first four tricks, dummy discarding a heart and East two clubs. West shifts to a club and declarer races off three clubs, ending in dummy, West discarding a diamond (hopefully).

Now the queen of hearts is led from dummy. East sees the queen and jack, so he follows the rule of covering the LAST equal honor he can see and plays low. If the jack is led next East covers and West's ten becomes high. Notice that if East covers the queen, South wins and finesses dummy's nine on the way back -- to lose no heart tricks and make his contract.

In other words, the main reason for not covering a queen is that the player with the queen may have QJ9, and by covering prematurely you expose partner to a finesse.

Now let's go back to our two original positions:

North (Dummy)
C. A32

West (You)
C. K54

South
C. Q

Now perhaps you can see why West should not cover the queen. South may well have QJ9 and East the guarded ten. However, if West has K10x or even K9x, he can cover since declarer cannot possibly have the one feared holding: namely, QJ9 with or without extended length.

Now for the most frightening one of all:

North (Dummy)
C. A32

West (You)
C. Q54

South
C. J

Should West cover? Only if he wants to be branded a beginner for the rest of his life! South is known to hold the ten (if he knows how to play bridge), and at least half the time he holds the king as well. Let's take each case separately.

```
                    North (Dummy)
                    C. A32

West (You)                              East
C. Q54                                  C. K96

                    South
                    C. J1087
```

If West covers the jack, dummy wins and a club is led
toward the closed hand. East can take no more than his
king, and South loses exactly one club trick. However,
if West plays low to the first trick East wins the king.
Later, if South leads the ten, West covers and East's
nine is promoted to a second trick.

Furthermore, South may have started with J1098 and an
original cover makes it easy for him to establish the
suit; whereas, if West ducks South must find a way back
to his hand to repeat the finesse. And if West judges
that South cannot get back to his hand a second time,
he will not even bother to cover the ten, thus making
it impossible for South to realize his fourth club.
Hand re-entry possibilities have to be considered even
when declarer leads the second equal honor. If second
hand judges that declarer started with three or four
equal honors he must refuse to cover even the second
lead of the suit. But relax, that last line was for
experts only. Your job is simply not to cover the jack.
Look how bad you would look here:

                    North (Dummy)
                    C. A32

West (You)   East
C. Q54   C. 76

                    South
                    C. KJ1098

South leads the jack to test your nervous reaction. If
you hesitate or cover you are a dead duck. But if you
realize that it is almost never right to cover the first
honor, and play low smoothly, chances are excellent that
South will rise with the ace and finesse East for the
queen. Even with Qx it is almost always right to duck
in this position. You would be surprised at how many
players (who have not read this book) cover the jack.

Covering honors in the trump suit

Second hand must be extremely careful about covering
honors in the trump suit, because in most cases partner
is marked with shortness and promotion is impossible.

                    North (Dummy)
                    C. A54

West (You)
C. Q32

                    South
                    C. J

South has bid and rebid clubs and leads the jack. No
West in his right mind covers. Partner could well have
the singleton king! Assume for the moment you duck and
the jack does, in fact, lose to the king. Later South
reenters his hand and leads the ten. Should you cover?

Again let common sense dictate. How many clubs does
your partner have at this point? At most one, so there
can be no point in covering. The only reason to cover
the second honor from the closed hand is in the hopes
that partner has the third equal. When this is obviously
impossible, do not cover. Another way to look at this
problem:

```
                        North
                        C. A54

West (You)                              East
C. Q32                                  C. K

                        South
                        C. J109876
```

Assume for a moment that South is the dummy and leads
the jack. Surely you do not cover with all those equals
staring at you. East wins the king and later the ten is
led from dummy. Again there can be no possible point in
covering, so once more you play low.

Now reverse the position and assume North is the dummy.
If West visualizes the club holding, perhaps from the
bidding, he has no trouble ducking twice.

```
                        North (Dummy)
                        C. AK97
West (You)
C. Q32

                        South
                        C. J
```

South leads the jack; should West cover? In the trump
suit it is unthinkable. True, South could have Jxxx and
be making some fancy play, and by covering your partner
will probably score his 10x, but chances are greater
that South has J10xx or J10xxx and is simply trying to
bait you. In a side suit, however, cover in the hopes
of promoting a possible 10xx or even 108xx in partner's
hand. Again the length factor enters into the decision.

Let's conclude our discussion of second hand play when
the dummy plays _after_ we do with this typical example:

```
Both sides vul.        North
Dealer South           S. 1072
                       H. A832
                       D. AKQ2
                       C. 109

West                                        East
S. KJ93                                     S. A85
H. Q5                                       H. 764
D. 1043                                     D. 9876
C. 5432                                     C. Q76

                       South
                       S. Q64
                       H. KJ109
                       D. J5
                       C. AKJ8
```

South	West	North	East
1C	Pass	1D	Pass
1H	Pass	4H	All pass

Opening lead: Three of spades

West leads the unbid suit and strikes gold. East wins
the ace and returns the suit, the defense collecting
the first three spade tricks. At trick four West shifts

to a small diamond. Declarer wins the jack and plays
the jack of hearts. If West is not ready for this play
the defense crumbles. Obviously it is right for West
to play the five. South will probably rise with the
ace and finesse the ten on the way back (his proper
percentage play). Notice how aggravating it is to East
if West covers. Prevent dandruff - learn when not to
cover!

B. WHEN DUMMY IS TO THE RIGHT

This is a bit tougher. When dummy leads an
honor should second hand cover? Again the
same reasoning applies:

1. Only if a trick can possibly be pro-
    moted for either you or your partner;
    and as usual LENGTH CONSIDERATIONS
    are vital.

2. If there are two or more equal honor
    cards in dummy second hand covers the
    LAST equal; not the second equal as
    is sometimes done when the honors are
    led from the concealed hand.

                    North (Dummy)
                    C. J104

                                East (You)
                                C. Q76

The jack is lead from dummy; should East
cover? No. Cover the last equal if you

are going to cover at all. Again, if
South has not bid the suit East ducks
the jack and covers the ten, catering
to South having AK8x. If that is the
holding, South might decide to finesse
the eight, allowing partner to score a
trick with his 9xx. However, if the jack
loses to the king and the ten is led next,
cover if you suspect partner has at least
two more cards but play low if you do not.

But, if the jack loses to the ACE you are
marked with the queen, so you might as
well cover the ten in the hope that partner started with A9x. (If the jack loses
to the king declarer still does not know
who has the queen.)

If there is only one honor card in the dummy, it
is usually proper to cover -- unless either your
own length or partner's lack of length precludes
promotional possibilities.

<u>North</u> (Dummy)
C. J4

<u>East</u> (You)
C. Q52

If the jack is led from dummy in a side suit it
is usually right for East to cover. But if East

has Kxxx he can insure a trick for himself
by _not_ covering. If South has preempted
the suit it would be the height of insanity
for East to cover, for West is marked with
shortness.

```
Neither side vul.            North
Dealer South                 S. J4
                             H. AQ
                             D. A8765
                             C. AK86

        West                                     East
        S. K                                     S. Q52
        H. J982                                  H. K10653
        D. Q109                                  D. 42
        C. QJ1043                                C. 972

                             South
                             S. A1098763
                             H. 74
                             D. KJ3
                             C. 5


        South        West         North        East
        3S           Pass         6S           All pass
```

Opening lead: Queen of clubs

Dummy wins and leads the jack of spades. If East covers,
both partner and the defense fall apart. But if East and
South both play low, West wins; and if he shifts to a
heart the hand is defeated. East should not even cover
the jack with Qx once South has announced at least a
seven card suit. South may have started with K109xxxx
and decide to play the king when the jack is not covered.
(His percentage play is low, however.)

One of the tougher situations for second hand to fathom is one we've all been through:

North (Dummy)
C. A10987

West   East (You)
C. 62   C. Q543

South
C. KJ

Assume hearts are trumps and the diagram suit is, as usual, clubs. South leads the king, the jack to the ace and finally the ten from dummy. Should East cover?

Yes, if:

1. Dummy has no side entry.

2. Declarer is about to discard a loser that is readily cashable by the defense (i.e., if declarer ruffs and partner overruffs, he can cash a trick).

No, if:

1. Trumps have been removed and there is a side entry to dummy. (This is the most common situation.)

2. Partner has worthless trumps.

3. There are no immediate tricks to be taken by the defense -- even if the ten is covered, ruffed and overruffed by partner.

Both sides vul.   North
Dealer North   S. Q
                     H. AKJ103
                     D. KQJ4
                     C. QJ4

        West   East
        S. J10832   S. A9764
        H. 54   H. Q876
        D. 52   D. 7
        C. K653   C. 872

                     South
                     S. K5
                     H. 92
                     D. A109863
                     C. A109

        North   East   South   West
        1H   Pass   2D   Pass
        4D   Pass   4NT   Pass
        5D   Pass   6D   All pass

Opening lead: Jack of spades

East wins and shifts to a club. South judges to rise
with the ace, hoping to discard club losers on dummy's
hearts. Two rounds of trumps are drawn and the ace,
king, jack of hearts are played. Here it is clearly
correct for East to play low. West has no more trumps
and dummy has a reentry. If East covers, South claims.
(He ruffs, enters dummy with a trump, and discards the
losing clubs on the hearts.) If East plays low smoothly
South must guess the heart position.

In the trump suit second hand must consider the possibility of overruffing dummy before spending an honor upon an
honor.

Both sides vul.   North
Dealer South   S. 654
                   H. KQ876
                   D. Q1098
                   C. 3

West   East
S. J32   S. A10987
H. 10432   H. AJ9
D. 65   D. K32
C. Q972   C. J4

                   South
                   S. KQ
                   H. 5
                   D. AJ74
                   C. AK10865

South	West	North	East
1C	Pass	1H	1S
2D	Pass	3D	Pass
4C	Pass	4D	Pass
5D	All pass		

Opening lead: Deuce of spades

East wins the ace and returns the suit. South plays the
ace of clubs and ruffs a club at tricks three and four.
At trick five the queen of diamonds is led from dummy.
East must not cover because he wishes to retain his king
to overtrump dummy the next time a club is led. If East
covers, South wins, ruffs another club and loses only
one more heart trick. If East refuses to cover, declarer
must ruff one more club in dummy before extracting trumps.
East overruffs to defeat the hand one trick.

And finally, these common positions:

                    North (Dummy)
                    C. J4

                                        East (You)
                                        AQ3

Dummy leads the jack; what should East do? In these
cases it is almost always right to play the ace. This
forces declarer to return to dummy to repeat the finesse
against the queen. If East plays low and the jack holds,
the lead remains in dummy and East will have made life
too convenient for declarer.

However, even this rule has an exception. (I'm sure
you're glad to hear that.)

                    North (Dummy)
                    C. J4

    West   East (You)
    C. 76   C. AQ3

                    South
                    C. K109852

Assume South is trying to establish his club suit and
has no outside entries to HIS OWN HAND. If East wins
the first club, later declarer can lead the four from
dummy, finesse the ten, and take five club tricks.
However, if East either plays low or the queen the
first time and wins the ace the second time, South
will presumably have no way to get back to his remaining good clubs.

If East has AQxx, the ace is usually best when the jack is led. (But low and then the ace is better if declarer has no hand entries.)

Thousands of tricks have been lost by naive defenders in this situation:

```
                    North (Dummy)
                    S. J2

West                                East (You)
S. 8643                             S. A109

                    South
                    S. KQ65
```

Dummy leads the jack. If East plays low (he should not think South is finessing because he himself owns the ten), South can come to three tricks by leading a second round of the suit; if East ducks again, declarer can win and then lead a <u>low</u> spade from his hand. If East plays the ace on the jack, like a man, then West must make a fourth round trick.

However, it could be right to play low:

```
                    North (Dummy)
                    S. J2

West                                East (You)
S. 763                              S. A109

                    South
                    S. KQ854
```

If the South hand is known to be weak it could well be right for East to duck the jack and win the second round of the suit. If South has no hand entries he can take no more than one spade trick -- assuming this is a no trump contract, of course.

The following position is much clearer, yet many defenders cannot force themselves to make the right play.

<pre>
                      North (Dummy)
                      S. J32

West   East (You)
S. 95   S. A1087

                      South
                      S. KQ64
</pre>

Dummy leads the jack (no trump or suit) and East should know that declarer probably has the king-queen (although he could hold Q9xx) because East holds the ten. East should play the ace, holding declarer to two tricks rather than the three he will take if East ducks and the suit is played twice more from dummy.

Obviously, the bidding and declarer's hand entries must be considered when deciding whether or not to cover; nevertheless, these combinations should be understood.

Keep in mind that in every example up to now either declarer or dummy has led an honor card. We have yet to discuss second hand's problem when a low card is led from dummy toward declarer's hand, or vice versa.

II. WHEN DECLARER LEADS A LOW CARD TOWARD DUMMY SHOULD SECOND HAND WIN THE TRICK IF HE CAN?

1. If this is the setting trick or if second hand can see that this trick along with other established tricks will defeat the contract, he normally wins.

2. If the dummy has a broken honor combination it is almost always right for second hand to play low and allow declarer to guess which honor to play from dummy. The most common of these are:

a.
$$\underline{\text{Dummy}}$$
KJx

$$\underline{\text{West}} \text{ (You)}$$
Axx

$$\underline{\text{Declarer}}$$
x

b.
$$\underline{\text{Dummy}}$$
Q10x

$$\underline{\text{West}} \text{ (You)}$$
Kxxx

$$\underline{\text{Declarer}}$$
x

c.
$$\underline{\text{Dummy}}$$
KQ10

$$\underline{\text{West}} \text{ (You)}$$
Axxx

$$\underline{\text{Declarer}}$$
x

             d.   Dummy
                                   __AJ9__

West__ (You)
KQxx

                         Declarer__
                         x

In each of these four cases it is usually correct

for second hand to play low the first time the

suit is led toward the dummy.

In "a" partner frequently has the queen and you

can take your ace the next time.

In "b" partner must have either the ace or jack

or both, so let him win the first trick -- unless

you have some compelling reason for wanting to

gain the lead. (If declarer had both the ace and

the jack, he would lead the suit from dummy orig-

inally.)

In "c" it is frequently correct to duck twice.

If declarer has two, three, or four small cards he

frequently plays the king the first time and the

ten the second (thinking you have the jack and your

partner the ace), and your partner scores his jack.

In "d" declarer will usually insert the nine if you

play low, and partner will probably win the trick

with his ten.

Strangely enough, when declarer leads up to a
king-queen combination on the board, even though
he has no guess, it is usually right for second
hand to play low holding the ace -- even though
he suspects a singleton is being led!

<pre>
                        North
                        S. KQ6
                        H. QJ1052
                        D. A
                        C. 7652

West   East
S. A10843   S. J975
H. 4   H. 6
D. KQ102   D. 76543
C. KQ8   C. J43

                        South
                        S. 2
                        H. AK9873
                        D. J98
                        C. A109
</pre>

Assume South gets to a wildly optimistic six
heart contract and West leads the king of diamonds. A trump is led to the closed hand, and
at trick three South leads his singleton spade.

If West rises with the ace, South discards two
clubs on the two top spades and actually makes
his slam. However, if West plays low South
does not lose a spade trick; but instead he
loses two club tricks.

Naturally, if West leads the king of clubs instead of the king of diamonds he rises with the ace of spades because he has the setting trick, the queen of clubs, in his own hand.

III. WHEN DECLARER LEADS A LOW CARD TOWARD DUMMY AND SECOND HAND CANNOT WIN THE TRICK.

1. Nine times out of ten second hand simply plays low, remembering to give the count signal when necessary. He should give the count signal whenever declarer leads up to a strong or fairly strong honor combination, particularly when second hand has a number of small cards.

Dummy
KQJ104

West (You)
83
875
9753
87532

Declarer
6

In each case it is practically automatic for West to play the underlined card when declarer leads up to this strong suit. This is to help partner know when to take the ace and what the distributional situation is in the suit.

Note: It is important only for the WEAKER of the two defending hands to give the count signal when declarer leads up to strength in the dummy.

2. Second hand does not "force" honors out of the dummy (with few exceptions).

North (Dummy)
C. K105

West (You)
C. Q876

South
C. 2

Assuming declarer leads the deuce in the above diagram, second hand should not play the queen to force the king out of the dummy. That play is strictly for early beginners. Nine times out of ten, the card that second hand wanted to force out will be played anyway; or if dummy inserts a low honor partner is right there to take the trick. If partner cannot take the trick, then sacrificing your high card will have been for naught.

3. If second hand has two equal honors and dummy has only one, second hand can "split his honors" to insure taking one trick; but even then it is sometimes better not to split.

North (Dummy)
C. K105

West (You)
C. QJ62

South
C. 3

If South leads the three toward the dummy West
must judge whether or not to "split" by playing
the jack. Splitting insures at least one trick
even if declarer has the ace. On the other hand,
if you think declarer's intention is to play the
king it is better to play low -- especially if
partner has the ace.

But:
                    North (Dummy)
                    C. AK104

West (You)
C. QJ62

                    South
                    C. 3

In this situation splitting won't help. Dummy
has your honor cards well covered. Play low.
Declarer seldom inserts the ten, and if he does
you have lost nothing. (If you split your honors
you give the show away. Declarer wins, returns
to his hand, and finesses the ten the next time.)

But if declarer knows what you have because of a
previous winning finesse, split -- to make things
more inconvenient for him.

                    North (Dummy)
                    C. AQ93

West (You)   East
C. KJ52   C.76

                    South
                    C. 1084

South leads the eight, you play low, dummy plays low, and the eight holds. Next, when South plays the ten, cover with the jack. South knows you hold at least the jack (and probably the king), and by covering you force him to return to his hand to repeat the finesse. If you play low the ten will hold, and declarer will still be in his hand to play the suit a third time.

4. When dummy has a suit headed by the AJ10, and no side entries, it is usually right for second hand to play high with Qx, Qxx, Kx or Kxx when the suit is led by the declarer (particularly against no trump).

North (Dummy)
C. AJ1032

West (You)   East
C. K54   C. Q98

South
C. 76

All too often South leads low to the ten, losing to the queen, and later low to the jack, taking the remaining four tricks. However, if West plays the king the first time, South is held to one trick! Watch. Declarer wins the king with the ace and leads the jack to force out the queen. East wins, but now poor South cannot get back to dummy to enjoy

his established suit. (Sometimes East will be
afraid to win the second trick for fear that
South started with three small rather than two.)

If South ducks the king (hoping West has KQx) and
later finesses the jack, he takes _no_ tricks!

Notice that in each of these situations dummy has
been visible, making second hand play easier.
When declarer leads low toward the closed hand
second hand tries to play similarly.

Dummy
C. 874

East (You)
C. QJ5

South
???

If this is a side suit being led from dummy East
plays low because for all he knows declarer has
AK10. However, if dummy has, for example, A84
East can safely split his honors to insure one
trick.

IF SECOND HAND PLAYS AN HONOR WHEN DUMMY HAS NO
HONOR CARDS, SECOND HAND USUALLY HAS THREE ADJA-
CENT HONORS, NOT TWO. (MOST EXPERTS PLAY THE
HIGHEST IN THIS SITUATION TO ALERT PARTNER TO
THEIR STRENGTH.)

<pre>
                         Dummy
                         C. 874

                                                    East (You)
                                                    C. QJ102
</pre>

If dummy leads the suit East plays the queen.

West knows that East is unlikely to split with

two equal honors (although East may have KQ),

and assumes he has the QJ10.

IV.   SOME OTHER SITUATIONS IN WHICH SECOND HAND PLAYS HIGH.

1.   When second hand can see the setting tricks.

<pre>
Both sides vul.   North
Dealer South   S. J76
                       H. K109
                       D. KQ74
                       C. J103

      West   East
      S. Q10842   S. A53
      H. J43   H. 8652
      D. 86   D. 1032
      C. Q42   C. A76

                       South
                       S. K9
                       H. AQ7
                       D. AJ95
                       C. K985

      South   West   North   East
      1NT   Pass   3NT   All pass
</pre>

Opening lead: Four of spades

East wins the ace and returns the five to South's king,

noticing the fall of West's deuce to indicate a five card

suit.   When declarer crosses to dummy with a red suit and

leads the jack of clubs, East rises with the ace to take

the setting tricks in spades.   (South had no intention of

finessing the jack of clubs. He knew that the opponents

had the setting tricks in spades and he was simply trying

to steal a club trick from East. South might have the KQ

of clubs and make the same play, for that matter.)

2. When declarer is out stealing.

```
Both sides vul.            North
Dealer South               S.  AQ3
                           H.  32
                           D.  AKQ109
                           C.  876

        West                                    East
        S.  J1086                               S.  975
        H.  A1054                               H.  QJ97
        D.  J3                                  D.  852
        C.  J53                                 C.  A94

                           South
                           S.  K62
                           H.  K86
                           D.  764
                           C.  KQ107

        South       West        North       East
        Pass        Pass        1D          Pass
        2NT         Pass        3NT         All pass
```

Opening lead: Jack of spades

Dummy's queen wins the first trick and at trick two a

small club is nonchalantly played from dummy. If ever

a man was stealing a ninth trick this is it!

East knows from the lead that South has three spade

tricks and can see five diamond tricks staring him in

the face, for eight. Unless partner has the ace-ten

of hearts there is no defense. (If declarer has the

ace of hearts he has nine tricks and the defenders are just playing for practice anyway.)

East must rise with the ace of clubs and shift to the queen of hearts if he wishes to live with himself for the next week.

3. When partner leads from strength vs. no trump. It is frequently imperative that you return partner's suit as quickly as possible while he still retains an outside entry.

Neither side vul.
Dealer South

North
S. 72
H. AQJ
D. J10987
C. A43

West
S. QJ1098
H. 9853
D. A2
C. 105

East
S. 643
H. 1072
D. K3
C. J9876

South
S. AK5
H. K64
D. Q654
C. KQ2

South	West	North	East
1NT	Pass	3NT	All pass

Opening lead: Queen of spades

South wins the second spade, leads a heart to dummy, and then a diamond. East must rise, hoping partner has the ace. If East wins the FIRST diamond trick he can return his remaining spade, knocking out declarer's ace, so that when West wins the SECOND diamond he can run his spades. But if West wins the first diamond and clears spades, East will have no more spades to return when he wins the second diamond.

The corollary to this play (retaining the entry in the hand that has the long suit until the suit has been established) can be seen on this hand.

```
Both sides vul.          North
Dealer South             S. J1065
                         H. KQJ3
                         D. 543
                         C. K4

        West                             East
        S. 873                           S. Q942
        H. 62                            H. A987
        D. A97                           D. J8
        C. QJ762                         C. 1093

                         South
                         S. AK
                         H. 1054
                         D. KQ1062
                         C. A85
```

South	West	North	East
1NT	Pass	2C	Pass
2D	Pass	3NT	All pass

Opening lead: Six of clubs

Declarer ducks the first club and wins the second on the table. At trick three a diamond is led to the king. If West takes this trick, removing his last entry before his clubs have been established, the defense has no further chance. However, if West ducks smoothly, it is South who is in trouble. If he leads a heart at trick

-204-

four to get to dummy in order to lead a second diamond, the hand blows up in his face.

East wins the first heart (important for East to use his entry NOW, even at the expense of giving dummy an extra heart trick, which could be prevented by holding up until the third round) and returns his last club, establishing partner's suit while he still has the ace of diamonds. Declarer can take no more than eight tricks. Contrast this to the ten declarer takes if West wins the first diamond.

4. When declarer has stripped the hand (vs. a suit contract primarily) and is about to duck a trick to your partner, who will be endplayed.

Neither side vul.
Dealer South

North
S. 762
H. A43
D. 105432
C. K6

West
S. AQ103
H. J98
D. J
C. J8743

East
S. J85
H. KQ10765
D. 6
C. Q109

South
S. K94
H. 2
D. AKQ987
C. A52

South	West	North	East
1D	Pass	2D	2H
4D	4H	5D	All pass

Opening lead: Eight of hearts

South wins the ace, ruffs a heart, cashes the ace of diamonds, enters dummy with the king of clubs, ruffs the last heart, and plays ace and a club, ruffing in dummy.

At this point the hand is completely stripped, and if South can pass a spade to West (by inserting the nine) he can insure his contract. However, East is still with us (hopefully). He can see that three spade tricks are needed to defeat the hand, so he must hope that his partner has AQ10. When a spade is led from dummy East plays the jack, and South loses three spade tricks.

5. When declarer is obviously trying to get to his own hand to discard a loser on a winner from his hand.

East-West vul.
Dealer East

North
S. K
H. 9742
D. 62
C. KJ10752

West
S. Q10432
H. 6
D. AQJ8
C. 983

East
S. 9765
H. A3
D. 7543
C. A64

South
S. AJ8
H. KQJ1085
D. K109
C. Q

East	South	West	North
Pass	1H	1S	2H
2S	4H	All pass	

Opening lead: Three of spades

Dummy wins the king (marking the ace with South) and leads a trump. East must be alert. He must rise and shift to a diamond in order to prevent South from discarding a losing diamond on the ace of spades. Another contract goes down the drain.

6. When declarer can be bamboozled without fooling partner. There are certain card combinations that offer an alert second hand defender an opportunity to make an enemy of declarer for life. (Nobody likes to be fooled.) Here are a few of the most common:

North (Dummy)
1082

West   East (You)
765   AJ9

South
KQ54

This could be the trump suit or more likely a side suit at no trump. In any case dummy leads the deuce. Sitting East you must play the jack!

If declarer has the king and partner the queen you have lost nothing; and if declarer has the queen and partner the king you have also lost nothing. But if declarer has both the KQ you can count on making a trick with your nine.

Assume you play the jack and declarer's king holds.
What will he think? He will think that you have
either AJ doubleton or a singleton jack. In either
case his best play is low to the eight ... he
thinks! The play would be equally effective if
declarer had a five card suit headed by the KQ.
Here is a very similar one:

<pre>
                North (Dummy)
                1082

West   East (You)
A43   J9

                South
                KQ765
</pre>

Again when dummy leads the deuce you should play
the jack. Again you can practically count on
making your nine on the way back as declarer will
surely play you for a singleton jack after West
wins the ace. Give South AQ765 and your partner
the king and you will also make your nine the
second time the suit is played against a good
declarer.

Many of the great plays we have been discussing
here don't work against declarers who don't know
what they are doing.

And finally:

North (Dummy)
1082 or J82

West   East (You)
A43   Q9

South
KJ765 or K10765

When dummy leads low East must play the queen!
Don't worry, you'll make the nine the second
time the suit is led and that will be one more
trick than you would have taken had you played
the nine the first time.

SECOND HAND PLAY   LESSON HANDS

I. East-West vul.   North
    Dealer South   S. Q5
                                H. Q93
                                D. 10954
                                C. J765

        West   East
        S. 10832   S. K976
        H. KJ10765   H. 82
        D. A62   D. K3
        C. none   C. 109432

                                South
                                S. AJ4
                                H. A4
                                D. QJ87
                                C. AKQ8

        South   West   North   East
        2NT   Pass   3NT   All pass

    Opening lead: Ten of hearts

II. Both sides vul.   North
    Dealer South   S. Q4
                                H. A72
                                D. KQ1075
                                C. K64

        West   East
        S. none   S. K2
        H. QJ84   H. K9653
        D. A642   D. J98
        C. QJ1072   C. A83

                                South
                                S. AJ10987653
                                H. 10
                                D. 3
                                C. 95

        South   West   North   East
        4S   All pass

    Opening lead: Queen of clubs

III. Both sides vul.   North
      Dealer East   S. 432
                            H. 43
                            D. AJ1086
                            C. Q72

      West   East
      S. K9865   S. 107
      H. 109   H. Q8765
      D. K92   D. Q75
      C. J96   C. K104

                            South
                            S. AQJ
                            H. AKJ2
                            D. 43
                            C. A853

      East   South   West   North
      Pass   1C   Pass   1D
      Pass   2NT   Pass   3NT
      All pass

      Opening lead: Six of spades

IV. East-West vul.   North
     Dealer South   S. 752
                            H. AQJ95
                            D. 1087
                            C. 86

      West   East
      S. QJ1043   S. 986
      H. 104   H. K8732
      D. none   D. AQ5
      C. J97532   C. 104

                            South
                            S. AK
                            H. 6
                            D. KJ96432
                            C. AKQ

      South   West   North   East
      2C   Pass   2H   Pass
      3D   Pass   4D   Pass
      4NT   Pass   5D   Pass
      6D   All pass

      Opening lead: Queen of spades

KEY PLAYS

I. Dummy wins the opening lead and a small diamond is played.
    East must rise with the king to return his remaining heart.
    If he does not, the hand can be made. If West wins the
    first diamond the defense collapses; and if neither East
    nor West wins the first diamond trick South can shift his
    attention to spades to collect nine tricks.

II. Whether the defenders shift to a heart after cashing two
    clubs or play three rounds of clubs, declarer should at-
    tempt to steal a diamond before eventually leading the
    queen of spades from the table trying to tempt East to
    cover. If East plays low smoothly (no point in covering
    on this bidding) South, with eleven spades between the
    two hands, will probably rise with the ace. BUT SOUTH
    MUST GIVE EAST A CHANCE TO MAKE A MISTAKE.

III. South wins the first spade with the QUEEN (so that West
    does not know who has the jack) and leads a diamond.
    West must play the king. South can overcome this play
    if he takes all the right views from here on (he can
    eventually force East to lead away from the king of
    clubs by throwing him in with a heart), but don't bet
    on it. However, if West woodenly plays a low diamond
    at trick two the defense collapses, unless East is
    clever enough to duck with his queen. (Don't bet on
    that either.)

IV. Declarer wins the spade, enters dummy with a heart, and leads a diamond. East must rise with the ace. East can see that if he wins the ace of diamonds and exits with anything but a low heart, it will be impossible for South to get to dummy to repeat the diamond finesse even though he knows East has the guarded queen. East sees that he can overtrump a third round of clubs, which is the only possible way South has of getting to dummy. If East ducks the diamond, and South does too, the lead remains in dummy and South can lead a second diamond to make his slam.

I.   Both sides vul.   North (Dummy)
     Dealer South   S. KQ10
                            H. J108543
                            D. 76
                            C. K4

          West (You)
          S. A65
          H. 2
          D. 9853
          C. J10987

          South   West   North   East
          1H   Pass   4H   All pass

Opening lead: Jack of clubs

Partner wins the ace and queen of clubs, then shifts
to the queen of diamonds, which declarer wins with the
ace. Declarer plays the ace of hearts, partner following, then the king of diamonds and a diamond, ruffing
in dummy, partner playing the deuce and ten.

A spade is led toward dummy. Plan your defense. Do
you take this trick? If you duck, the king wins; then
if declarer enters his hand with a trump (partner discarding) and plays a second spade, what do you do?

II. Both sides vul.   North (Dummy)
     Dealer South   S. 653
                              H. AKQ2
                              D. Q52
                              C. 953

                                              East (You)
                                              S. 82
                                              H. J987
                                              D. K987
                                              C. A64

     South   West   North   East
     1C   Pass   1H   Pass
     1NT   Pass   2NT   Pass
     3NT   All pass

Opening lead: Seven of spades

Declarer wins the ten, enters dummy with a heart,

West playing the trey, and plays a low club. Plan

your defense.

III. Neither side vul.   North (Dummy)
     Dealer West   S. 74
                               H. A5
                               D. AKQ1098
                               C. Q32

                                              East (You)
                                              S. 65
                                              H. J876
                                              D. 6532
                                              C. K65

     West   North   East   South
     2S*   3D   Pass   3NT
     All pass

     * Weak

Opening lead: King of spades

Partner's king wins and he continues with the jack, which

declarer wins with the ace. A diamond is led to dummy

followed by the queen of clubs. Do you cover?

IV. Both sides vul.   North (Dummy)
     Dealer South   S. 876
                              H. 2
                              D. J964
                              C. AQ632

                                              East (You)
                                              S. KQ4
                                              H. J983
                                              D. Q1085
                                              C. J9

          South   West   North   East
          1S   Pass   2S   Pass
          3H   Pass   3S   Pass
          4S   All pass

Opening lead: King of diamonds

West continues with the ace and a diamond, South ruffing

the third round. South cashes the ace of hearts and

leads the four of hearts, West playing the seven and

six, ruffing in dummy. A spade is led from dummy.

Which spade do you play?

I.

North
S. KQ10
H. J108543
D. 76
C. K4

West
S. A65
H. 2
D. 9853
C. J10987

East
S. J983
H. 6
D. QJ102
C. AQ65

South
S. 742
H. AKQ97
D. AK4
C. 32

West should plan to duck both spades and hope that
South misguesses. Obviously the only way to defeat
this contract is to try for two spade tricks, and
ducking twice gives you the best chance.

II.

North
S. 653
H. AKQ2
D. Q52
C. 953

West
S. KJ974
H. 1063
D. 1063
C. K2

East
S. 82
H. J987
D. K987
C. A64

South
S. AQ10
H. 54
D. AJ4
C. QJ1087

East must win the ace of clubs and return a spade.
This has the dual effect of clearing the spade suit

and retaining partner's entry. Hopefully, he will
be able to win the second club trick and run his
now established spades. If partner has no side entry
the hand cannot be defeated, unless, of course, his
spades are AQ974.

III.

North
S. 74
H. A5
D. AKQ1098
C. Q32

West
S. KQJ832
H. Q109
D. 7
C. 874

East
S. 65
H. J876
D. 6532
C. K65

South
S. A109
H. K432
D. J4
C. AJ109

Don't cover. Even though covering may well promote
a possible ten in partner's hand, you know declarer
cannot afford to take the club finesse into a hand
that has four more good spades! If declarer has the
ace of clubs (which he obviously does) he is no more
going to take this finesse than the man in the moon.
He is simply trying to steal overtricks from you.
Play low and watch him go up with the ace.

IV.

North
S. 876
H. 2
D. J964
C. AQ632

West
S. 105
H. 10765
D. AK7
C. 10874

East
S. KQ4
H. J983
D. Q1085
C. J9

South
S. AJ932
H. AKQ4
D. 32
C. K5

Play low. South apparently does not have any more losing hearts to ruff or else he wouldn't be drawing trumps. His trump holding may be what you see in the diagram, in which case he is planning to play low, and your partner will win the ten. Your remaining king-queen will be the setting trick. Besides, you would look mighty foolish splitting your honors if your partner turned out to have the singleton jack!

VIII. THIRD HAND PLAY

In general, it is third hand's play to the first trick (or tricks) that shapes the course of the defense. Third hand must be familiar with what is expected of him, and the opening leader must be familiar with the possibilities available to his partner.

GENERALLY, THIRD HAND PLAYS HIGH WHEN PARTNER LEADS LOW, AND THERE ARE NO HONOR CARDS IN DUMMY. WITH TWO OR THREE CARDS OF EQUAL RANK THIRD HAND PLAYS THE LOWER OR LOWEST EQUAL.

North (Dummy)
S. 943

West   East (Third hand)
S. A1082   S. KJ6

South
S. Q75

Assume West leads the deuce of spades against a no trump contract. East plays the KING, not the jack. If he plays the king and returns the jack, South cannot take a spade trick. If East plays the jack originally he makes a friend of South for life.

If East's spade holding is KQ6 he plays the QUEEN the first time -- the lower equal.

THIRD HAND MUST PAY ATTENTION TO DUMMY'S SPOT CARDS WHEN CONSIDERING A PLAY FROM EQUALS.

                    North (Dummy)
                    S. 943

West   East (Third hand)
S. 2   S. a. J106
                                           b. J108

In "a" East plays the ten to the first trick (lower equal).

In "b" East plays the eight, because with the nine in dummy the

eight is equal to the ten. (If East plays the ten he denies

possession of the eight.)

If third hand follows these rules, the opening leader can often

deduce every unseen card by simply perusing the first trick!

                    North (Dummy)
                    S. 1075

West (You)   East
S. Q6432   S. 9

                    South
                    S. K

West leads the three of spades, partner's nine losing to declar-

er's king. What is going on?

Obviously, South has the ace, for East would have played that

card had he held it. Also, East must have the jack (an equal

of the nine with the ten in dummy) because South would have

taken the trick with the jack if he held AKJ. Also, South must

have the eight because East would have played the eight holding

J98 (lowest equal). Therefore, the entire configuration is:

                    North (Dummy)
                    S. 1075

West   East
S. Q6432   S. J9

                    South
                    S. AK8

See if you can work this one out:

                    North (Dummy)
                    S. 1075

West (You)   East
S. Q6432   S. 8

                    South
                    S. A

Again, West leads the three, and East's eight forces the ace.
Where is every missing card?

This is what you should have come up with:

                    North
                    S. 1075

West   East
S. Q6432   S. J98

                    South
                    S. AK

THIRD HAND MUST CONSIDER THE LEAD BEFORE AUTOMATICALLY PLAYING
THIRD HAND HIGH, OR RETURNING PARTNER'S SUIT.

                    North (Dummy)
                    S. 843

West   East (Third hand)
S. 9   S. K10652

West's lead of the nine marks declarer with AQJ. In this case
it is incorrect for East to play the king. He should play low

forcing declarer to use a dummy entry to repeat the finesse.

When partner leads his lowest card against a no trump contract he is presumed to have a four card suit. Third hand uses this information to steer the defense.

```
Both sides vul.              North
Dealer South                 S. QJ95
                             H. Q106
                             D. 76
                             C. 8432

        West                                        East
        S. 872                                      S. 1064
        H. 542                                      H. J983
        D. K982                                     D. A3
        C. KJ9                                      C. Q1065

                             South
                             S. AK3
                             H. AK7
                             D. QJ1054
                             C. A7

        South        West          North          East
        2NT          Pass          3C             Pass
        3D           Pass          3NT            All pass
```

Opening lead: Deuce of diamonds

East wins the first diamond and realizes that declarer has a five card diamond suit, since partner is marked with four. Rather than establish South's long suit, East shifts to his lowest club at trick two. South plays low and West wins the nine and returns the king to unblock the suit. When West gets in with the king of diamonds he leads his jack of clubs to defeat the hand one trick. (West knows that South has only two clubs because East's first club was the five, his lowest,

showing a four card suit. That is why West can safely plunk
down the king of clubs at trick three.)

THIRD HAND CAN USE THE RULE OF ELEVEN TO ADVANTAGE.

Both sides vul.
Dealer South

North
S. 98
H. J1092
D. AKJ2
C. Q65

West
S. AJ763
H. 854
D. 875
C. 74

East
S. Q105
H. A76
D. 43
C. J10932

South
S. K42
H. KQ3
D. Q1096
C. AK8

South	West	North	East
1NT	Pass	2C	Pass
2D	Pass	3NT	All pass

Opening lead: Six of spades

East plays the queen and South the king. At trick two South
crosses to a high diamond and leads the jack of hearts, trying
to steal a ninth trick. If East is alive and well he rises with
the ace and returns his ten of spades allowing West to run the
suit.

How does East know partner's spades are good? The rule of eleven
tells him. East subtracts the card his partner has led (the six)
from eleven, giving him an answer of five. This means that there
are five cards above the six in the three REMAINING hands (excluding the opening leader's). East can see two of these cards

in dummy and two in his own hand, leaving South with but one
card higher than the six. When South takes the first trick
with the king East knows that West's remaining spades are
ready to run. But how does East know that West has five spades?
Because South denied four spades when he rebid two diamonds over
North's two club Stayman response.

Another way to look at a fourth best lead is this: West is
known to have three cards higher than the six (because he is
leading his fourth highest card). East can see the 8, 9, 10,
Q and K after the first trick, which means that West must have
the AJ7, since those are the only three cards higher than the
six unaccounted for.

Using the rule of eleven can often save the day for the defenders in this extremely common situation:

Both sides vul.   North
Dealer South   S. 1054
                               H. A832
                               D. KQ6
                               C. Q43

            West   East
            S. AQ962   S. J87
            H. K954   H. J10
            D. 32   D. J1054
            C. 76   C. J1092

                          South
                          S. K3
                          H. Q76
                          D. A987
                          C. AK85

            South   West   North   East
            1NT   Pass   3NT   All pass

Opening lead: Six of spades

Dummy plays low and East uses the rule of eleven to determine that South has exactly one card higher than the six. It obviously cannot be the nine for that would give partner AKQ and he would hardly lead the six from that holding. South, therefore, has either the ace, king or queen of spades and in no case is it right for East to play the jack. In fact, if East plays the jack South makes the hand!

South tests both minor suits ending in his hand and when neither suit breaks exits with a spade. West perforce wins the spade exit, cashes four spades, but must lead away from the king of hearts at trick twelve to allow South to make his game.

However, if East had retained the jack of spades at the critical juncture when South exits with a spade, East, not West can win the trick, cash his minor suit winners and then return his remaining spade to West to actually defeat the hand two tricks.

THIRD HAND MUST REALIZE THE VALUE OF RETAINING COMMUNICATIONS WITH PARTNER'S HAND.

```
Neither side vul.              North
Dealer East                    S. KJ2
                               H. AQ5
                               D. 76
                               C. QJ1094

        West                                        East
        S. 9865                                     S. 743
        H. 98432                                    H. 76
        D. 82                                       D. AKJ1054
        C. K5                                       C. 82

                               South
                               S. AQ10
                               H. KJ10
                               D. Q93
                               C. A763

        East        South         West          North
        2D*         2NT           Pass          3NT
        All pass
```

* Weak Two Bid

Opening lead: Eight of diamonds

In order to use his diamonds later, East must play the ten at
trick one, conceding a trick to South's known queen WHILE RE-
TAINING A DIAMOND IN PARTNER'S HAND. When West wins the club
he returns a diamond to defeat the contract.

From East's point of view, West must hold two diamonds in order
to defeat the contract, so EAST ASSUMES WEST HAS A SECOND DIAMOND.
Notice that if East has a certain outside entry (an ace, or a king
in back of a long suit headed by the ace), he can afford to play
third hand high and continue the suit, driving out the queen.
Eventually he gets in with his outside entry and runs his suit.
However, with no CERTAIN outside entry East must retain communications with his partner's hand.

This type of play is extremely common at no trump; here are some other similar combinations for third hand to recognize. (Assume third hand has no outside entry.)

                        North (Dummy)
                        S. 765

West   East (Third hand)
S. 83   S. AQJ1042

                        South
                        S. K9

West leads the eight of spades and East plays the ten.

                        North (Dummy)
                        H. 765

West   East (Third hand)
H. 94   H. AJ1032

                        South
                        H. KQ8

West leads the nine and East plays the three. If East and West each have one entry card and West uses his first he can return his remaining heart allowing East to clear the suit. (See chapter on "Second Hand Play".) Later when East gets in with his entry he can run his suit. If East wins the first heart and returns the suit West will not be able to play a heart when he gets in.

Third hand must be familiar with this exceptional position:

Both sides vul.
Dealer South

North
S. 103
H. K82
D. AQJ74
C. K43

West
S. J8754
H. J953
D. 86
C. 98

East (Third hand)
S. AQ6
H. Q106
D. K92
C. J1076

South
S. K92
H. A74
D. 1053
C. AQ52

South	West	North	East
1C	Pass	1D	Pass
1NT	Pass	3NT	All pass

Opening lead: Five of spades

East must play the QUEEN at trick one. The play loses nothing
if West has the king, but if South has the king it prevents
South from holding up. Follow the play. East plays the queen
and South wins the king. (He dares not duck for fear that West
has the AJ, in which case he won't score his king at all.)

The diamond finesse loses and East plays the ace and a spade.
East-West score four spades and a diamond to defeat the hand
one trick.

Now let's see what happens if East plays the ace of spades at
trick one. East returns the queen and South wins the THIRD
spade. When the diamond finesse loses to East he has no more
spades to return, and South makes his contract easily.

A similar situation exists when partner, for once in his life, leads your suit rather than his:

North (Dummy)
S. 104

West   East (You)
S. J82   S. AQ763

South
S. K95

Perhaps spades is the only unbid suit or perhaps partner receives your vibrations. In any case, when partner leads the deuce of spades you should play the queen. Declarer will hardly be able to hold up (partner may have led from some combination headed by the ace-jack), and if partner has an entry and realizes his own brilliance he will plunk down the jack and then lead his remaining card to you and your beaming smile.

Play the ace the first time and declarer simply holds up until the third round, and your partner's brilliance and your smiles are in vain.

WHEN DUMMY HAS ONE HONOR CARD AND THIRD HAND HAS A HIGHER HONOR CARD, THIRD HAND NORMALLY SAVES HIS HONOR UNLESS THE HONOR IS PLAYED FROM DUMMY. HOWEVER, THIRD HAND MUST HAVE A CARD AS HIGH AS THE NINE TO INSERT IF THE HONOR IS NOT PLAYED FROM DUMMY.

                              North (Dummy)
                              C. J76

West   East
C. Q832   C. K105

                              South
                              C. A94

West leads the deuce of clubs, dummy plays low and East plays

the ten. East has an honor card higher than dummy's (the king)

and a card high enough to insert (the ten).

                              North (Dummy)
                              S. J76

West   East
S. AQ43   S. K82

                              South
                              S. 1095

West leads the three, dummy plays low and East plays the king

because he does not have a card as high as the nine to insert.

(AN IMPORTANT EXCEPTION TO THIS RULE: WHEN THIRD HAND HAS THE

ACE AND DUMMY THE JACK OR TEN, THIRD HAND PLAYS THE ACE.)

Third hand must also do some guessing in this common position

when defending a SUIT contract:

                              North (Dummy)
                              D. Q43

West   East (Third hand)
D. 5   D. A106

                              South
                              D. ???

West leads the five against a suit contract and dummy plays low.

What should East play? The rule says play the ten (best vs. no

trump, since you don't mind losing to a doubleton jack), but
the rule didn't hear the bidding or see the rest of dummy.

If West is leading from the king-jack the ten will win the
trick and is surely best. However, if West is leading from
five to the king and declarer has the doubleton jack then the
ace is obviously right. But West may be leading from three
or four to the jack-nine in this position:

                         North (Dummy)
                         D. Q43

        West   East (Third hand)
        D. J975   D. A106

                         South
                         D. K82

Then East does better to play the ten and wait for West to re-
gain the lead. When West later leads the jack through dummy's
queen, South takes but one trick. If East plays the ace prematurely South takes two tricks.

It might be added that third hand play also varies in the following position depending upon whether the contract is a suit
or no trump:

                         North (Dummy)
                         S. Q43

        West   East (Third hand)
        S. 5   S. A96

At no trump, if dummy plays low East plays the nine; but vs. a
suit contract East plays the ace, although the nine is right if
West has led from J10.

THIRD HAND MUST BE CAREFUL ABOUT PLAYING A JACK WHEN DUMMY HAS
A10 or K10 COMBINATIONS (PARTICULARLY VS. SUIT CONTRACTS).

                        North (Dummy)
                        C. A104

West   East (Third hand)
C. Q952   C. J83

                        South
                        C. K76

Defending a suit contract, West leads the deuce and dummy plays
low. East should play the eight. West cannot possibly have the
KQ and lead low, so South must have an honor. If that honor is
the king the eight might drive it out. If the honor is the queen
East saves a trick even if the eight loses to the nine!

                        North (Dummy)
                        H. A104

West   East (Third hand)
H. K752   H. J83

                        South
                        H. Q96

Defending a suit contract, West leads the deuce; dummy plays the
four and East the eight. South wins the nine but can subsequently
take only the ace if the defense abandons the suit.

Vs. no trump it is never quite clear whether to play the jack or
the eight.

If partner has led from both the king and queen the jack is obviously best, but if he has led from only one honor then the eight is best. You pays your money...

A somewhat similar situation arises when third hand has the Q9x or Q8x and dummy the K10x or A10x.

<pre>
                        North (Dummy)
                        S. K104

        West   East (Third hand)
        S. 5   S. Q9
                                             Q8
                                             Q93
                                             Q83
                                             Q953
                                             Q853
</pre>

Vs. a suit contract it is clear to play the eight or nine if dummy plays low, for partner is unlikely to be underleading the ace; he is much more likely to be underleading the jack. (However, if from the bidding you suspect that partner has the ace, play the queen.)

Vs. no trump play the queen unless you have specifically the queen and the nine, in which case the nine usually works out better. (However if you are sure partner has the ace, play the queen.)

                    North (Dummy)
                    S. A104

West   East (Third hand)
S. 5   S. Q9
                                          Q8
                                          Q93
                                          Q83
                                          Q953
                                          Q853

Vs. suit play the eight or nine if no discards are available
to declarer on side suits; if there is length to fear in dummy, play the queen.

Vs. no trump play the queen from the Q8 combinations, but the
nine from the Q9 combinations.

Instead of memorizing a bunch of rules about the Q9 try to take
the whole hand into consideration. If there are no long suits
upon which declarer can discard losers, play the nine; if there
are long suits hanging about play the queen (hoping partner has
underled the king). Also, keep in mind that the better your
partner the more likely he is to underlead a king rather than a
jack. (If he has underled both, your play is immaterial.)

Finally, before leaving our Q9 combinations forever do not forget this one:

                        North
                        S. 103

West   East
S. A862   S. Q95(4)

                        South
                        S. KJ7

West leads low against a no trump contract and dummy plays low.
If West has underled both the ace and king the queen is the
proper play, but if West has underled the ace the nine saves
a trick.

Interchange the eight and nine in the East-West hands and the
eight is best here but much more risky. If declarer started
with A9x and you play the eight you had better have this book
nearby to defend yourself.

Also if the jack and ten are interchanged in the North-South
hands East's play of the nine still saves one trick but loses
one partner if declarer has Jxx. Vs. suit always play the queen.

If it will make anyone feel any better, this one happened to me
while I was writing this chapter:

                        North
                        C. J82

West   East   (Author when
C. AK543   C. Q9   he can't
                                                             see all
                                                             four hands

                        South
                        C. 1076

Against one no trump by South, all pass, my partner led the four
of clubs. Dummy played low and guess which one I played? Right!

I played the nine, which is correct if partner has led from the A10 or K10 but wrong if he has led from the AK. Nobody is perfect and I am finishing this chapter regardless.

ENTRY CONSIDERATIONS SOMETIMES PRECLUDE THIRD HAND FROM PLAYING HIGH.

Both sides vul.
Dealer South

North
S. 1093
H. KQJ9
D. 654
C. 764

West
S. 42
H. 7653
D. J987
C. Q85

East
S. J75
H. A84
D. 1032
C. 10932

South
S. AKQ86
H. 102
D. AKQ
C. AKJ

South	West	North	East
2C	Pass	2D	Pass
2S	Pass	3S	Pass
4D	Pass	4H	Pass
4NT	Pass	5C	Pass
6S	All pass		

Opening lead: Deuce of spades

Dummy plays the nine and if East plays the jack South makes the slam. South draws a second high trump from his hand and then proceeds to knock out the ace of hearts. Dummy's remaining spade is an entry to the established heart suit.

On the other hand, if East, who knows he has control of dummy's length, plays low at trick one and wins the second round of hearts (West giving the count signal, of course) declarer must lose a club as well as a heart.

Another case in point:

```
                        North
                        S. 983
                        H. 763
                        D. A87
                        C. 10432

        West                            East
        S. 72                           S. K104
        H. J82                          H. K1054
        D. 10654                        D. J932
        C. J976                         C. 85

                        South
                        S. AQJ65
                        H. AQ9
                        D. KQ
                        C. AKQ
```

No bidding is given because the final contract of 6S is so lousy I don't want to be associated with the sequence.

However, if West leads a trump and dummy plays the eight East must play the <u>ten</u> or else South makes his slam.

South now lacks the entries to finesse you out of your major suit kings although your partner doesn't seem to mind if he does. Play any other spade and declarer will pin a medal on both you and your partner for putting up the most cooperative defense of the century.

Third hand must also be careful not to spend a high trump at trick one if he can foresee using that trump to overtrump dummy later in the play.

Neither side vul.   North
Dealer South   S. A764
                                     H. AJ75
                                     D. 4
                                     C. J1097

        West   East
        S. Q108   S. KJ32
        H. K1032   H. Q986
        D. QJ98   D. 72
        C. 32   C. Q54

                                     South
                                     S. 95
                                     H. 4
                                     D. AK10653
                                     C. AK86

        South   West   North   East
        1D   Pass   1H   Pass
        2C   Pass   2S   Pass
        3D   Pass   5C   Pass
        6C   All pass

Opening lead: Deuce of clubs

Once you overcome the spasms of hatred at seeing your partner's
trump lead you must cool off long enough to play low at trick
one. If you play the queen, declarer can make the hand easily
by ruffing two diamonds in dummy. However, if you duck the
opening lead you will be able to use your queen of trumps to
overruff dummy on the third round of diamonds. Eventually the
defense must also come to a spade and so the slam will be defeated in spite of your spasms.

THIRD HAND MUST BE AWARE OF VARIOUS OVERTAKING AND UNBLOCKING
POSSIBILITIES.   (SOME OF THESE PLAYS WERE DISCUSSED IN THE
SIGNALLING CHAPTERS.)

                        North (Dummy)
                        S. 753

West   East (Third hand)
S. KQ1086   S. A4

                        South
                        S. J92

Assume South is playing three no trump and West leads the king
of spades. East must overtake and return the four in order for
the defenders to collect their tricks. (East should make the
same play defending a suit contract. West is known to have the
queen, so East will be able to trump the third round if necessary.)

Third hand normally overtakes the lead of a queen with the ace
unless the jack is visible.

                        North (Dummy)
                        H. 654

West   East (Third hand)
H. Q   H. A872

                        South
                        H. ???

Defending a suit contract East normally wins the first trick to
prevent South from scoring a singleton king. Defending no trump,
East simply signals with the eight to indicate pleasure.

```
                        North (Dummy)
                        D. 654

West                                      East (Third hand)
D. Q                                      D. AJ82

                        South
                        D. ???
```

In this case East does not overtake the queen. At no trump it
is instant madness, and defending a suit contract it is likely
that West has Qx and declarer K109x. If East overtakes and returns the suit declarer may insert the ten and hold his losses
to one trick. If East simply signals with the eight he comes
to at least two tricks. (Naturally, if the lead is a singleton
and there are discards available it is conceivable to win the
ace and return the suit.)

Against both suit and no trump, third hand normally overtakes
a queen when holding a doubleton king.

```
                        North (Dummy)
                        S. 7652

West                                      East (Third hand)
S. QJ108                                  S. K4

                        South
                        S. A93
```

West leads the queen, and if East wishes to continue playing
with West he gently places the king on the queen. (Ladies like
to be treated gently.)

A shrewd defender must also be alive to the possibility of un-blocking to avoid an end play.

```
Neither side vul.              North
Dealer South                   S. QJ10
                               H. Q543
                               D. QJ4
                               C. 954

        West                                           East
        S. K943                                        S. 8765
        H. J10                                         H. 98
        D. AK92                                        D. 83
        C. KQ3                                         C. J10876

                               South
                               S. A2
                               H. AK762
                               D. 10765
                               C. A2

        South       West           North          East
        1H          Dbl.           2H             Pass
        Pass        Dbl.           Pass           2S
        3H          All pass
```

Opening lead: King of diamonds

West begins with three diamonds, East ruffing the third. East shifts to the jack of clubs at trick four, to South's ace. West should see an end play coming up. He knows South has the ten of diamonds on which one of dummy's clubs can be discarded; and he assumes South has five hearts. If South has the dia-grammed distribution he can win the ace of clubs, draw trumps, discard a club on the ten of diamonds, and exit with a club. If West is forced to win this trick he will have to play away from his king of spades or give declarer a ruff-sluff. But if East wins the club play he can lead a spade through South. Clearly, then, it is in West's best interest to throw a club honor under the ace (the king is the proper card).

THIRD HAND MUST USE TECHNIQUES OF LOGIC WHEN TRYING TO READ
AMBIGUOUS LEADS.

How can third hand tell whether the lead of a deuce is a singleton or fourth best?

How can third hand tell, when partner leads the three and then
plays the deuce, whether he has a doubleton or a five card suit?

How can third hand tell, when partner leads the queen, whether
he is leading top of a sequence or from a doubleton queen?

How can third hand tell, when partner leads a middle spot card,
whether it is top of a doubleton or fourth best? (For example,
the seven is led from 74 as well as KJ973, not to mention Q97
or even occasionally 752.)

Almost every one of these questions can be answered by going
back to the bidding, looking closely at your own, dummy's, and
declarer's spot cards that are played to the first trick, and
asking yourself what type of lead partner is most apt to make
on the given bidding sequence. In other words, you can seldom
read the lead just by looking at the card itself.

Let's consider a few examples and you will see how easy it is.
(After five years of practice.)

Assume South has bid three suits, indicating shortness in diamonds. Partner leads the deuce of diamonds and you and dummy
each have four. Obviously partner is not leading a singleton

because that would place declarer with four diamonds, which we know is not possible. Therefore, it is most likely that declarer has a singleton and partner a four card suit.

Declarer has opened one spade and rebid two spades over partner's two club response. This is raised to game and partner leads the three of hearts.

<pre>
                        North (Dummy)
                        H. J105

West   East (You)
H. 3   H. AK7

                        South
                        H. ???
</pre>

You take the king and ace and partner follows with the deuce. Does partner have a doubleton? If he did, how many hearts would that give declarer? That would give declarer five hearts, which is inconsistent with the bidding; so you assume partner has five and declarer a doubleton.

When partner leads an honor card he either has a sequence or is short suited. Obviously, if he has bid the suit he is leading from a sequence. If you have bid the suit he is more likely to be leading from a singleton or doubleton; but if he has supported the suit the lead of the queen, for example, could be from QJx. If, however, you can see the honor directly beneath the one partner has led you know your partner is leading from shortness.

For example the lead of the jack can be from J109x, J108xx, J10x, Jx or J. If you can see the ten in either your hand or dummy you know partner must be leading from shortness.

The lead of a middle spot card is not always easy to read. Against no trump it tends to be fourth best. However, if the rule of eleven tells you that this cannot be the case, you must consider other possibilities.

North (Dummy)
H. AQ7

West
H. 6
              East (You)
              H. K102

Your partner leads the six of hearts against a no trump contract and dummy plays low. Using the rule of eleven you discover that South has no card higher than the six and you play the ten. South produces the jack!

What has happened? What has happened is that your partner's lead of the six is not fourth best from some holding such as J986, but rather a bust lead from something like 654 or 6543. Had you K109 rather than K102 you would know immediately from the rule of eleven partner's lead was not fourth best.

OTHER CONSIDERATIONS TO HELP THIRD HAND READ PARTNER'S LEAD:

1. Partner figures to underlead aces against suit contracts only when dummy is known to have the stronger hand, usually having bid no trump; then the king is more likely to turn up in dummy than in declarer's hand.

2. If dummy has bid no trump, and you have overcalled a suit, partner is apt to lead the queen or jack from Qxx or Jxx, hoping to trap a king in dummy. Therefore, this is one time you cannot be sure the lead of an honor card is from shortness even though you can see the honor card directly beneath the one partner has led.

3. When you or partner is known to be long in trump, partner is more apt to lead a long suit than a short one.

4. When partner and you have each bid the same suit and partner leads another, it is usually for one of two reasons: (1) He has the ace of the bid suit and is afraid to set up a possible king in declarer's hand or (2) He has a short suit and trump control. Obviously if you have the ace of the bid suit "2" is very likely. Also, the opening leader may have a strong sequence in an unbid suit when he does not lead the suit the partnership has been bidding.

5. When dummy is known to have a long suit partner will tend to make aggressive leads. If partner makes a passive lead he is announcing to one and all that he does not fear dummy's length.

THIRD HAND MUST TRAIN HIMSELF TO OVERTAKE WHENEVER HE HAS THE
NECESSARY SPOT CARDS AND HE WANTS THE LED SUIT TO BE CONTINUED.

                         North (Dummy)
                         C. 832

West   East (Third hand)
C. J   C. KQ1094

                         South
                         C. A765

West leads the jack, which East knows is either a singleton or a
doubleton (because he is looking at the ten). East overtakes
with the queen to insure a continuation of the suit in case South
ducks.

THIRD HAND MUST REMEMBER TO UNBLOCK FROM Qx, Jx, or 10x WHEN
DUMMY WINS THE TRICK WITH Ax, Kx, OR Qx.

Both sides vul.   North
Dealer South   S. 63
                         H. Q7
                         D. Q1054
                         C. KQJ32

        West   East
        S. 7   S. KQ1082
        H. A108532   H. J4
        D. 632   D. A98
        C. 987   C. 1065

                         South
                         S. AJ954
                         H. K96
                         D. KJ7
                         C. A4

        South   West   North   East
        1NT   Pass   3NT   All pass

Or, for those who are offended by South opening 1NT with a five
card major:

-247-

	South	West	North	East
	1S	Pass	2C	Pass
	2NT	Pass	3NT	All pass

Opening lead: Five of hearts

Assuming dummy plays the queen (the correct play any time West has the ace of diamonds, and the losing play any time West has exactly six hearts and no ace of diamonds), third hand should drop the JACK!

Now when East wins the ace of diamonds he can return the four of hearts, allowing West to run the suit. If third hand plays the four of hearts at trick one, clutching the jack, then when he wins the ace of diamonds and returns the jack of hearts, declarer can duck and will make his contract.

Similar combinations are:

<pre>
                        North (Dummy)
                        S. J4

        West   East (Third hand)
        S. AK973   S. 102

                        South
                        S. Q865
</pre>

West leads the seven against a no trump contract. If dummy plays the jack East must unblock the ten. If East does not, and later gets the lead, his ten will block the run of his partner's suit.

                          North (Dummy)
                          S. A4

West   East (Third hand)
S. KJ932   S. Q5

                          South
                          S. 10876

West leads the three and dummy plays the ace. East should drop

the queen. If he does not, when he later gets the lead his

queen will prevent partner from running his good spade tricks.

Third hand should also be familiar with this unblocking position

(usually vs. a suit contract):

                          North (Dummy)
                          H. A762

West   East (Third hand)
H. 3   H. K5

                          South
                          H. ???

West leads the three and dummy plays the ace. East should real-

ize that partner is a big favorite to hold the queen. (If de-

clarer has the queen he normally plays low from dummy.) It is

often correct in this situation for East to unblock the king.

(See Chapter on "Inferences".)

THIRD HAND SHOULD BE FAMILIAR WITH SOME BASIC DECEPTIVE MANEUVERS.

North (Dummy)
D. 32

West   East (Third hand)
D. J986   D. AK54

South
D. Q107

West leads the six against a no trump contract. Third hand knows
this to be a four card suit because he can see all the lower spot
cards. Third hand should play the king (or ace) and return the
four. If South plays the ten the defenders take all four tricks.
Notice that East can safely underlead his ace-king because he is
sure South has at least three. Do not confuse it with this situation:

North (Dummy)
D. 32

West   East (Third hand)
D. J10754   D. AK96

South
D. Q8

West leads the five. East wins, noticing that the four is missing.
If West has that card declarer must have a doubleton, so East's
better continuation, by far, is his remaining honor.

<pre>
                    North (Dummy)
                    S. 7653
</pre>

<pre>
        West   East (Third hand)
        S. 4   S. AKQ102
</pre>

West leads the four of spades against a suit contract. East reads the lead as a singleton or low from three or four. (The bidding usually clarifies which it is.)

East's normal play is to win the queen (the lowest equal). But if East is planning on continuing the suit in any case it cannot hurt to win the ace (although West will temporarily think that South has the king). Why?

If South trumps the opening lead West will know East's holding, but South will not know that East has all those high honors. (He will think that West has the king if East plays the ace, and may misplace some other high cards later in the hand.) If South does not trump East continues with the queen. If South trumps, again West knows the situation. If South follows to the second spade, West should be aware that his partner remains with the king from declarer's failure to play it. In any event he will see the king at the next trick.

This type of deceptive play (trying to misplace high honors for declarer) is done mainly with AK or AKQ combinations.

Neither side vul.   North
Dealer East   S. 75
                                     H. K643
                                     D. QJ
                                     C. AKJ87

        West   East
        S. 106432   S. AKQJ8
        H. Q98   H. 7
        D. 762   D. 8543
        C. 94   C. 1065

                            South
                            S. 9
                            H. AJ1052
                            D. AK109
                            C. Q102

        East   South   West   North
        Pass   1H   Pass   2C
        2S   3D   Pass   4H
        Pass   4NT   Pass   5D
        Pass   6H   All pass

Opening lead: Three of spades

As it turns out six clubs is cold while six hearts needs some
good fortune in the trump suit. However, that is not the point.
The point is that if East wins the first spade with the jack,
marking himself with all four spade honors (West would never
underlead an ace against a slam), South will know from East's
original pass that West must have the queen of hearts. (With
the top spade honors and the queen of hearts East would have
an opening bid.)

Therefore, in order to conceal his super strength in spades
East should win the first trick with the ace and return the
queen, the same way he would play if he started with AQJxx(x).

When South ruffs the second spade West will not be fooled but South might. He may well assume West started with the king of spades and, perhaps, East the queen of hearts, or at least he may play hearts to be 2-2.

In any case a defender who passes originally and then turns up with a solid suit is as much as telling the declarer that he has no side honor cards. A word to the wise.

Third hand also has a duty when it comes to playing combinations like AK, KQ or QJ doubleton.

If third hand is sure to win the trick and plans to continue the suit he should play the higher equal first. Then when he returns the remaining honor partner will recognize it as a doubleton because of the abnormal order of the play.

Obviously with AK doubleton the ace is taken first but with the other two combinations care must be taken.

North
H. 864

West
H. J9732

East
H. KQ

South
H. A105

Against either suit or no trump West leads the three of hearts. East, particularly against suit, knows that South has the ace and, therefore, East may not win the trick. Therefore, his proper play is the queen so as not to deny the king.

However, if the ace is in dummy and this is the position:

```
                            North
                            H. A105

West                                               East
H. J9732                                           H. KQ

                            South
                            H. 864
```

If dummy plays low and East plans to continue the suit he should win the king and then continue with the queen to show a doubleton. This, in turn, will help West count the hand and may result in East getting a ruff in certain situations vs. a suit contract.

For example:

```
Neither side vul.          North
Dealer North               S. A75
                           H. K753
                           D. 84
                           C. KQ85

          West                                     East
          S. 96432                                 S. KQ
          H. A6                                    H. 42
          D. 1052                                  D. QJ97
          C. J97                                   C. A10432

                           South
                           S. J108
                           H. QJ1098
                           D. AK63
                           C. 6
```

North	East	South	West
1C	Pass	1H	Pass
2H	Pass	4H	All pass

Opening lead: Three of spades

Dummy plays low and East wins the king. When he continues with the queen the whole world and hopefully West will know that East started with a doubleton.

-254-

If declarer crosses to the ace of diamonds to make the sneaky play of the jack of hearts, West must conceal a smirk, rise with the ace and give his partner a spade ruff. The ace of clubs polishes South off.

If East plays his spades in reverse order, and South falsecards with the jack on the second round, West will assume that East has the ten and may well duck the jack of hearts (assuming declarer plays the same way) hoping partner has the queen, since no spade ruff should be available.

When holding the doubleton KQ, QJ or J10 and dummy wins the first trick, the higher card should be played.

```
                        North
                        D. AK65

        West                             East
        D. 10932                         D. QJ

                        South
                        D. 874
```

West leads the deuce and dummy wins the king or ace. East should drop the queen. Playing the queen does not promise the jack in this situation but playing the jack denies the queen.

WHEN PARTNER LEADS THE WRONG SUIT. (SO WHAT ELSE IS NEW?) Sometimes you will have mentioned a weak suit and partner will make the mistake of trusting you and leading your suit. If you can tell from the lead that partner is also weak you must make an unusual play in third seat...low.

                         North
                         D. Q107

West   East
D. 95   D. J432

                         South
                         D. AK86

West leads the nine of diamonds against a no trump contract,
you, East, having bid the suit. Dummy plays the ten and you
should play the deuce! There is no holding in your partner's
hand, given the lead of the nine, whereby covering with the
jack will help. Furthermore, if you cover, your partner will
think you have another high honor and may continue the suit.

Similarly:

                         North
                         D. 654

West   East
D. 107   D. Q9832

                         South
                         D. AKJ

With East having opened the bidding one diamond, South winds up
playing a spade contract and West leads the ten of diamonds.
You should play low in the East chair for two reasons:

   1. You can tell from the lead that declarer has the AKJ,
       and if he happens to have the seven as well you give
       up a trick by playing the queen.
   2. If you play the queen and declarer wins the ace part-
       ner will think you have KQ and may subsequently err on
       defense.

In this situation the queen promises the king.

And finally:

North
C. A32

West
C. 94

East
C. J8765

South
C. KQ10

West leads the nine of clubs and dummy plays low. If East plays the jack in this situation he would be promising the queen, since there is no point in playing the jack if he does not have the queen. Obviously, East should play low.

(However, if East wants to purposely fool West into continuing the suit he can play the jack at trick one.)

Third hand's responsibility to return the proper card in the suit partner has led cannot be minimized. The rule is simple yet many players play a lifetime without knowing it.

WHEN RETURNING PARTNER'S SUIT, WITH TWO CARDS REMAINING PLAY THE HIGHER; WITH THREE OR MORE CARDS REMAINING PLAY THE ORIGINAL FOURTH HIGHEST.

North (Dummy)
S. 75

West
S. 6

East (Third hand)
S. A103
S. A1032
S. A10432

West leads the six of spades (suit or no trump) and East wins the ace. If East decides to return a spade he returns: the ten in the first case, the deuce in the second, and the three in the third. We will see in the quiz section how West relies

on these plays to determine declarer's honor holding and dis-

tribution.

Returning the correct card is an invaluable defensive tool.
It often acts an an effective unblocking device, enabling the
defenders to run a suit:

                        North (Dummy)
                        S. 76

West   East (Third hand)
S. A9832   S. KQ5

                        South
                        S. J104

West leads the three of spades vs. a no trump declaration. East

wins the queen and is careful to return the king. East-West now

have no trouble running the first five tricks. Try running the

suit if East returns the five instead of the king.

                        North (Dummy)
                        S. 864

West   East (Third hand)
S. A93   S. KQ72

                        South
                        S. J105

West leads the three of spades and East wins the queen. At

trick two he returns the deuce, his original fourth best. West

wins the ace and returns the nine, allowing East to take two

more tricks with the king and seven.

Even when holding worthless cards, third hand is expected to

return the proper spot.

North (Dummy)
S. 64

West
S. K

East (Third hand)
S. 932
S. 8732

South
S. 5

West leads the king vs. no trump; East plays the deuce and declarer the five. West shifts and later East gets the lead. In the first case, with the 93 remaining, East's proper return is the nine, the higher of his two remaining cards. In the second case, having already played his lowest card, East's proper return is the three, his lowest remaining card. If you consistently follow these rules partner will always know how many little cards you started life with.

Finally, third hand may be playing before the dummy instead of after (later in the hand). He will follow the same general rules, but must be doubly careful about watching partner's spot cards:

North (Dummy)
S. Q54

West
S. AJ107

East (Third hand)
S. 963

South
S. K82

At some point in the hand, East shifts to the nine of spades and South plays low. What should West play? Since the nine marks the king in declarer's hand, West plays the seven and waits to capture the king with his ace. That is the same play he would make if South were the dummy and East had led the nine. Remember, when third hand has an honor higher than dummy's he does not waste his honor if he has a nine or better to insert.

Now consider this somewhat similar situation:

                         North (Dummy)
                         S. Q54

West   East
S. AJ102   S. 3

                         South
                         S. ???

During the course of the hand East shifts to the three of spades. Declarer plays low. What should West do? This time East is marked with an honor from his lead of the three. Since the only missing honor is the king, East must have that card; therefore West should play the ace and return the jack. (One of the few times the original fourth best is not returned.) To make this clearer, let's turn the hand around and assume South is the dummy:

                         North (Declarer)
                         S. Q54

West   East
S. AJ102   S. K873

                         South (Dummy)
                         S. 96

Now, looking at two small in dummy, West doesn't hesitate to play third hand high when his partner leads the three.

I. Both sides vul.
    Dealer North

                        North
                        S. K53
                        H. QJ7
                        D. AQJ82
                        C. 102

West   East
S. J862   S. A109
H. 52   H. 643
D. 9643   D. K5
C. A43   C. 98765

                        South
                        S. Q74
                        H. AK1098
                        D. 107
                        C. KQJ

North   East   South   West
1D   Pass   1H   Pass
2H   Pass   4H   All pass

Opening lead: Deuce of spades

II. Neither side vul.
     Dealer South

                        North
                        S. J74
                        H. KQ109
                        D. 732
                        C. 653

West   East
S. Q863   S. K102
H. 82   H. A763
D. 864   D. QJ109
C. J974   C. 102

                        South
                        S. A95
                        H. J54
                        D. AK5
                        C. AKQ8

South   West   North   East
2NT   Pass   3NT   All pass

Opening lead: Three of spades

III. Both sides vul.   North
      Dealer North   S. AKQ
                                 H. 75
                                 D. 87654
                                 C. KJ9

           West   East
           S. 432   S. 8765
           H. Q9432   H. J86
           D. AK   D. 32
           C. 865   C. A432

                                 South
                                 S. J109
                                 H. AK10
                                 D. QJ109
                                 C. Q107

           North   East   South   West
           1D   Pass   2NT   Pass
           3NT   All pass

      Opening lead: Three of hearts

IV.   North-South vul.   North
      Dealer West   S. 1065
                                 H. 974
                                 D. AKQJ9
                                 C. 73

           West   East
           S. 32   S. Q4
           H. KQ108   H. A5
           D. 1065   D. 87432
           C. Q842   C. 10965

                                 South
                                 S. AKJ987
                                 H. J632
                                 D. none
                                 C. AKJ

           West   North   East   South
           Pass   Pass   Pass   1S
           Pass   2D   Pass   3S
           Pass   4S   All pass

      Opening lead: King of hearts

I. East plays the NINE of spades at trick one, which loses to the queen. South draws trumps and runs the ten of diamonds to East's king. East returns the NINE of clubs (showing no interest), West wins and returns the jack of spades. East-West take two spades, a diamond, and a club.

II. East plays the TEN of spades at trick one. Later West gives East the count signal in hearts (by playing the eight first) and East wins the THIRD heart. Declarer can take no more than eight tricks.

III. South wins the first heart and plays a diamond to West. (Or a spade to dummy and a diamond to West.) West can tell from East's play of the jack at trick one that South's original heart holding was AK10. Since West cannot safely continue hearts, he shifts to the EIGHT of clubs (showing no interest). East wins and returns the EIGHT of hearts (higher of two remaining cards). West clears the heart suit and waits to get in with a diamond to run the hearts, defeating the hand two tricks.

IV. East overtakes the opening lead and returns the suit. West wins the ten and queen, East discarding a LOW CLUB (showing no interest). West continues a fourth heart, allowing East to overtrump dummy.

THIRD HAND PLAY   PROBLEMS

I. You are East defending a no trump contract. Partner leads

the three of hearts. Which heart do you play with each of

the following holdings? (Dummy plays the five.)

North (Dummy)
H. 97<u>5</u>

West   East (You)
H. 3   a. H. KJ2
                                        b. H. AJ84
                                        c. H. KQ8
                                        d. H. K108
                                        e. H. 1084
                                        f. H. AQ2
                                        g. H. QJ8
                                        h. H. QJ102
                                        i. H. QJ108
                                        j. H. KJ108
                                        k. H. 842
                                        l. H. KQJ6
                                        m. H. QJ

II. You are East defending a suit contract and your partner

leads the three of hearts. (Spades are trumps.) Which

heart would you normally play with each of the following

holdings? (Dummy plays low.)

North (Dummy)
H. K8<u>4</u>

West   East (You)
H. 3   a. H. AJ9
                                        b. H. Q107
                                        c. H. A5
                                        d. H. QJ62
                                        e. H. AQJ
                                        f. H. 752
                                        g. H. A1097
                                        h. H. A72
                                        i. H. J10
                                        j. H. J106
                                        k. H. AQ102
                                        l. H. 1097
                                        m. H. J95

III. You are East defending a no trump contract. Your partner
has led the three of hearts; in each case you have played
correctly to trick one, and you have won the trick. Assuming you plan to return partner's suit, which card do
you return?

                        North (Dummy)
                        H. 97<u>5</u>

West   East (You)
H. 3   a. H. A106
                                          b. H. AK82
                                          c. H. AJ82
                                          d. H. KQ2
                                          e. H. AJ8
                                          f. H. KQJ
                                          g. H. QJ108

Using the methods we have discussed for third hand play,
put yourself in the West position and try to answer the
questions beneath each diagram.

IV.   North (Dummy)
                        S. 86

        West (You)   East
        S. J75<u>3</u>2   S. 10

                        South
                        S. K

You lead the three of spades against a suit contract.
Partner plays the ten and declarer the king.

    a. Who has the ace?

    b. Who has the queen?

    c. Who has the nine?

V.
North (Dummy)
S. 765

West (You)   East
S. Q84<u>3</u>2   S. 10

South
S. K

You lead the three of spades against a no trump contract.
Partner plays the ten and declarer the king.

   a.   Who has the ace?

   b.   Who has the jack?

   c.   Who has the nine?

VI.
North (Dummy)
H. 862

West (You)   East
H. A94<u>3</u>   H. J

South
H. K

You lead the three of hearts against a no trump contract.
Partner plays the jack and declarer the king.

   a.   Who has the queen?

   b.   Who has the ten?

VII.
North (Dummy)
H. 76

West (You)   East
H. AQ8<u>3</u>2   H. 10

South
H. J

Again you lead the three of hearts against no trump.
Partner plays the ten and declarer the jack.

   a.   Who has the king?

   b.   Who has the nine?

VIII.   North (Dummy)
                               D. 765

       West (You)   East
       D. K1042   D. 9

                               South
                               D. Q

This time you lead the deuce of diamonds against no

trump. Partner's nine loses to declarer's queen.

   a. Who has the ace?

   b. Who has the jack?

   c. Who has the eight?

IX.   North (Dummy)
                               D. 1062

       West (You)   East
       D. Q7543   D. 9

                               South
                               D. A

You lead the four of diamonds vs. a suit contract. Dummy

plays low, partner the nine, and declarer the ace.

   a. Who has the king?

   b. Who has the jack?

   c. Who has the eight?

X.   North (Dummy)
                               C. 1054

       West (You)   East
       C. K832   C. J

                               South
                               C. A

You lead the deuce of clubs vs. a suit contract. Partner

plays the jack and declarer the ace.

   a. Who has the queen?

   b. Who has the nine?

XI.
North (Dummy)
C. 95

West (You)
C. J8632

East
C. Q

South
C. K

You lead the three of clubs vs. a no trump contract.
Partner plays the queen and declarer the king.

a. Who has the ace?

b. Who has the ten?

c. If declarer had taken the trick with the ace
    who would you assume had the king?

XII.
North (Dummy)
S. Q82

West (You)
S. J763

East
S. 10

South
S. A

You lead the three of spades against a suit contract.
Dummy plays low, partner the ten, and declarer the ace.

a. Who has the king?

b. Who has the nine?

XIII.
North (Dummy)
S. K75

West (You)
S. 10862

East
S. J

South
S. Q

You lead the deuce of spades vs. a suit contract. Dummy
plays low, partner the jack, and declarer the queen.

a. Who has the ace?

b. Who has the nine?

XIV.   North (Dummy)
                                    H. Q75

        West (You)   East
        H. 96   H. J

                                    South
                                    H. A

You lead the nine of hearts vs. a suit contract. Dummy

plays low, partner the jack, and declarer the ace.

    a. Who has the king?

    b. Who has the ten?

In each of the following diagrams you will be able to

see TWO cards that your partner, third hand, has played:

the card that he has played to the first trick (under-

lined once) then the card he has returned (underlined

twice). After each problem, answer the questions

to see how clever you are.

XV.   North (Dummy)
                                    H. 65

            West (You)   East
            H. Q10742   H. A3

                                    South
                                    H. 89

        a. Who has the king?
        b. Who has the jack?

XVI.   North (Dummy)
                                    H. 42

        West (You)   East
        H. A10765   H. K9

                                    South
                                    H. 8Q

        a. Who has the jack?
        b. Who has the three?

XVII.

                                    North (Dummy)
                                    S. 76

West (You)   East
S. AJ82   S. K3

                                    South
                                    S. 510

a. Who has the queen?

b. How many spades did East have originally?

XVIII.

                                    North (Dummy)
                                    S. 76

West (You)   East
S. KJ82   S. A9

                                    South
                                    S. 310

a. Who has the queen?

b. How many spades did East have originally?

XIX.

                                    North (Dummy)
                                    C. J7

West (You)   East
C. K1043   C. A8

                                    South
                                    C. 56

a. Who has the queen?

b. Who has the nine?

c. How many clubs did East have originally?

XX.
                              North (Dummy)
                              D. 64

West (You)   East
D. A1082   D. Q3

                              South
                              D. 59

a. Who has the king?

b. Who has the jack?

c. How many diamonds did East have originally?

d. Do you think you have answered enough questions?

I. a. The king.   Third hand high when there are no

                                    honors in dummy.

    b. The ace.   Same as "a".

    c. The queen.   With equal high cards third hand

                                    plays the lower or lowest equal.

    d. The king.   Same as "a".

    e. The eight.   With the nine in dummy the eight

                                    is as good as the ten.

    f. The queen.   To prevent declarer from making a

                                    hold up play. One of the few ex-

                                    ceptions to "a".

    g. The jack.   Same as "c".

    h. The ten.   Same as "c".

    i. The eight.   Same as "c" or "e".

    j. The king.   Same as "a".

    k. The deuce.   With three small cards (lower than

                                    the nine) third hand does not play

                                    high.

    l. The jack.   Same as "c".

    m. The jack.   Same as "c".

II. a. The jack.   When third hand has an honor higher

                                    than dummy's honor he usually plays

                                    his next highest card, if it is a

                                    nine or higher.

b. The queen.   When third hand has no card higher
                than dummy's honor, he plays as if
                there were only small cards in the
                dummy.

c. The ace.   With no card as high as the nine to
                insert third hand plays high, even
                though he has an honor card higher
                than dummy's.

d. The jack.   Same as "b".

e. The jack.   Always win a trick on defense with
                the lower or lowest equal (unless
                you purposely wish to fool either
                your partner or the declarer). If
                you play the queen, partner assumes
                declarer has the jack.

f. The deuce   With three small cards (lower than
                the nine) third hand plays low.

g. The seven.   Retaining the ace over the king.
                The seven is equal to the nine or
                ten when the eight is in dummy.

h. The ace.   Same as "c".

i. The ten.   Lower equal even with doubletons.

j. The ten.   Same as "b".

k. The queen.   Partner probably has the jack, but
                no reason to take a chance. If
                partner does have the jack nothing
                has been lost.

l.   The seven.   Equal to the nine or ten with the
                       eight in dummy.

m.   The jack.   Same as "b".

III.   a.   The ten.   With two remaining cards return
                        the higher.

b.   The ace.   Declarer probably has a doubleton,
                       for partner appears to have a four
                       card suit (he led his lowest card).
                       Declarer might well have Qx.

c.   The deuce.   Original fourth best with four or
                       more cards.

d.   The king.   Same as "a".

e.   The jack.   Same as "a".

f.   The king.   After having played the lowest card
                       in a sequence, play the highest
                       next.

g.   The queen.   Same as "f". (You should have
                       played the eight at trick one.)

IV.   a.   Declarer.

b.   Declarer.

c.   Declarer.   (Third hand never owns the card
                       directly beneath the one he plays.)

V.   a.   Declarer.

b.   Partner.   (If declarer had the jack he would
                       have taken the trick with that card.)

c.   Declarer.

VI. a. Can't tell.   Declarer could be trying to fool
you with KQ, or partner could have
the queen.

b. Declarer.

VII. a. Declarer.

b. Declarer.

VIII. a. Declarer.

b. Declarer.

c. Declarer.

IX. a. Declarer.

b. Partner.   Same as V "b".

c. Declarer.

X. a. Partner.

b. Declarer.   With the ten in dummy, partner
would have played the nine if he
owned it.

XI. a. Can't be sure.   Either player could have the ace,
for partner would probably play
the queen from the ace-queen vs.
no trump.

b. No way of knowing. (That was a trick question.)

c. Probably declarer. Because if his only stopper were
the ace he might have made a
hold up play.

XII. a. Can't tell.   Partner would play the ten from

king-ten as well as from 10x or

10xx.

b. Declarer.

XIII. a. Can't tell.   Partner would play the jack from

the ace-jack as well as from a

holding that did not include the

ace.

b. Can't tell.

XIV. a. Partner.   He can tell from your lead that

you have nothing in the suit.

With a holding headed by the jack

he should play low.

b. Declarer.

XV.   a. Declarer.   If partner has both the ace and

king he plays the king originally.

b. Declarer.   If partner has AJ3 he returns the

jack.

XVI. a. Declarer.   If partner has KJ9 he returns the

jack.

b. Partner.   If declarer has QJ83 he could not

have afforded to play the eight.

XVII. a. Declarer.   Partner's play of the king has denied the queen.

b. Two or four.   Probably four unless declarer has bid the suit. If partner has two declarer has five.

XVIII. a. Declarer.   For two reasons: (1) Holding an ace-queen combination, third hand usually plays the queen; and (2) if East has AQ9 he returns the queen to unblock the suit.

b. Two or three.   Probably three. If East has two then declarer has five and the bidding might have revealed that.

XIX. a. Declarer.

b. Declarer.   If partner has A98 he returns the nine. If partner has AQ98 he plays the queen originally.

c. Very likely three.

XX. a. Partner.   Declarer would have taken the trick otherwise.

b. Declarer.   Partner's play of the queen denies the jack.

c. Four.   He has returned his lowest card showing either two or four, but it must be four because you know he still has the queen.

d. Most definitely.

IX. INFERENCES

You are driving along, it is a sunny day and you approach a busy intersection that has a traffic light. The only trouble is that the sun is shining in your eyes and you can't see the signal, but you see that all the other cars in front of you and along side of you are going through the intersection. What color is the light? Of course, it must be green.

Assuming you weren't killed going through the intersection, you have just made an inference, or a logical assumption, that the light must have been green, based on what the other cars were doing.

This is the same type of reasoning one applies at the bridge table on every single hand, particularly on defense. Your inferences are necessarily based on the fact that declarer is playing logically; and, similarly, the declarer makes inferences based on what the defenders are doing. It goes without saying that if you are defending a hand and declarer doesn't know what he is doing he might send you crashing through an intersection when the light is red!

Let's start out with some simple examples of inferences and work our way to more difficult ones.

Let's say you are defending a spade contract, and between your hand and dummy you can see ten diamonds. You lead the king of hearts and partner overtakes. Obviously he is not void in diamonds or else he would have allowed you to hold the lead.

Again, spades are trumps, and dummy comes down with a side suit in diamonds of AQ10xx. After you make your opening lead you fear that perhaps declarer has the king of diamonds and soon the diamonds will be run off, declarer discarding losers.

But wait! Your partner wins the opening lead and shifts to a trump. Obviously he doesn't fear the diamond suit, so the inference is that your partner has strong diamonds.

Another very common defensive inference is when third hand can judge what is going on in an unseen suit from what is not led. We all know that perhaps the most attractive lead in the game is the king from the ace-king. (Some players lead the ace, conventionally.)

Assume spades are trumps and partner leads a diamond. Dummy comes down with three little hearts and you, East, have four hearts to the queen. You can immediately infer that your partner does not have the ace-king of hearts. Either declarer has them both or they are divided. If your partner has bid, the honors are probably divided.

To a somewhat lesser extent you can draw the same inference when a king-queen is missing in a side suit. If your partner leads another suit it is safe to say that he does not hold both the king and queen of the missing suit.

Still another third hand inference is when partner leads a trump even though dummy has advertised a long or fairly long side suit. The inference here is that partner is well-heeled in that side suit.

Another comes when your partner has bid a suit yet leads another. The reason is usually that he has something like the ace-queen in his suit and is reluctant to lead it.

However, if both you and your partner have bid the same suit yet he leads another, one of three things is probably happening: Either he has the ace of the suit and is afraid to bang it down and set up a possible king in declarer's hand, or more likely, he either has a sequence in another suit or is leading a short suit, with trump control.

Now for some others.

We will start out assuming you are defending a heart contract and you have decided to lead a spade from your king.

<u>North</u> (Dummy)
S. AQ5

<u>West</u> (You)
S. K10732

Let's say dummy plays the ace. How many spades would you expect declarer to have? Right, one, or else declarer would have finessed.

Now let's say declarer plays the queen. Who has the jack? The answer is that your partner has the jack, because if declarer had it he would have played low from dummy.

Now that you have the idea, try this one:

North (Dummy)
S. QJ10

West (You)
S. K765

Hearts are still trumps and early in the hand declarer initiates spades by leading low towards the dummy. Who has the ace? Why? Partner must have the ace or else declarer would have taken a spade finesse by leading the queen from dummy.

Here's another breather:

North (Dummy)
S. Q105

West (You)
S. J3

You lead the jack of spades; declarer plays low from the dummy and wins the trick with the ace. Who has the king? This time you should figure declarer for the king, otherwise he would have covered the jack with the queen.

How about this one:

North (Dummy)
S. 1065

West (You)
S. KQ83

Still defending against hearts you lead the king of spades, partner plays the deuce and declarer allows you to hold the trick. What is going on here? Does declarer have the ace-jack?

The answer to this one is that the declarer does not have the
ace-jack because with the ten in the dummy he would have taken
the king, thus insuring himself a second trick with the jack
and ten. The most likely possibility is that your partner has
Jxx and declarer Axx. In any event, you know that your partner
must have one high honor in spades.

Now this (hearts still trumps):

North (Dummy)
S. 53

West (You)
S. Q106

Early in the play declarer leads a spade from the dummy and plays
the nine, you winning the ten. What is going on here? Does declarer have both the ace and king? No, of course not, or else he
would have played the ace-king and started ruffing spades. Does
partner have the ace-king of spades? Unlikely, since he would
not have ducked the first spade lead off the table with that
holding. Therefore, the ace-king must be split. Does declarer
have the king and partner the ace? Hardly; if declarer had the
king with a doubleton on the table he would have played the king.
Therefore, partner has the king and declarer the ace. Declarer
probably has three or four spades headed by the ace and is simply
ducking a round of spades preparatory to ruffing one or two on
the table.

Speaking of ruffing on the table: Put yourself in the West position defending six hearts after declarer has opened with an artificial two clubs and bid hearts strongly.

```
                          North
                          S. 3
                          H. J1054
                          D. 6543
                          C. 6543

West
S. KJ98
H. 32
D. 872
C. KQ102
```

You lead the king of clubs which declarer wins. Declarer plays
two high trumps, partner discarding two spades, and now plays the
ace of spades and ruffs a spade. A third trump is played to declarer's hand and he proceeds to run all of his trumps and the
ace-king of diamonds, forcing you to remain with one card. Do
you save your king of spades or your queen of clubs?

Perhaps you are thinking you would like to see your partner's
signals on these plays. Well it is not necessary.

Declarer must have a club and not a spade. If he has a spade
left he is a lunatic because he could have ruffed the spade on
the table before drawing all of the trumps.

Defenders must always assume that when declarer does not trump
losers on the table when there is a short suit and sufficient
trumps, it is simply because he does not have any losers in that
suit.

Declarer's hand was: S. Ax   H. AKQxxxx   D. AK   C. AJ

True, you did not defeat the contract by saving properly, but in tournament bridge you would have earned some points from the players who have not read this chapter. Besides, the next time it may be the setting trick you are clutching.

Now let's switch to no trump, but you are still leading spades:

                        North (Dummy)
                        S. Q6

        West (You)
        S. J9432

You lead the three of spades, dummy plays the queen, partner the king and declarer the ace. Who has the ten?

Almost certainly your partner. If declarer had A10x or A10xx the proper play from the dummy is low, to insure two tricks. Declarer might hold A10 doubleton, however.

Now let's take a look at something similar from the other side of the table:

                        North (Dummy)
                        S. Q6

                                East (You)
                                S. K1074

Partner leads the three of spades against no trump and dummy plays low. What's going on? Well if declarer has Ax or Axx he would have played the queen from the table. Therefore, declarer does not have the ace but must have the jack. Your proper play is the king, as declarer may have Jx.

How about this one?

North (Dummy)
S. A105

West (You)
S. K763

This time it doesn't matter whether hearts are trumps or it is
no trump. Early in the hand declarer leads a small spade to
his queen and your king. Who has the jack? Your partner must
have the jack, because if declarer had the queen-jack he would
have finessed spades by leading an honor from his hand.

How about this?

North (Dummy)
S. KQJ105

West (You)
S. 763

Declarer is playing a no trump contract and there are plenty of
entries to the table, yet declarer never touches spades. Who
has the ace? Declarer should have the ace or else he would have
established the suit early. As a defender you should assume declarer has five spade tricks. The same would hold true if dummy
has a strong suit missing the king such as: AQJ10x or AQJxxx.
If declarer does not play this suit it is almost always because
he has the king and is trying to conceal his strength.

Here's a common one that comes up mainly at suit contracts.

North (Dummy)
S. A76

West (You)
S. K10432

You lead a small spade and declarer takes the ace. Who has
the queen? Almost certainly your partner has the queen or

else why didn't declarer allow the lead to ride to his queen?
Later in the hand if you need your partner on lead it should
be safe to underlead your king a second time.

Defenders can also make distributional inferences from what has
and has not been bid. For example, assume a competitive auction
where spades have not been mentioned. The lead is made and dummy comes down with two spades and you, in third seat, have three
spades.

The eight outstanding spades are almost certainly divided 4-4.
If anyone had five spades the suit would surely have been bid.

Here's another similar inference. After the bidding sequence
1NT - 3NT partner leads the deuce of hearts, showing a four card
suit. Dummy comes down with a doubleton spade and you have a
doubleton spade. How are the nine invisible spades divided?
Declarer must have five and partner four. If partner had five
he would not have led from a four card heart suit.

Another. Partner leads the deuce of hearts against the same
bidding and then turns up with a singleton diamond. What is
partner's distribution? He must be 4-4-1-4. The reason is
that since he has led from a four card heart suit it is reasonable to infer that he does not have a five card suit.

Perhaps the most valuable inference available to the defenders
is the way the declarer attacks a hand. Is he drawing trumps?
Is he trying to ruff losers in the dummy? Is he trying to set

up a side suit? Every play declarer makes has some bearing on
his hand. The better you are at drawing inferences, the quicker
you will figure out what is concealed in the hidden hand.

Defenders are also required to make distributional inferences
from both declarer's and dummy's bidding as to trump length,
possible singletons, etc.

For example, if you heard the following bidding:

North	South
1H	1NT
2H	

You would have to assume that unless North is an inexperienced
player he has a six card heart suit, as it is folly to rebid a
five card major over a one no trump response.

Other bidding is even more explicit:

North	South
1S	2C
2H	2NT
3C	3NT
Pass	

What can you infer about this sequence of bids? You should assume
that dummy has a singleton diamond, for a player who bids two suits
and then supports (not prefers) a third should have a singleton in
the fourth suit. What about the South hand? South is presumably
aware of North's distribution yet persists in no trump. Clearly
South must have excellent diamonds, for he is facing a known
singleton. Let's assume you are West and you must make an opening lead against this sequence of bids and this is your hand:

S. 763   H. J10   D. A542   C. J1065.   Which card would you select?

Your reasoning should follow these lines. The normal club lead is out, since partner must be short in clubs. The diamond lead is un-attractive because of the lack of intermediate cards (a determining factor when leading into strength). You should settle on the jack of hearts because your partner must have at least four, more likely five, hearts. How do you know this?

Defenders always assume that if the opponents have an eight card major suit fit they will find it in the bidding. Therefore, it is impossible that North-South have eight hearts between them, so they have seven or less. If they have seven hearts partner has four and if they have six, partner has five. Bridge is actually a very sim-ple game!

Figuring out partner's distribution from the opponents' bidding can lead to some very successful defenses. For example assume you have the following hand sitting West:

S. A4   H. 10875   D. 9764   C. QJ10

The bidding has gone like this:

North	South
1D	2S
2NT	3D
3S	4NT
5D	6S
Pass	

What should you lead? Your normal lead is the queen of clubs ... but not on this bidding. They have each bid diamonds and there is an excellent chance that your partner has a singleton. With the ace of trumps as a certain entry your lead should be a diamond.

Sometimes, turning the tables to see what inferences declarer makes helps us to understand defensive play even more.

The first clue to a defender's holding comes from not only the opening lead but from the amount of time it takes to make the lead. For example, put a defender on lead against a no trump contract with this:

a)   S. QJ1093
         H. A43
         D. 65
         C. Q87

and the queen of spades will practically singe a hole in the tablecloth.

b)   S. 8643
         H. KQ3
         D. J10
         C. 10432

But give the same defender hand b) and the opening lead will come much more slowly. You can rest assured that he does not have a clear cut lead and the opening lead may well be from a short suit.

The lead of a deuce can be most revealing:

North
S. 1093
H. 653
D. Q1054
C. QJ3

South
S. A74
H. AKQ10
D. AK6
C. 987

South plays three no trump and West leads the deuce of spades, presumably from a four card suit. South takes the third spade and plays the ace, king of hearts upon which West discards a club. Now what?

West has led from a four card spade suit and has turned up with a singleton heart. That means that he has eight minor cards. The assumption is that West has four cards in each minor because with a five card suit he probably would have led it in preference to a four card suit.

South should, therefore, play the ace, king, and finesse the ten of diamonds in order to get to dummy to take the marked heart finesse.

A trump lead against a suit contract carries certain inferences. Since it is dangerous to lead a trump if there is a possible long suit on the table, the inference is that the opening leader has that suit under control. For example:

South	North
1S	2C
2S	4S

If West leads a trump against this bidding you can bet your bottom dollar that West has good clubs and is not afraid that declarer is going to use that suit for discards.

Another inference that can be made when a trump is led is that the opening leader is strong in declarer's second suit:

South	North
1S	1NT
2H	3H
4H	Pass

A trump lead against this auction is indicative of a strong spade holding.

Short suit leads also carry inferences. Normally when a player has four trumps he does not try for a ruff, but leads his long suit instead.

Therefore, if a short suit is led the inference is that the trumps are not breaking badly, but the real danger is defensive ruffs. This is particularly true in doubled contracts when one fears insidious trump divisions.

Another inference to be drawn is that when your weakest suit is not led the opening leader must have a very unattractive holding in that suit.

Dummy
xxx

You
Jxx

For example, if West has bid that suit and leads something else it is odds on that West has the AQ and East the K.

The assumption is, when you are missing the AKQ of a suit and it is not led, that the opening leader has neither the AK nor the KQ. If the stronger bidding was to your left you can bet that the A and K are split between the two hands.

The stronger the defenders (the more logical they play) the more inferences declarer can make. For instance, consider this dummy:

North
S. J10x
H. x
D. 9xxx
C. AQ108x

The bidding has proceeded:

South	North
1S	2S
3S	4S

West leads the queen of hearts to East's ace and East returns a trump, not a diamond. The presumption is that East must be strong in clubs or else he could not have risked declarer discarding all of his diamond losers on the clubs.

Another inference that can be put to use with reasonable certainty is that if a player has a singleton in an unbid suit he will lead it. Therefore, if you are faced with this combination of cards in an unbid suit:

Dummy
S. AQ94

You
S. K1032

If anyone is likely to have a singleton spade it is East because West did not lead a spade. Therefore, you should lead the ace and then low to the king to guard against Jxxx in the West hand.

Still another handy inference is that against suit contracts most players will not underlead aces, particularly when the stronger of the two hands is the declarer.

For example, if this were your holding in a side suit:

Dummy
S. K4

You
S. J105

if a small spade is led the best play is low from dummy, since the ace is probably with East. This inference is not as clear if the dummy has bid no trump and the king is more or less marked there, making the underlead of the ace more attractive.

Declarer should also make distributional inferences from what the defenders have and have not bid.

For example, if one defender has bid a suit and the other supported, and you become the declarer and have a total of six cards in that suit, you should assume that the original bidder had four and the partner three.

Furthermore, if the opponents are in the bidding and do not mention a major suit and later you become the declarer and see that you have a total of only five cards in this major suit, you should assume that their cards are divided 4-4. The reason is that if either opponent had five of the major he would surely have mentioned the suit. This leads us into this deal, which you might have seen before because I often use it to illustrate these two points:

```
East-West vul.                    North
Dealer West                       S. Kxx
                                  H. xxx
                                  D. Q10xx
                                  C. K9x

                                  South
                                  S. Ax
                                  H. Axx
                                  D. xxx
                                  C. AJ108x

        West        North        East         South
        1D          Pass         1H           2C
        2H          3C           All pass
```

Opening lead: King of diamonds

West continues with the ace of diamonds upon which East discards a spade; a third diamond is led, you inserting the ten, and East ruffs and returns the queen of hearts. How do you play the clubs?

West started with five diamonds because East failed at trick two; hearts must be 4-3 because East bid them and West supported; spades must be 4-4 because the opponents were in the bidding and the suit was never mentioned. West, therefore, started with four spades, three hearts, five diamonds and a singleton club.

Declarer should rise with the heart ace, lead a club to the king and finesse the jack of clubs on the way back. The ace of clubs will draw the last trump and one of the losers in hearts can be parked upon the queen of diamonds.

The manner in which the defenders handle their strength is also indicative of their holding in the suit.

For example, consider this typical no trump stopper:

Dummy
S. xxx

You
S. Axx

If the queen is led and East signals, the presumption is that East started with Kxx; but if East overtakes the queen with the king, then the inference is that East is unblocking with Kx. This can be very important, particularly to duplicate players. Consider the following deal:

Dummy
S. xxx
H. KQx
D. Al09xx
C. Kx

South
S. Axx
H. Axx
D. QJxx
C. AQx

South	North
1NT	3NT
Pass	

West leads the queen of spades and East plays the king. Plan the play. You should assume East has Kx of spades, and hold off one round. Now if the diamond finesse loses East will have no more spades and you will make five no trump.

If you duck a second round of spades you will find yourself losing two spades and a diamond, making only four no trump. Inconsequential to the rubber bridge player but a matter of life and death to the tournament player.

The thought arises that it would be a good play for East to play the king on the queen with Kxx to make declarer think that East had a doubleton and only hold up one round instead of two.

My reply is that for years I have been begging players to play the king from king doubleton when their partner leads the queen, with minimal success. Therefore, if one is the declarer and the king is placed upon the queen it does not pay to worry about Kxx!

Digressing for a moment from inferences to discuss the hold up play at no trump; consider this deal:

> North
> S. xx
> H. AJ109
> D. QJx
> C. Axxx
>
> South
> S. Axx
> H. KQ
> D. A1098xx
> C. Kx

If South is playing three no trump in a tournament and a spade is led, South should not hold up for even one round! Whenever a contract depends upon a finesse and that finesse is going into the opening leader's hand it does not pay to hold up at all. Furthermore, if the diamond finesse works South makes seven and the hold up play will cost a couple of tricks.

Contrast this to how the hand should be played at rubber bridge. Not only should South hold up in spades twice, but the diamond finesse should not even be attempted. South should lay down the ace of diamonds to cater to the possibility of the singleton king in the West hand with an original holding of five spades. (If spades are 4-4 nothing can defeat the contract.)

One final no trump inference. Whenever a defender has an established suit and then begins to discard that suit, it is a sure sign he has no certain entry.

Therefore, if you are the declarer and are missing the ace and queen of another suit you can bet your last cent that the defender who is discarding his established suit is protecting the queen and does not hold any ace.

Along this same vein, it is much easier to discard from a suit where one holds the ace than the queen. Therefore, when missing the ace and queen of a particular suit and one defender seems to have no trouble with his discards in that suit it is because he has the ace.

In conclusion, let it be noted that expert players are expert for this reason - they are able to make more inferences.

As suits are being bid and played around the table, you too should be on the alert to be making the types of inferences that were discussed in this chapter. Maybe you can even discover some others. Just try not to go through any red lights!

INFERENCES   LESSON HANDS

I.   East-West vul.   North
     Dealer South   S. 10
                                 H. 10976
                                 D. 5432
                                 C. 6543

     West   East
     S. KJ8743   S. Q9652
     H. 2   H. 43
     D. 76   D. J1098
     C. J1097   C. Q8

                                 South
                                 S. A
                                 H. AKQJ85
                                 D. AKQ
                                 C. AK2

     South   West   North   East
     ----   ----   -----   ----
     2C   Pass   2D   Pass
     2H   Pass   4H   Pass
     7H   All pass

     Opening lead: Jack of clubs

II. East-West vul.   North
     Dealer North   S. AQ104
                                 H. 53
                                 D. Q7654
                                 C. 76

     West   East
     S. 76   S. 32
     H. AQ64   H. J1098
     D. K10   D. J92
     C. A9853   C. QJ42

                                 South
                                 S. KJ985
                                 H. K72
                                 D. A83
                                 C. K10

     North   East   South   West
     -----   ----   -----   ----
     Pass   Pass   1S   Dbl.
     3S   All pass

     Opening lead: Six of spades

III. Both sides vul.   North
      Dealer South   S. J32
                                     H. A84
                                     D. 64
                                     C. AQ1098

           West   East
           S. 1084   S. Q976
           H. Q1062   H. K73
           D. AQ32   D. 109
           C. 73   C. 6542

                                     South
                                     S. AK5
                                     H. J95
                                     D. KJ875
                                     C. KJ

           South   West   North   East
           1NT   Pass   3NT   All pass

      Opening lead: Deuce of hearts

IV.   Neither side vul.   North
      Dealer South   S. 983
                                      H. K2
                                      D. Q7654
                                      C. 1098

           West   East
           S. AQ10   S. J7652
           H. QJ10765   H. A943
           D. 98   D. K
           C. 52   C. 763

                                     South
                                     S. K4
                                     H. 8
                                     D. AJ1032
                                     C. AKQJ4

           South   West   North   East
           1D   2H*   Pass   4H
           5C   Pass   5D   All pass

           * Weak Jump Overcall

      Opening lead: Queen of hearts

-299-

I.   After South draws trumps and tests diamonds he has no alter-
      native but to play off all his winners and hope the defend-
      ers discard clubs. West should realize that if South had
      any losing spades he would have trumped them in dummy, so
      he should discard spades and save clubs.

II.   If declarer draws trumps and plays the ace of diamonds (a
      low diamond is better) West must unblock the king, for he
      should infer that if declarer had the jack of diamonds he
      would have finessed. West does not want to be thrown in
      with his doubleton king of diamonds to lead away from
      either hearts or clubs. If he unblocks, East wins the
      third diamond and can lead both clubs and hearts through
      declarer's kings to defeat the contract.

III. East wins the first heart and returns the suit. Although
      it may be tempting to switch to a diamond, East must
      reason that nine diamonds are missing, and if partner
      had five he would probably have led one in preference
      to a four card heart suit. Obviously declarer has five
      diamonds and East should continue hearts.

IV.   Declarer should duck the opening lead to avoid a possible
      spade play through his king. East should realize from
      the bidding that declarer is 5-5, with one heart and two
      spades. (Partner should have a six card suit for his two

level jump overcall.) Therefore East must overtake the
queen with the ace and immediately return a spade before
declarer can discard dummy's spades on his own clubs.

The following situations occur frequently at the bridge table. See if you can infer what is going on by what you see. (Remember you are to assume that declarer is playing logically.)

I.
North (Dummy)
S. J74

West (You)   East
S. KQ102   S. 5

South
S. 6

Defending a suit contract, you lead the king of spades. Partner plays the five, and declarer the six.

  a.   Who has the ace?

  b.   Why?

II.
North (Dummy)
S. KJ9

West (You)
S. A1043

In the middle of a hand, with hearts trumps, declarer leads the king of spades from dummy, both partner and declarer playing low.

  a.   Who has the queen?

  B.   Why?

III.
North (Dummy)
S. AJ2

West (You)   East
S. 10863   S. Q

South
S. K

Defending no trump you lead the three of spades; dummy plays the jack, partner the queen, and declarer the king.

    a. Who has the nine?

    b. Why?

IV.
                  North (Dummy)
                  S. Q1062

West (You)   East
S. K97   S. 3

                  South
                  S. A

Spades are trump and South leads the ace, partner playing the three.

    a. Who has the jack?

    b. Why?

V.
                  North (Dummy)
                  D. J7654

West (You)
D. Q103

                  South
                  D. 2

Playing a no trump contract, South leads a low diamond toward dummy early in the hand.

    a. Would you normally play low or the queen?

    b. Why?

VI.
                  North (Dummy)
                  S. 10983

West (You)   East
S. KQJ4   S. 2

                  South
                  S. 5

Defending no trump, you lead the king of spades. Partner
plays the deuce and declarer the five.

    a. Who has the ace?

    b. Why?

VII.
                   North (Dummy)
                   S. K4

West (You)   East
S. Q9863   S. 2

                   South
                   S. 5

Defending a suit contract, you lead the six of spades.
Dummy plays the king, partner the deuce, and declarer
the five.

    a. Who has the jack?

    b. Why?

VIII.
                   North (Dummy)
                   S. KJ

West   East (You)
S. 6   S. A95

After South has shown a strong hand during the bidding,
and hearts have become trump, West leads the six of
spades. Dummy plays the king.

    a. Who probably has the queen?

    b. Why?

IX.   North (Dummy)
                             S. K4

West (You)   East
S. J9832   S. 5

                             South
                             S. 6

Defending no trump, you lead the three of spades. Dummy

plays the king, partner the five, and declarer the six.

   a. Who has the queen?

   b. Why?

X.   North (Dummy)
                             S. A65

West   East (You)
S. Q   S. K10732

After you have bid spades and partner has not supported,

he leads the queen of spades against a suit contract.

Dummy plays low.

   a. Who has the jack?

   b. Why?

   c. Would your answer be any different if this

       were no trump?

I. a. East.

     b. With the jack in dummy South would win the ace (if he had it), and later lead toward the jack for an additional trick.

II. a. South.

     b. If South did not have the queen he would have started spades by leading <u>toward</u> dummy's holding.

III. a. East.

     b. If South had any combination including the K9 his normal play would be low from dummy, which wins anytime the opening leader has led from either the ten, the queen, or both. (If South has K9x and plays low from dummy, and if East produces the ten, South can always finesse the jack later.)

IV. a. East.

     b. If South had the jack he would have started the suit from dummy, intending to finesse.

V. a. Low.

     b. Playing low loses only when South has the AK; unlikely.

VI. a. East.

     b. If South had the ace he would have taken the trick, for dummy's 1098 would provide a second stopper. (East apparently has A2 doubleton and could not afford to overtake.)

VII. a. East.

     b. If South had the AJx he would play low from dummy.

VIII. a. South.

     b. Good defenders generally do not underlead aces when the stronger hand is to their right. Good declarers know this. Therefore, any time South has shown strength during the bidding and an opening lead comes through a KJ combination it is almost always right to play the jack. The fact that South played the king from dummy is an indication that he has the queen (or is not a very good declarer).

IX. a. South.

     b. If partner had the queen he would signal with a higher spot card. For example, if he held Q75 his play to the first trick should be the seven. With Qx he would normally unblock the queen.

X. a. West.

     b. If declarer had the jack he would win the ace in dummy in order to be able to lead toward the jack later.

     c. No. For the same reason.

X.   COUNTING DECLARER'S DISTRIBUTION

There are at least five ways to count declarer's distribution.

     1.   The bidding.

     2.   Partner's leads.

     3.   Partner's signals.

     4.   The fall of the cards.

     5.   Common sense.

The bidding tells you the most about the makeup of declarer's hand. You must listen, you must infer, and you must know a little bit about bidding yourself to draw the proper inferences. To illustrate, let's take some easy sequences and work into more difficult ones.

Assume you are West and are listening to South's bidding. South opens the auction with three spades. How many spades do you figure South has? Of course, South probably has seven. Remember that figure when the defense starts.

What if South opens four spades? South probably has seven or eight spades. What if South opens with a weak two bid in spades? South almost certainly has a six card suit. What if South opens one spade?

When an opponent opens one of a major, assume he has a five card suit even though the partnership opens four card majors! The reason is that the majority of the time it will be a five card suit. If it is only four, subsequent bidding usually reveals it.

Besides, many players will not open with a four card major, so it pays to assume five FOR THE TIME BEING.

Once you assume an opening bid of one heart or one spade is based upon a five card suit, and you know from experience that a second suit is almost always a four carder, you are on your way. Listen to this one:

South	North
1S	1NT
2H	Pass

You should assume South has five spades and four hearts until you learn otherwise. Without these assumptions it is impossible to play an intelligent defensive game. South may clarify his hand even more if given the opportunity to make more than two bids.

South	North
1S	2C
2H	2NT
3C	3H
4H	Pass

Presumably South has shown five spades and four hearts, his delayed support in clubs indicates a three card holding, so the entire table knows that South started with 5-4-1-3 distribution. Furthermore, everyone should realize that South is playing a 4-3 heart fit.

Responder obviously doesn't have four hearts (he would have raised immediately) so you know by simply looking at your hand how many trumps your partner has, and the moment dummy comes down you know everyone's distribution.

When the opener rebids his suit it is not always clear whether
he has a five card or a six card suit, but knowing the opponents'
system and keeping your ears open help considerably.

    A.   South   North
	South	North
A.	1S	1NT
	2S	

	South	North
B.	1S	2H
	2S	

In "A" South has skipped over every other suit to rebid his own,
a marked indication of a six card suit (assuming South knows how
to bid). In "B" South has not skipped over a single suit, which
means that he may hold either five or six spades. This is the
rule:

THE MORE SUITS OPENER SKIPS OVER TO REBID HIS ORIGINAL SUIT THE
MORE LIKELY HE IS TO HAVE A SIX CARD SUIT.

The reason for this rule is simply that good bidders do not skip
over secondary four card suits to rebid their original suit unless it is a six carder, and even then it is optional.

Now consider this sequence:

South	North
1S	2C
2H	2NT
3S	4S

What is South's most likely distribution? Remember, responder
also assumes the original major opening is a five card suit, so

opener does not rebid a five carder unless he has no other option or the suit is unusually strong and can play opposite a small doubleton. (This is true even if you play four card majors.)

In this sequence South clearly has six spades and four hearts.

Of course we are all familiar with the sequence in which opener rebids his second suit. But even these can be a bit tricky if you have wax in your ears.

	South	North
A.	1H	1S
	2D	2NT
	3D	

	South	North
B.	1D	1S
	2H	2NT
	3H	

In "A" South started with a higher ranking suit and rebid a lower ranking suit twice. South will normally have five hearts and five diamonds, although it is possible for South to have six hearts and five diamonds, or even five hearts and six diamonds and a hand not strong enough to reverse. Assume five hearts and five diamonds.

In the second case South started with a lower ranking suit and rebid a higher ranking suit twice. South cannot have 5-5 distribution or else he would have opened one heart. South must have six diamonds and five hearts.

Jump rebids promise six or seven card suits - never five.

South	North
1H	1S
3H	

South has at least six hearts, and if he had jumped directly to four hearts he would probably have seven.

Rebidding no trump after opening a major does not deny a five card major.

South	North
1H	2C
2NT	3NT
Pass	

The defenders should assume that South has five hearts and very likely 5-3-3-2 distribution. However, if the bidding proceeds:

South	North
1H	2C
2NT	3H
3NT	Pass

the inference is that South has only four hearts since North has shown three card support with ruffing values and South has de-clined the invitation to play the hand in hearts.

Even when declarer makes a jump shift the defenders should assume 5-4 distribution until they learn otherwise.

South	North
1S	1NT
3H	4H

South is assumed to hold five spades and four hearts.

What inferences about declarer's distribution can the defenders draw after a minor suit opening?

Naturally it is a bit tougher to gauge declarer's distribution after a minor suit opening, particularly one club, because of the possibility of a three card suit. Now it becomes very important to know something of your opponents' system. Do they or don't they? Will they or won't they open the bidding with a four card major? If they say seldom it means they won't at gunpoint.

Will they open the bidding with a three card diamond suit? You are entitled to know these things beforehand. Inquire.

In general, assume a minor suit opening contains a four card suit. Furthermore, if it is rebid by a good player he is almost certain to have six, while Mr. and Mrs. John Average will rebid five card minors as quickly as possible to show partner it was not a short club or a short diamond. You have to know your customers when it comes to making assumptions from the bidding.

When opener rebids one no trump after a one club opening on this sequence:

South	North
1C	1D
1NT	

the inference is that South does not have a four card major. Indeed many players would not dream of skipping over a four card major with the South hand on this sequence. On the other hand, some players will skip over a four card major and rebid one no trump if their distribution is precisely 4-3-3-3 or 3-4-3-3. I would.

The point is that if you are really serious about making reasonable distributional assumptions you have to know something about the peculiarities of the players involved.

Don't be taken in by sequences like these:

South	North
1C	1H
1S	1NT
2S	

South is not showing a short club! South must have five spades and therefore either five or six clubs. The fact that South bids his second suit twice merely emphasizes the length of his first suit.

Indeed, the more suit bidding the opener does the more distributional his hand, and the likelihood of a short club is practically nil.

South	North
1C	1H
1S	1NT
2H	2S

If South is bidding intelligently his most likely distribution is four spades, three hearts, one diamond and five clubs. A second possibility is four spades, three hearts, two diamonds and four clubs. Notice that a three card club suit is not even considered once South bids three suits.

WHEN A PLAYER BIDS THREE SUITS HE IS SHORT IN THE FOURTH SUIT, USUALLY HOLDING A SINGLETON. IT THEREFORE STANDS TO REASON THAT HIS FIRST BID SUIT CANNOT BE A THREE CARDER EVEN IF IT IS CLUBS.

Two notable exceptions to this:

1. Some players holding this hand:

> S. K10xx   H. AJx   D. xxx   C. AQx

will bid as follows:

Opener	Responder
1C	1H
1S	1NT
2H	

2. Others with this type of hand:

> S. AQxx   H. KQxx   D. xx   C. Kxx

will bid:

Opener	Responder
1C	1D
1H	1S
2S	

In both cases, particularly (1), they have performed a masterpiece of concealing their distribution.

Many bidding sequences promise balanced hand patterns; for example, opening bids of one, two or three no trump, or direct responses of either two or three no trump. The distribution of the no trumper's hand will invariably be either (a) 4-3-3-3 (b) 4-4-3-2 or (c) 5-3-3-2.

Sometimes the bidding and/or partner's lead will furnish enough clues to determine the exact distribution.

Opener	Responder
1NT	2C
2S	3H
3NT	

Opener has shown four spades and denied three hearts. Therefore his distribution must be 4-2 in the majors and 4-3 in the minors.

Sometimes the opening lead will pinpoint the minor suit distribution immediately.

Opener	Responder
1NT	2C
3S	3NT
Pass	

Opener has shown a five card spade suit, so his distribution must be 5-3-3-2.

Partner's leads can even be more revealing. Say partner leads a deuce against a no trump contract. Later he turns up with a singleton in a side suit. His most obvious distribution is 4-4-4-1 otherwise he would have led from a five card suit. Once you know partner's distribution you also know declarer's.

Opener	Responder
1NT	2C
2D	2S
2NT	3NT

Opener has denied a four card major and does not have three card spade support. Therefore, he must have two spades and three hearts. Now assume partner leads the deuce of clubs; you hold A9 and dummy the 84. Partner has four clubs and you and dummy each have a doubleton, leaving declarer with five clubs. So his entire distribution, starting with spades, must be 2-3-3-5.

Or:

	Opener	Responder
	1NT	2C
	2D	3NT
	Pass	

Assume opener turns up early in the hand with a doubleton diamond. You should realize that he has five clubs and three cards in each major. (He has denied a four card major and would not open one no trump with two doubletons.)

Also keep in mind the difference between these two similar sounding sequences:

	Opener	Responder
A.	1S	2NT

	Opener	Responder
B.	1S	2C
	2H	2NT

In "A" responder must have a balanced hand and presumably 13-15 high card points, although players have been known to hold 12.

In "B" responder has fewer high card points (10-12) and need not have balanced distribution. He is quite likely, for example, to have a singleton spade.

The same reasoning applies if responder's second bid is three no trump, as opposed to an immediate response of three no trump. An immediate response is a point or two stronger (16-17) and promises balanced distribution; a three no trump rebid shows 13-15 and could well contain a singleton in a bid suit.

If the responder becomes the declarer, what new distributional inferences are available:

	Opener	Responder
A.	1D	1H
	2H	Pass

	Opener	Responder
B.	1D	1H
	2H	4H
	Pass	

What can we infer about responder's heart length? In "A" we can't tell for sure how many hearts responder has - only that he has a weak hand.

In "B" we know responder has at least five hearts since he would not unilaterally commit the partnership to a major game contract with fewer than eight trumps. (Opener's raise in most systems can show either three or four card support.)

If opener's raise guarantees four hearts (in some systems it does), then responder could have a four card heart suit. Another point you must know about your opponents' system.

When responder receives a major suit raise and then branches off into no trump, there is a strong inference that his major is a four carder.

Opener	Responder
1C	1H
2H	2NT
3NT	

Responder has four hearts and opener three. If opener returns to three hearts and responder either passes or bids four hearts you can be sure the opponents are playing a 4-4 fit.

IT IS OF THE UTMOST IMPORTANCE TO KNOW HOW MANY TRUMPS THE OPPO-NENTS HAVE BETWEEN THEM WHEN DEFENDING A SUIT CONTRACT.

When responder bids two suits, assume the first suit has five cards and the second suit four. If responder jumps in his own suit without support, assume a six or seven card suit. The more suit bidding the responder does the more distributional his hand.

	Opener	Responder
A.	1C	1S
	2C	2H

	Opener	Responder
B.	1C	1S
	2C	3S or 4S

	Opener	Responder
C.	1C	1S
	2C	2H
	2NT	3C
	3S	4S

In "A" responder presumably has five spades and four hearts, although he could have five spades and five hearts. Remember, with two five card suits the responder bids the higher ranking suit first.

In "B" responder has either six or seven spades.

In "C" responder has five spades, four hearts, three clubs and one diamond. It is also very likely that the opponents are playing a 5-2 spade fit, for opener would certainly have supported sooner with three cards.

WITH TWO OR MORE FOUR CARD SUITS RESPONDER NORMALLY BIDS THE CHEAPEST, OR LOWER RANKING, SUIT FIRST.

Opener	Responder
1C	1H
2H	2NT
3NT	Pass

The inference, as mentioned before, is that responder has four hearts. Also, it is unlikely that responder has four diamonds, but possibly four spades.

Opener	Responder
1D	1S
2S	2NT
3NT	Pass

Responder has four spades and not four hearts, for his normal response is one heart with four of each major.

Opener	Responder
1S	2H
2S	2NT
3NT	Pass

Responder has five hearts.

A TWO LEVEL RESPONSE IN HEARTS GUARANTEES A FIVE CARD SUIT. A TWO LEVEL RESPONSE IN A MINOR CAN BE MADE ON A FOUR CARD SUIT.

Finally, if the original response is two or three no trump you know the responder's hand is balanced.

Opener	Responder
1S	2NT
3H	3NT
Pass	

Opener has five spades and four hearts and responder a doubleton spade, since he would give preference with three card support on this bidding. Once it is assumed that responder has two spades, it is clear that responder has three hearts, since he would not respond two no trump with two doubletons, and he obviously does not have four hearts.

This is the killer:

<pre>
          Opener   Responder
          1S   1NT
          Pass
</pre>

Responder can have anything ranging from a balanced hand to one with a void in partner's suit and a weak six card side suit! One must be very careful when defending against this sequence, as responder frequently turns up with unexpected length.

Once the bidding has revealed the distribution of two of declarer's suits, the opening lead may tell all about a third. Once you know three you know four:

<pre>
East-West vul.   North
Dealer South   S. Q7
                            H. K432
                            D. Q876
                            C. AQ7

          West   East
          S. 10432   S. 65
          H. J6   H. Q75
          D. K53   D. AJ92
          C. J853   C. K942

                            South
                            S. AKJ98
                            H. A1098
                            D. 104
                            C. 106

          South   West   North   East
          1S   Pass   2NT   Pass
          3H   Pass   4H   All pass
</pre>

Opening lead: Three of diamonds

East and West assume for the time being that declarer has five spades and four hearts, although they may change their minds once the play develops.

When East sees the opening lead, West's smallest card, he assumes a four card suit headed by at least one honor, and his first thought is that declarer is probably 5-4-1-3.

In any case, East wins the first trick with the jack and returns the deuce, his original fourth best. When declarer follows, both East and West have a count on declarer's hand. East knows that West has led from three diamonds to an honor, and West knows that East started with four. So declarer is marked with 5-4-2-2 distribution.

West wins the second diamond and immediately shifts to a club before declarer can discard dummy's clubs on good spades. This defense defeats the contract one trick.

Partner's signal at trick one, along with the bidding, is often enough to give an alert defender a full count on declarer's hand.

Both sides vul.   North
Dealer South   S. AQ3
                    H. A105
                    D. J74
                    C. Q1063

West   East
S. 1094   S. KJ82
H. 76   H. 984
D. 865   D. Q109
C. AK875   C. 942

                    South
                    S. 765
                    H. KQJ32
                    D. AK32
                    C. J

South	West	North	East
1H	Pass	2NT	Pass
3D	Pass	3H	Pass
4H	All pass		

Opening lead: King of clubs

East-West begin by assuming declarer has five hearts and four
diamonds. When West sees East's deuce of clubs at trick one
he reads it as low from a three card suit when declarer follows. This gives declarer an original distribution of 3-5-4-1
and a spade shift is called for before declarer leads the queen
of clubs from dummy, discarding one spade, and then uses the
ten of clubs to discard another.

At trick two West shifts to the ten of spades. If dummy's
queen is played East must win and return a spade (or a trump),
but not a club. If a club is returned South discards a spade
and later two more diamonds on dummy's established clubs.
Help!

The count signal on defense is a great help in counting the hand. To review this signal for the last time: When DECLARER or DUMMY leads a suit for the first time the defenders can, if they wish give each other (and declarer) a count on the suit by playing high-low with a doubleton, low from odd (three or five cards) and second high from four if it can be afforded, otherwise third high.

For example, assume declarer is playing a heart contract; this is the layout of the spade suit and there are trumps in dummy.

```
                        North (dummy)
                        S. 63

        West                            East
        S. J542                         S. Q987

                        South (Declarer)
                        S. AK10
```

Assume that South plans to trump his ten of spades in dummy, and plays the ace-king. West follows with the 5-4 and East with the 9-8 (third highest should be played after second highest to show four, although most players don't do this). Now when South ruffs the ten of spades in dummy and both defenders see each other follow they know that each other's high-low showed a four card suit and declarer has no more spades. (East, for example, may have to discard later in the hand and he can safely discard his queen of spades knowing declarer does not own the jack.)

This may sound easy enough, but defenders have been known to forget that when declarer or dummy initiates a suit the only signal they can give is the count signal. In an effort to show strength they often mislead partner as to the count.

<pre>
                        North (Dummy)
                        S. 43

    West   East
    S. 86   S. KJ972

                        South
                        S. AQ105
</pre>

Again spades is a side suit and declarer leads the four from dummy. East should play the deuce (lowest from odd). The deuce does not mean that East is weak in spades, it simply means he has an odd number. If East, for example, panics and plays 7-2 he is showing an even number of spades, which might confuse West. West, on the other hand, plays 8-6 to show a doubleton.

Before proceeding further with the count signal, there are a few points to keep in mind.

1. Playing against a weak (blind) declarer, by all
    means give as many count signals as you can.
    He surely won't notice, so you and partner can
    merrily tell each other secrets about your dis-
    tribution without worrying about an eavesdropper.

2. Against a strong declarer (like yourself) be a
   little more prudent. Save the signal for times
   when declarer leads up to dummy's length or when
   you have a particularly weak hand and can help
   partner (who has all the missing strength) by
   giving him the count. He, on the other hand,
   does not have to worry about giving you count
   because you will seldom take a trick if your
   hand is very weak. One more example:

                    North (Dummy)
                    S. KQJ10

West   East
S. 8743   S. A92

                    South
                    S. 65

South leads a spade toward dummy in a diamond contract. West
plays the seven. East reads this as either two or four spades.
He surely can tell from the bidding that South does not have
four spades (which he would have if the seven were from a doubleton), and so he assumes that West has four spades. With that in
mind East wins the second spade trick, making it tougher for South
to reach dummy's remaining spades. Also, if West were to discard
a spade early in the play he would discard the seven, the same
card he would play if the suit were led. This high-spot discard
when holding worthless cards is done only when dummy has great
strength. Usually a high-spot discard indicates strength rather
than distribution.

Here is another typical situation in which a defensive player
must rely on the bidding as well as his partner's count signal:

                          North (Dummy)
                          S. KQJ10

West   East (You)
S. 2   S. A76

                          South
                          S. 3

South leads the three of spades up to dummy's holding and West
plays the deuce, showing either three or five (an odd number).
How can East tell?

If South has shown a balanced hand during the bidding he is
unlikely to have a singleton so West's deuce cannot be from
five; so it must be from three, meaning that South also has
three spades. East is usually best advised to win the third
round, particularly at no trump with no sure dummy entry visible.

On the other hand, if, during the bidding, South has shown a red
two suiter he is presumably short in spades. In that case it is
very likely that West's deuce is from five and declarer does, in
fact, have a singleton spade. East will usually be best advised
to win the first spade, particularly at a suit contract where he
may lose his ace if declarer turns out to have a singleton.

Another review: Some of the plays we saw in the chapter on
Third Hand Play are really going to help you count a hand.

                        North (Dummy)
                        S. 76

West   East
S. KJ43   S. Q1052

                        South
                        S. A98

South is playing a club contract and West leads the three of

spades to East's queen and South's eight. East returns the

deuce of spades, his original fourth best to give West the

count. Had East Q92, he would return the nine to show a three

card holding. Also remember that if South chooses to win the

first trick, and if East is forced to discard later in the hand,

IF HE DISCARDS A SPADE IT SHOULD BE THE SAME ONE HE WOULD HAVE

RETURNED. This gives West the count.

                (FOR SERIOUS MINDED PLAYERS ONLY)

Expert defenders have developed the following method to help

partner with the count of the hand.

                        North (Dummy)
                        S. Q4

            West   East
            S. 1052   S. KJ9873

                        South
                        S. A6

East has bid spades and West leads the deuce to the queen, king,

and ace. Later in the hand East wishes to discard a spade; which

one should he discard? Traditionally East has discarded his eight,

his original fourth best. However, this is confusing as he would

also discard the eight if his original holding were KJ986.
Assuming West knows that East has some length in the suit, he
still won't know whether East started with five or six spades
after the play of the eight.

The better way is to discard the three, the lowest card. By
agreement this shows an original holding of either four, six,
or eight (rare). An expert West will know the entire spade
distribution immediately upon seeing that three.

Therefore, if the discard of the lowest remaining card, AFTER
THE SUIT HAS BEEN PLAYED ONCE, shows an original holding of an
even number of cards, the discard of a high spot, AFTER THE
SUIT HAS BEEN PLAYED ONCE, shows an original holding of an odd
number of cards - three or five (or seven).

North (Dummy)
S. Q4

West   East
S. 1052   S. KJ983

South
S. A76

Assume diamonds are trump, spades have never been mentioned, and
West strikes upon the lead of the deuce of spades to the queen,
king, and ace. Early in the hand East wishes to discard a spade.
He should discard the nine to show an original holding of an odd
number. Even a non-expert West might be able to figure East for
five spades rather than three. (If East has three spades, then
South has five and surely would have mentioned the suit.)

This signal can be invaluable in situations where partner has
made a preemptive opening and it is difficult to determine his
exact length.

North (Dummy)
S. J10

West
S. 72

East
S. KQ986543

South
S. A

Assume that East has opened four spades and South is playing
the hand. West leads the seven of spades to the ten, queen,
and ace. At this point, from West's point of view, East could
have started with either seven or eight spades. But assume that
East discards the three at his first opportunity. Now West knows
that East started with an even number, most likely eight since an
original preempt at the four level is not often made with a six
card suit.

In each of these examples declarer has won the first trick and
the defender with length has discarded from his long suit to
give partner the count. What if the player with length wins
the trick and wishes to return the suit?

Now there could be trouble because of a conflict of signals.
Defending a suit contract the player with length does not always
give count on his return. If he suspects a singleton his return
is suit preference oriented, so that partner knows which suit to
return after ruffing.

However, if the defender with length knows that his partner will not be trumping, he can give the count in the same fashion as he did when discarding.

```
                         North (Dummy)
                         S. 105

West                                      East
S. Q82                                    S. AJ9743

                         South
                         S. K6
```

East has bid spades, West has supported, but South becomes declarer. West leads the deuce of spades to the ace and declarer's six. Traditionally, East has returned the seven of spades (his original fourth best) and West was left in the dark as to the original holding. (East could have AJ974 and South K63.)

However, a modern East returns the three, showing an original holding of an even number. West should be able to work out from the bidding whether East started with four or six spades.

The beauty of this method is that it is almost impossible for declarer to false card to prevent the defenders from getting the count.

```
                         North (Dummy)
                         S. 74

West                                      East
S. K103                                   S. AJ865

                         South
                         S. Q92
```

East has bid spades, West supported, and South plays a touchy heart contract wherein the defenders have to adopt a passive defense (not breaking new suits).

West leads the three to East's ace and South's nine. East returns the eight (showing an odd number) to the queen and king. At this point West knows South has another spade and he can safely continue the suit, knowing that a ruff-sluff is not being donated.

Playing the old way East would return the six of spades; and if South had false carded with the nine earlier and then played the queen it would be impossible for West to discern the original spade position, for East might well have started with AJ8652 and a third spade might be giving South, that tricky devil, a ruff-sluff.

```
                      North (Dummy)
                      S. 72

West                                          East
S. KQ10863                                    S. 954

                      South
                      S. AJ
```

West leads the king of spades vs. a suit contract to South's ace. Early in the hand West discards the three of spades to show an original holding of an even number. A competent East can work out from the bidding whether West started with four or six spades.

```
                      North (Dummy)
                      S. 1042

West                                          East
S. KQ987                                      S. 653

                      South
                      S. AJ
```

In this very similar situation West leads the king of spades to South's ace. Again West must make an early discard. This time

West discards the nine of spades (not the eight, which could be from KQ98) to show an original holding of an odd number.

We have seen that from the other side of the table (when East held the long suit) the first discard can clarify length in preemptive situations.

                            North
                            S. J10

West   East
S. KQ986543   S. 72

                            South
                            S. A

West has preempted spades, showing either seven or eight, and leads the king. Later he discards the three to show an original holding of an even number. Had West's original spade holding been KQ98654, his first discard would be the nine to show an original holding of an odd number.

Keep in mind that this particular form of count signal is made by a player who has either led an honor or played an honor when his partner has led the suit.

You are almost ready to play with the big boys. Now all you have to do is put it all together.

Both sides vul.   North
Dealer North   S. 432
                                         H. QJ102
                                         D. K65
                                         C. KQ4

              West   East (You)
              S. Q8   S. AK76
              H. K9   H. 53
              D. QJ1043   D. 982
              C. 9832   C. J1075

                                         South
                                         S. J1095
                                         H. A8764
                                         D. A7
                                         C. A6

              North   East   South   West
              Pass   Pass   1H   Pass
              3H   Pass   4H   All pass

Opening lead: Queen of diamonds

Follow the play from the East position. Dummy wins the first
trick and the queen of hearts goes to partner's king. At this
point you don't have a count on any suit.

Partner returns the ten of diamonds to declarer's ace, so you
still don't know if declarer has any more diamonds. Keep cool;
your moment is coming. Declarer leads a trump to dummy and your
partner plays the nine, the highest missing spot card, meaning
he has no more hearts. So you know declarer started with five
hearts. Now South ruffs a diamond in his hand, so you know he
started with two diamonds. Then declarer plays three rounds of
clubs, discarding a spade from his hand. Now the count is complete. Declarer started with 4-5-2-2 distribution and remains
with three spades.

When a spade is led from dummy you must play low, hoping partner
has Jx (and declarer with a presumed Q109 misguesses) or that
partner has Qx, in which case you would block the suit if you
won the trick. You see how important it is to stay with these
hands? If you don't, at the end of a hand such as this you will
be defending like a lost sheep.

I. Neither side vul.   North
    Dealer South   S. 1032
                               H. AK107
                               D. AQ4
                               C. 962

    West   East
    S. AKQJ654   S. 98
    H. J986   H. 432
    D. none   D. 532
    C. Q4   C. A10753

                               South
                               S. 7
                               H. Q5
                               D. KJ109876
                               C. KJ8

    South   West   North   East
    3D   4S   5D   All pass

    Opening lead: King of spades

II. East-West vul.   North
    Dealer South   S. 9
                              H. AJ7
                              D. Q984
                              C. KJ532

    West   East
    S. QJ654   S. 102
    H. 54   H. 632
    D. AKJ7   D. 103
    C. Q7   C. A109864

                              South
                              S. AK873
                              H. KQ1098
                              D. 652
                              C. none

    South   West   North   East
    1S   Pass   2C   Pass
    2H   Pass   2NT   Pass
    3H   Pass   4H   All pass

    Opening lead: King of diamonds

III. Both sides vul.   North
      Dealer East   S. 1042
                              H. 10653
                              D. K5
                              C. AJ86

      West   East
      S. 93   S. A865
      H. K42   H. 7
      D. A7642   D. J983
      C. 942   C. Q1075

                              South
                              S. KQJ7
                              H. AQJ98
                              D. Q10
                              C. K3

      East   South   West   North
      Pass   1H   Pass   2H
      Pass   4H   All pass

      Opening lead: Nine of spades

IV.   Both sides vul.   North
      Dealer South   S. QJ65
                              H. A43
                              D. A2
                              C. AJ43

      West   East
      S. 32   S. 74
      H. QJ109   H. 852
      D. J8764   D. KQ1095
      C. 72   C. Q98

                              South
                              S. AK1098
                              H. K76
                              D. 3
                              C. K1065

      South   West   North   East
      1S   Pass   3C   Pass
      4C   Pass   4S   Pass
      4NT   Pass   5S   Pass
      5NT   Pass   6C   Pass
      6S   All pass

      Opening lead: Queen of hearts

KEY PLAYS

I. After ruffing the second spade, drawing trumps, and discarding a club on a heart, South leads up to his KJ of
clubs. If East is counting he knows at this point that
declarer has two clubs, and plays low without hesitating.
If South misguesses the club position he loses the hand.
If East plays the ace there is no problem.

II. East signals with the ten of diamonds and West plays the
ace and a diamond, East trumping dummy's nine. East knows
from the bidding that South is 5-5 in the majors and has
seen South produce three diamonds. Obviously South is
void in clubs. A trump shift is clearly called for since
both declarer and partner are marked with five spades.
The trump return ruins South's crossruff and he must come
up one trick short.

III. East knows from the bidding that South has at least five
hearts and, therefore, not five spades. In other words,
the nine of spades is NOT a singleton, so it must be a
doubleton. East signals with the eight, and later when
West wins the king of hearts he returns his remaining
spade to get a ruff. The ace of diamonds is the setting
trick.

IV. South draws trumps, plays the ace and ruffs a diamond, and then two more rounds of hearts throwing West on lead. West counts South for four clubs and knows that a ruff-sluff won't help South. West returns a red card and South still has to go-a-hunting for the queen of clubs. COUNTING IS ONE DEFENSE AGAINST STRIP AND END PLAYS.

COUNTING DECLARER'S DISTRIBUTION   PROBLEMS

I. What do you assume South's major suit distribution to
    be from the bidding:

      a.   <u>South</u>   <u>North</u>

	South	North
a.	1NT	2C
	2S	3H
	3NT	Pass
b.	2NT	3C
	3D	3H
	3NT	Pass
c.	1S	2D
	2S	2NT
	3H	4H
	Pass	
d.	1S	2C
	2H	3C
	3S	4S
	Pass	
e.	1S	2H
	2NT	3NT
	Pass	
f.	1H	1NT
	2S	2NT
	3S	4S
	Pass	
g.	1H	1NT
	2S	2NT
	3H	4H
	Pass	
h.	1C	1D
	1H	1S
	2S	4H
	Pass	

-340-

i. | South | North |
|---|---|
| 1S | 2C |
| 2H | 3S |
| 3NT | Pass |

II. Playing a suit contract, declarer leads up to a heart side suit on the table.

North (Dummy)
H. KQJ8

West (You)
a. H. 752
b. H. 10763
c. H. 97652
d. H. 10953
e. H. 102

Which heart do you play in each case?

III.   North (Dummy)
                          S. 54

West   East
S. 1087   S. KJ632

                          South
                          S. AQ9

South is playing a heart contract and leads a spade from dummy, finesses the queen, plays the ace, and then trumps the nine in dummy. How do East-West play their spades if they decide to give each other the count signal?

IV. Both sides vul.   North (Dummy)
     Dealer South   S. 52
                              H. KQ54
                              D. A76
                              C. 7654

          West (You)
          S. 763
          H. A1072
          D. QJ98
          C. Q10

          South   West   North   East
          1S   Pass   1NT   Pass
          4S   All pass

Opening lead: Queen of diamonds

Dummy plays low, partner the deuce and declarer the three.

You continue with the eight of diamonds to dummy's ace,

partner's king, and declarer's four. Declarer draws three

rounds of trumps, partner discarding the nine of hearts on

the third round.

     a. What is declarer's entire distribution?

     b. If declarer leads a low heart at this point, what

         do you do?

V. East-West vul.   North (Dummy)
    Dealer North   S. A72
                                  H. J1065
                                  D. KQ1086
                                  C. 9

                                              East (You)
                                              S. J954
                                              H. AQ82
                                              D. 4
                                              C. Q865

North	East	South	West
Pass	Pass	1D	1S
3D	4S	5D	All pass

Opening lead: King of spades

Dummy wins and a spade is ruffed at trick two. A diamond is led to dummy, partner furnishing the jack, and
another spade is ruffed in the closed hand. Declarer
now plays the king, ace, and four of clubs, ruffing in
dummy, partner playing the 2-3-7 in that order.

a. What is declarer's original distribution?

b. What heart do you play when the jack is led
    from dummy?

VI. Both sides vul.   North (Dummy)
     Dealer North   S. 1065
                              H. 643
                              D. A2
                              C. KQ1098

                                             East (You)
                                             S. AJ983
                                             H. J752
                                             D. QJ9
                                             C. J

     North   East   South   West
     Pass   Pass   1C   Pass
     3C   Pass   5C   All pass

Opening lead: King of spades

Declarer ruffs the second spade lead, enters dummy
with a club, partner playing the four, ruffs another
spade and then plays the ace, king and ruffs a diamond, partner playing 3-6-7 in that order.

   a. What is declarer's entire distribution?

   b. When a low heart is played from dummy
       which heart do you play?

VII.   Neither side vul.   North (Dummy)
        Dealer West   S. 87
                                   H. J72
                                   D. A965
                                   C. KJ94

                                                  East (You)
                                                  S. KJ9643
                                                  H. 53
                                                  D. 2
                                                  C. AQ103

        West   North   East   South
        Pass   Pass   1S   4H
        4S   5H   All pass

Opening lead: Ace of spades

Declarer ruffs, plays the ace and ten of hearts to

dummy's jack, partner following, and ruffs dummy's

remaining spade. Declarer now leads a low club to

dummy's jack and your queen, partner playing the

deuce.

    a.   What is declarer's distribution?

    b.   What do you play at this point?

I. a. Four spades and two hearts.   Holding three hearts, South raises to four hearts.

    b. Three spades and two hearts.   With three hearts, South raises to four hearts.

    c. Six spades and four hearts.   With five spades and four hearts, hearts are rebid immediately.

    d. Six spades and four hearts.   The difference between "c" and "d" is that in "c" South is showing a weaker hand.

    e. Five spades and two hearts.   With three hearts South usually raises immediately. South might even have a singleton heart, but never a void.

    f. Six hearts and five spades.   South has shown five spades by rebidding them, and if he held only five hearts he would have opened the bidding with one spade.

g. Six hearts and four spades.

South already promised five hearts and four spades so there is no point in rebidding hearts without six cards in the suit.

h. Four hearts and four spades, and presumably four clubs.

Although playing five card major openings, South could have 4-4-2-3.

i. Four spades and four hearts.

However, if North-South are playing five card majors South should have five spades and four hearts.

II. a. The deuce.

Low from odd.

b. The seven.

Second high from four.

c. The deuce.

Low from odd.

d. The five.

Third high from four if you can't afford second high.

e. The ten.

High-low from a doubleton if you can afford it.

III. West plays the 7-8-10 and East the 2-3-6. However, East may well falsecard with the king, a card he is known to hold.

IV.

North
S. 52
H. KQ54
D. A76
C. 7654

West
S. 763
H. A1072
D. QJ98
C. Q10

East
S. 94
H. J983
D. K2
C. J9832

South
S. AKQJ108
H. 6
D. 10543
C. AK

a. Declarer is marked with six spades from the play of
    the suit, four diamonds from partner's failure to
    signal at trick one, and one heart from partner's
    discard signal. Notice that East gambles by dis-
    carding the nine of hearts to give partner the
    count, even though it costs a trick if declarer
    has the ace. The reason he can be so frivolous
    is that if declarer has the ace of hearts he has
    at least ten tricks anyway.

b. West should rise on the heart play, exit with a
    club, and wait for his two diamond tricks. Notice
    that South could have made this hand had he cashed
    his two high clubs before leading the heart.

V.   North
                                S. A72
                                H. J1065
                                D. KQ1086
                                C. 9

West   East
S. KQ1086   S. J954
H. K7   H. AQ82
D. J   D. 4
C. J10732   C. Q865

                                South
                                S. 3
                                H. 943
                                D. A97532
                                C. AK4

a. Declarer is marked with 1-3-6-3 distribution

    from the way he is playing the hand, as well

    as from partner's count signal in clubs.

b. You should play a low heart hoping partner

    has the king, in which case you can take three

    tricks. If you play the ace or queen you block

    the suit. Strangely enough, if you are defend-

    ing six diamonds and the play comes up the same,

    you should cover the jack with the queen, play-

    ing partner for 9x of hearts. Of course he has

    to unblock the nine under declarer's presumed

    king, but that's not your problem.

VI.   North
                        S. 1065
                        H. 643
                        D. A2
                        C. KQ1098

West   East
S. KQ74   S. AJ983
H. K109   H. J752
D. 108763   D. QJ9
C. 4   C. J

                        South
                        S. 2
                        H. AQ8
                        D. K54
                        C. A76532

a. Declarer should be 1-3-3-6. (You must assume
    that if partner had a second tiny trump declarer
    would have pulled it before messing around in
    the other suits.)

b. You must play the jack! You need two heart
    tricks, and if declarer has the AQx you cannot
    allow him to duck the trick into partner who
    will be endplayed, having to either lead from
    his king of hearts or give declarer a ruff-
    sluff.

VII.   North
                           S. 87
                           H. J72
                           D. A965
                           C. KJ94

          West   East
          S. AQ1052   S. KJ9643
          H. 64   H. 53
          D. Q87   D. 2
          C. 872   C. AQ103

                           South
                           S. none
                           H. AKQ1098
                           D. KJ1043
                           C. 65

a. Declarer should be 0-6-5-2 judging from partner's
    club play.

b. You should cash the ace of clubs and exit with a
    spade (or a club), giving declarer a ruff-sluff
    that will not help. Let declarer work out the
    diamond suit himself. You only need one more
    trick to defeat the contract.

XI. COUNTING DECLARER'S POINTS

ANALYZING NO TRUMP SEQUENCES FOR POINT COUNT RANGES

It is easy to zero in on declarer's point count if at some time during the bidding he bids no trump. Keep in mind that most no trump bids are limited, which means they will have a narrow range - usually three points.

Let's start by looking at some sequences in which opener becomes declarer after having bid no trump en route.

The simplest sequences of all are those that begin with either one or two no trump. The main point to remember is that not everyone uses the same ranges. The 16-18 range is not quite as common as it used to be. Gradually becoming more popular are 15-17 or 15-1/2 - 17-1/2. Of course, if your opponents are using weak no trumps, their range is 12-14. The Precision range is 13-15.

The opening bid of two no trump is not always the old standby 22-24. Most experts now use 20-22 or 20-21, with the artificial opening of two clubs followed by a rebid of two no trump to show hands in the 22-24 or 23-24 range. The point is that you must know your opponents' no trump ranges. In a tournament, of course, these ranges are listed on the convention cards, but it is sur-prising how many players do not bother to check before commencing the defense.

Consider these common sequences in which opener bids no trump and becomes declarer.

1. Opener   Responder
   1D   1H
   2NT   3NT
   Pass

Playing the modern game, opener has a count of 18-19 points, seldom 20. He may even have 16-17 with a six card suit.

2. Opener   Responder
   1D   2C
   3NT   Pass

A jump to three no trump over a two level response is equivalent in strength to a jump to two no trump over a one level response. It is not a signoff, but a hand slightly too strong to open one no trump.

3. Opener   Responder
   1D   1H
   1NT   Pass

This one is almost too much of an insult to include. Opener has 12-14 high card points, possibly 15, depending upon the opening one no trump range.

4. Opener   Responder
   1S   2C
   2NT   3NT
   Pass

This one is treated in a variety of ways by bridge experts. Some use it to show the same range as a rebid of one no trump; others use it to show extra strength, typically 15-17. You simply must ask. Also, it isn't a bad idea to ask your own partner (if it is a new one) how he or she plays this sequence.

5.   Opener   Responder

Opener	Responder
1S	2C
2D	2H
2NT	3NT
Pass	

Whenever responder bids the fourth suit he must have a fairly reasonable hand (upward of 10 high card points) and is asking opener for more information. When opener then makes a minimum bid in no trump he is showing a minimum hand, with typically five spades and four diamonds.

6.

Opener	Responder
1S	2C
2D	2H
3NT	Pass

This time opener has more than a minimum - typically 15-17 high card points, and again five spades and four diamonds.

Then there are sequences where it is necessary to know whether responder's last bid is forcing or invitational.

7.

Opener	Responder
1C	1D
1S	3D
3NT	Pass

If the jump to three diamonds is forcing it is difficult to know whether opener is dead minimum or has extra values. If the jump is not considered forcing opener has either a secondary diamond fit or slightly more than a bare minimum to go on. (In real life many players automatically rebid three no trump on this sequence because it sounds forcing to them.)

8. | Opener | Responder |
    |--------|-----------|
    | 1D | 1H |
    | 1S | 3D |
    | 3NT | Pass |

Again it depends upon whether or not the jump to three diamonds is considered forcing. If it is, opener could have a bare minimum; if not, opener should have a little extra.

Now take a look at a few sequences in which responder becomes the declarer and see what you can make of his point count.

First the obvious ones.

1. | Opener | Responder |
    |--------|-----------|
    | 1H | 1NT |
    | Pass | |

Responder holds 6-9 high card points, rarely 10. Furthermore, if the no trump response is made to a major suit opening bid there is a good chance that responder has an unbalanced hand pattern. He might even have a void in partner's suit! However, a response of one no trump to a one club opening does show a balanced hand. Some use this response to show 6-9, others 8-10, and still others 8/9-11! Find out.

2. | Opener | Responder |
|---|---|
| 1C | 2NT |
| 3NT | Pass |

Responder has 13-15 high card points and, of course, a balanced hand. On a sequence like this find out if responder can have a four card major or if their system forbids it.

3. | Opener | Responder |
|---|---|
| 1D | 3NT |
| Pass | |

Responder should have either 16-17 balanced or 16-18 balanced. Again, find out if a four card major can be held.

4. | Opener | Responder |
|---|---|
| 1H | 1S |
| 2C | 2NT |
| Pass | |

Most experts use the rebid of two no trump by the responder to show 11-12 high card points, perhaps 10 with a good five card suit. It is not forcing and here opener with a minimum elects to pass. If your opponents use this common rebid differently you should be alerted.

5. | Opener | Responder |
|---|---|
| 1H | 2D |
| 2H | 2NT |
| Pass | |

A rebid of two no trump by the responder shows the same strength whether the first response

is at the one or two level. Responder has
10/11-12 high card points, conceivably a
singleton heart.

6. Opener   Responder
   --   Pass
   1S   2NT
   Pass

A jump to two no trump by a passed hand shows
11-12 high card points, a balanced hand, and
is not forcing.

7. Opener   Responder
   1D   1H
   1S   3NT
   Pass

A second round jump to three no trump is equivalent to an original jump to two no trump. In
other words, responder has 13-15 balanced. Perhaps a five card heart suit or a small doubleton
in spades was his reason for not jumping to two
no trump immediately. Some poor souls get lost
on this sequence and have 16-18 points. This
is because they forget to jump shift or jump to
three no trump directly.

When opener's rebid shows extra strength it may get a little
"sticky" to determine responder's point count range.

8. | Opener | Responder |
    | --- | --- |
    | 1D | 1H |
    | 3D | 3NT |
    | Pass | |

Responder is apt to bid three no trump on a wing and a prayer hoping to bring in the diamonds plus a few morsels here and there. Then again he may have a reasonable hand - up to 12-13 high card points - and merely be taking a pessimistic view about a slam, perhaps holding a singleton diamond.

9. | Opener | Responder |
    | --- | --- |
    | 1D | 1H |
    | 3C | 3NT |
    | Pass | |

This time the responder has been forced to game. Opener has a hand in the 20 point range so responder could have 6-10 or conceivably 11 high card points. However, when defending against these unknown quantities, particularly at rubber bridge, assume opener is minimum and play to defeat the contract at all times. Unfortunately, at tournament play you cannot afford yourself the luxury of these assumptions, for preventing overtricks is just as vital as defeating the contract.

If responder bids a no trump game in the face of a multi-signoff sequence, play responder for an opening bid.

10. | Opener | Responder |
| --- | --- |
| 1H | 1S |
| 2H | 3C |
| 3H | 3NT |
| Pass | |

Opener couldn't be bidding weaker. Responder

who knows this still bids game. He is strong.

Probably in the 13-16 range.

ANALYZING POINT COUNT AT SUIT CONTRACTS

The easiest way to do this is to classify opener's hand into one

of four high card point groups:

The minimum opening bid: 11/12-15 high card points.

The intermediate opening bid: 15/16-18 high card points.

The Bomb: 18-21 high card points.

The Nuclear Bomb: More.

Most of the time opener's rebid will show his range (and distribu-

tion). Patience.

1. | Opener | Responder |
| --- | --- |
| 1H | 1S |
| 2H | Pass |

Opener is minimum with <u>six</u> hearts. (He skipped

over every suit to rebid his original one.)

2. | Opener | Responder |
| --- | --- |
| 1H | 1S |
| 2C | 2H |
| Pass | |

When opener bids two suits (without reversing)

he can either be minimum or intermediate. Wait

for his third call to find out which. In
this case he is minimum. If responder
passes two clubs you are forced to defend
in the dark.

3. | Opener | Responder |
    | --- | --- |
    | 1D | 1S |
    | 2H | 3D |
    | 3NT | Pass |

Opener is either intermediate or holds the
bomb. He has made a reverse bid to show
extra strength. He has presumably five
diamonds, four hearts and fewer than three
spades.

4. | Opener | Responder |
    | --- | --- |
    | 1S | 1NT |
    | 3H | 3S |
    | 4H | Pass |

This time opener definitely has the bomb.
He also has at least five spades and five
hearts. Responder probably has two spades
and three hearts.

RESPONDER'S RANGES FOR SUIT BIDDING

We slice up the responder as follows:

Minimum responding hand: 6-9 high card points.

Intermediate responding hand: 10-12 high card points.

Game-going responding hand: 12-15/16 high card points.

Slam invitational responding hand: 15/16-18 high card points.

"Forget it" responding hand: 19 or more high card points.

If responder's first bid is a new suit it is impossible to judge his range. However, the moment the opening bidder limits his hand responder must come out of the bushes.

1. | Opener | Responder |
    | --- | --- |
    | 1D | 1S |
    | 2C | 2S |
    | Pass | |

    Responder is minimum with a six card spade suit (or five very good ones).

2. | Opener | Responder |
    | --- | --- |
    | 1D | 1S |
    | 2D | 3S |
    | 4S | Pass |

    Responder is intermediate with at least six spades. Some play this sequence forcing to game, in which case responder's hand is either intermediate or game going.

3. | Opener | Responder |
    | --- | --- |
    | 1D | 1H |
    | 1NT | 4H |
    | Pass | |

    Responder is game going, with at least six hearts.

4. | Opener | Responder |
    | --- | --- |
    | 1D | 2H |
    | 3D | 3NT |
    | Pass | |

    Logically, responder should be in the slam invitational zone. However, some players still use this sequence to show the "forget it" hands. They seem to forget that if they have a "forget it" hand they should force the hand to slam and not give the opener a chance to pass.

MORE CLUES TO DECLARER'S POINT COUNT

1. An invaluable guide to judging the best defense is this: Once the dummy comes down, add your high card points to dummy's and then add that total to declarer's approximate count. (Remember declarer will usually have shown a range during the bidding.) Now subtract that total from 40 and you will know within a point or two your partner's strength. Actually it is much easier than it reads.

```
Both sides vul.          North (Dummy)
Dealer South             S. KQ93
                         H. 42
                         D. KQJ10
                         C. K52

       West                                        East (You)
       S. 72                                       S. J54
       H. Q1098765                                 H. 3
       D. 8                                         D. A753
       C. 763                                       C. QJ1098

                         South
                         S. A1086
                         H. AKJ
                         D. 9642
                         C. A4
```

South	West	North	East
1NT	Pass	2C	Pass
2S	Pass	6S!	All pass

Opening lead: Eight of diamonds

True, North's bidding was atrocious; for all he knows, the partnership can be missing two aces, but that's history. The idea is to defeat six spades.

Obviously, looking at the diagram it is easy. East wins the ace of diamonds and returns a diamond for West to ruff. What's the problem? The problem is that many East players (who have not read this chapter) shift to a heart at trick two, or the tempting queen of clubs, fearing that the lead is not a singleton. They are hoping when they switch that their partner has a trick in one of those suits.

Before making any play at all East should add his points to dummy's, which gives him a total of 22. Declarer figures to have about 16, which brings the total to 38. This means that the most partner can have is a queen. Using this as a basis for his defense, East sees that the best chance for a second trick lies in a diamond ruff rather than reaching for the impossible star.

2. Good defenders always keep track of the number of high card points declarer has already revealed. For example, if declarer shows 13-15 during the bidding and has produced 12 during the play, it is obvious he does not hold any missing ace.

It is almost impossible to defend accurately without doing this.

East-West vul.   North(Dummy)
Dealer North   S. KJ987
                   H. AKJ
                   D. 98
                   C. Q109

West (You)   East
S. A105   S. 432
H. Q98   H. 1076
D. J10765   D. K
C. K5   C. AJ6432

                   South
                   S. Q6
                   H. 5432
                   D. AQ432
                   C. 87

North	East	South	West
1S	Pass	1NT	All pass

Opening lead: Six of diamonds

Partner's king goes to declarer's ace. Already West
knows that South started with six high card points in
diamonds, not leaving room for too much more. (East's
play of the king denies the queen.)

At trick two South produces the queen of spades. Now
West knows about eight high card points, which means
the ace of clubs is marked in the East hand. Assume
West ducks the first spade and wins the second. He
can count eight sure tricks for declarer: two diamonds,
two hearts and four spades. Obviously, if there is any
hope of defeating this hand partner must have the ace-
jack of clubs with some length. It doesn't hurt to try.
At trick four West shifts to the king of clubs - not
very brave once you think about it, is greeted by an

-364-

encouraging six spot (encouraging because there are three lower spot cards missing), and continues with a club to defeat the contract one trick.

The only trouble with defending this well is that partner may never bid his suits, figuring you know he has them anyway!

In the previous example the opening leader was able to tell from his partner's play to the first trick the number of points declarer held in that suit.

Just as often, the partner of the opening leader can figure out declarer's high card holding in the suit led, particularly when an honor card is led.

East-West vul.   North (Dummy)
Dealer North   S. 43
                        H. AKJ2
                        D. AQJ10
                        C. Q98

West   East (You)
S. QJ107   S. 9862
H. 5   H. Q63
D. 986   D. K75
C. A10432   C. KJ6

                        South
                        S. AK5
                        H. 109874
                        D. 432
                        C. 75

North   East   South   West
1NT   Pass   2H   Pass
3H   Pass   4H   All pass

Opening lead: Queen of spades

Perhaps you don't agree with North's opening bid, but
that's not the problem here.

The moment West leads the queen of spades East knows
that South has the ace-king of spades, and, therefore,
no ace of clubs for his weak bidding. (East plays the
deuce of spades at trick one to let West in on the
secret. Do not give the count signal in this situation.
It is far more important to tell partner that you have
no honor in spades.)

At trick two a diamond is led to the queen and king.
A player who hasn't bothered to work anything out
will, at this point, return a spade. However, you
will return a club because you know your partner
has the ace. (Notice, if you do not return a club
declarer makes the hand by discarding a losing club
on dummy's fourth diamond after cashing two high
trumps.)

I. North-South vul.
    Dealer North

North
S. Q6
H. J854
D. QJ42
C. AKJ

West
S. 10987
H. K92
D. K5
C. 10854

East
S. J542
H. 7
D. A983
C. Q962

South
S. AK3
H. AQ1063
D. 1076
C. 73

North	East	South	West
1D	Pass	1H	Pass
2H	Pass	4H	All pass

Opening lead: Ten of spades

II. Both sides vul.
    Dealer North

North
S. KQJ
H. AJ3
D. K852
C. 763

West
S. A5
H. KQ10942
D. Q64
C. K5

East
S. 432
H. 876
D. 1097
C. J1092

South
S. 109876
H. 5
D. AJ3
C. AQ84

North	East	South	West
1D	Pass	1S	2H
2S	Pass	4S	All pass

Opening lead: King of hearts

III. Neither side vul.   North
     Dealer South   S. J104
                             H. J104
                             D. KQ
                             C. AKJ84

West   East
S. KQ2   S. A986
H. Q   H. 6532
D. 10842   D. 953
C. 109653   C. Q7

                      South
                      S. 753
                      H. AK987
                      D. AJ76
                      C. 2

South	West	North	East
1H	Pass	2C	Pass
2D	Pass	3H	Pass
4H	All pass		

Opening lead: King of spades

IV. Both sides vul.   North
     Dealer South   S. 632
                               H. Q84
                               D. A75
                               C. KQJ10

West   East
S. J1098   S. 754
H. A96   H. KJ75
D. 863   D. K102
C. 982   C. 765

                      South
                      S. AKQ
                      H. 1032
                      D. QJ94
                      C. A43

South	West	North	East
1NT	Pass	3NT	All pass

Opening lead: Jack of spades

I. After dummy wins the queen of spades and runs the jack of
    hearts to West's king, West, if he is at the party, real-
    izes that declarer is marked with AK of spades and AQ of
    hearts. West goes one step further and realizes that if
    South also has the ace of diamonds (1) the hand can never
    be defeated and (2) South would have bid more aggressively
    with 17 points and a strong five card suit. (South must
    have five hearts because he leaped to game without knowing
    that North had four hearts.) West shifts to the king of
    diamonds to defeat the contract.

II. This time West can count 28 high card points between his
    hand and dummy's, and knows that South has a strong hand
    (typically 11 or more high card points to leap to game
    after a single raise). Therefore, it is futile to look
    for any ace or king in partner's hand.

    A better plan is to defend passively. Win the ace of
    spades and exit with a spade. Later, if either a diamond
    or a club is finessed into your hand exit with the same
    suit, refusing to break any new suits for declarer, who
    you know has all of the missing high card strength.
    Playing this way, declarer will have to guess that you
    have a doubleton king of clubs and play ace and a low
    club to make the hand.

III. After cashing three spades, East ending on lead, East sees that South has no honor cards in the black suits and must have at least the ace of diamonds and the ace-king of hearts to justify an opening bid. East's best chance is to return a fourth spade, hoping partner has a singleton queen of hearts. He does! Declarer can still make the hand by ruffing high and banging down his remaining high trump, but if he does that, either you or your partner is sitting too close to the table. Much too close.

IV. Declarer wins the opening lead and plays the queen of diamonds. This gives East all the information he needs. He can tell from the lead that South has nine high card points in spades; and since declarer is ignoring the club suit he apparently has the ace. That comes to 13 points, and the queen of diamonds makes 15. Therefore, West must own the ace of hearts (unless South miscounted his points).

So ... after winning the king of diamonds East shifts to a low heart and the defenders score four hearts and a diamond, to defeat the hand one trick.

I. Within a range of three points estimate declarer's high card strength on these sequences. (Also, what do you know about declarer's distribution?)

a.

Opener	Responder
1H	1S
2H	4H
Pass	

b.

Opener	Responder
1H	1S
3H	4H
Pass	

c.

Opener	Responder
1C	1S
2S	3C
Pass	

d.

Opener	Responder
1D	1S
2NT	3D
3NT	Pass

e.

Opener	Responder
2C*	2D
2NT	3NT
Pass	

*Artificial and forcing

f.

Opener	Responder
2S*	4S
Pass	

*Weak Two Bid

g.

Opener	Responder
1D	1S
2H	2S
3NT	Pass

h.

Opener	Responder
Pass	1S
2C	Pass

i. | Opener | Responder |
|---|---|
| Pass | 1D |
| 1H | 2H |
| 2NT | Pass |

j. | Opener | Responder |
|---|---|
| 1D | 1H |
| 1S | 2H |
| 2NT | Pass |

k. | Opener | Responder |
|---|---|
| 1C | 1H |
| 3NT | Pass |

l. | Opener | Responder |
|---|---|
| 1S | 2D |
| 3C | 3S |
| 4S | Pass |

m. | Opener | Responder |
|---|---|
| 1D | 1S |
| 1NT | 4S |
| Pass | |

n. | Opener | Responder |
|---|---|
| 1C | 2NT |
| 3NT | Pass |

o. | Opener | Responder |
|---|---|
| 1D | 1H |
| 1S | 2NT |
| 3NT | Pass |

p. | Opener | Responder |
|---|---|
| 1D | 2H |
| 3H | 4H |
| Pass | |

q. | Opener | Responder |
|---|---|
| 1S | 2C |
| 2D | 3C |
| Pass | |

r. | Opener | Responder |
|---|---|
| 1D | 1S |
| 2C | 3S |
| Pass | |

s. | Opener | Responder |
|---|---|
| 1NT | 4NT |
| Pass | |

t. | Opener | Responder |
| --- | --- |
| 1D | 1S |
| 3C | 3S |
| 3NT | Pass |

u. | Opener | Responder |
| --- | --- |
| 1H | 1S |
| 4H | Pass |

v. | Opener | Responder |
| --- | --- |
| 2NT | 3C |
| 3H | 4H |
| Pass | |

w. | Opener | Responder |
| --- | --- |
| 1S | 2S |
| 3D | 3S |
| Pass | |

x. | Opener | Responder |
| --- | --- |
| 1H | 2C |
| 2D | 3NT |
| Pass | |

y. | Opener | Responder |
| --- | --- |
| 1H | 1NT |
| 2D | 2NT |
| Pass | |

z. | Opener | Responder |
| --- | --- |
| 1H | 1S |
| 2D | 2S |
| 2NT | 3S |
| Pass | |

II. Neither side vul.   North (Dummy)
     Dealer South   S. 109
                                H. 10765
                                D. QJ10
                                C. KJ98

          West (You)
          S. AJ2
          H. AJ2
          D. 765
          C. Q1076

          South   West   North   East
          1NT (15-17)   Pass   2NT   Pass
          3NT   All pass

Opening lead: Six of clubs

Dummy's eight wins. At trick two declarer leads
a club to the ace and then plays a club to the
jack and discards a spade on the king of clubs.
Partner follows to the first two clubs and discards the deuce of diamonds and the three of
spades on the third and fourth clubs.

Now the ten of spades is led to declarer's king,
partner playing the six. Plan your defense.

I. a. 11/12-14.   At least six hearts.

b. 14/15-17.   At least six hearts.

c. 12-14.   Three spades and at least four clubs.
Some play this sequence as forcing,
others do not.

d. 18-19.   Fewer than three spades.

e. 22-24.   Balanced.

f. 7/8-10.   At least six spades. Some open with
less but it is not recommended.

g. 19-20/21.   Five diamonds (at least), four hearts,
and fewer than three spades. With
17-18 opener rebids 2NT.

h. 9-11.   Could have four clubs, usually more.

i. 10-12.   Usually four hearts.

j. 17-18.   Either a secondary heart fit or a good
suit of his own (probably diamonds).

k. 15-17.   And a long solid club suit. Some play
that this shows 20-21, but those are
the ones who remember streetcars.

l. 15-17/18.   At least five spades. With more opener
makes a slam try.

m. 12-14/15.   At least six spades.

n. 13-15.   Balanced. Inquire if responder can have
a four card major. (It makes the defense
easier.)

o. 10-12.   Balanced. With only 10 points a five
                 card suit is likely.

p. 15-17/18.   Obviously a light jump shift. At least
                 five hearts.

q. 8-10.   At least six clubs, often seven.

r. 9-11.   At least six spades. Some play this
                 sequence forcing, others do not.

s. 15-16.   Balanced. With more opener goes to
                 slam.

t. 18-20   Not much in spades. At least five
                 diamonds and four clubs.

u. 16-18/19.   At least six or seven hearts. The
                 more hearts the fewer points.

v. 20-22.   At least four hearts. Some play
                 22-24, others 21-22, still others
                 21-23. Find out.

w. 15-17.   At least five spades. Declarer has
                 made a game try and responder has
                 signed off. If declarer were stronger
                 he would bid four spades.

x. 13-15.   Fewer than three hearts.

y. 9-10.   Typically double stoppers in the unbids.

z. 5-7.   At least six or seven spades, but a
                 very weak hand.

II.

                        North
                        S. 109
                        H. 10765
                        D. QJ10
                        C. KJ98

West   East
S. AJ2   S. 8763
H. AJ2   H. KQ43
D. 765   D. 982
C. Q1076   C. 52

                        South
                        S. KQ54
                        H. 98
                        D. AK43
                        C. A43

Judging from partner's discards he has no strength in
either diamonds or spades. This, in turn, marks South
with the ace-king of diamonds and the king-queen of
spades. Along with the ace of clubs this gives South
a grand total of at least 16 high card points, and
NINE tricks if he has four diamonds.

Since South is marked with no more than 17 high card
points, partner must have both the king and queen of
hearts. You should play the ace and then the jack of
hearts to unblock in case partner has four hearts.
If partner has only three hearts nothing is lost;
he can return a spade before cashing a third heart
and still defeat the hand in case declarer has something like: S. KQxx   H. xxx   D. AKx   C. Axx

Incidentally, an expert declarer leads a spade at trick two before he cashes good clubs which allow informative discards to be made, which in turn allow at least one defender to count declarer's points and tricks.

However, this declarer was just testing to see if you had learned your lesson. Did you?

There are four factors to consider when counting declarer's tricks:

I. THE BIDDING.

Compare these two bidding sequences:

a. | South | North |
    |-------|-------|
    | 1NT | 2NT |
    | 3NT | Pass |

b. | South | North |
    |-------|-------|
    | 1C | 1D |
    | 3C | 3D |
    | 3NT | Pass |

You hold:

S. KQ6   H. J10432   D. Q52   C. 73

What do you lead?

Against sequence "a" lead the three of hearts. Why? Because there are no long suits in either hand and declarer will usually have to fight for nine tricks, normally by giving up the lead two, three, or four times. Perhaps you can establish your hearts before he can establish his tricks in the other suits.

However, against sequence "b" it is incorrect to lead the three of hearts. Here's a hand where both players have long suits, and the chances are that you will get in only once, if at all. Clearly you must try for tricks quickly, and the best chance is to lead the king of spades.

This same type of reasoning is used anytime either
dummy or declarer is known to have a LONG STRONG
suit. Attack! When neither player has a long
suit, make a more passive lead - perhaps fourth
best from your longest suit.

II.   THE LEAD.

Partner's opening lead, particularly if it is an
honor card, clearly let's you, in third seat, count
declarer's tricks in the suit led.

Assume you are defending a no trump contract in the
following two diagrams:

                          Dummy
                          S. 75

        West   East
        S. Q   S. A82

West leads the queen of spades and East immediately
knows that declarer has exactly one spade trick coming.

                          Dummy
                          S. 75

        West   East
        S. J   S. A82

This time West leads the jack of spades. Assuming you
play that the lead of the jack denies a higher honor,
you know that declarer is entitled to two spade tricks.

If you do not use this convention you would not be able to count declarer's tricks, for partner might have led from KJ10. (See "Leads vs. No Trump Contracts".)

```
                      North
                      S. 82

West                                    East
S. J1076                                S. A94

                      South
                      S. KQ53
```

West leads the six; East steps up with the ace and returns the nine to South's king. Which card should West play? West should play the jack, denying the queen, and giving East a chance to count declarer's tricks. If West plays the seven, true, he gives East the count, but it is more important for East to know who has the queen.

```
                      North
                      S. 54

West                                    East
S. Q9873                                S. 1062

                      South
                      S. AKJ
```

West leads the seven and East's ten fetches South's jack. At this point West knows that South is entitled to three spade tricks. East, however, cannot read the position.

Assuming East gets the lead and returns the six, West plays the queen.

WHEN THE OPENING LEADER PLAYS AN HONOR UNDERNEATH DECLARER'S HONOR, IN A SUIT THE OPENING LEADER HAS ALREADY LED, HE DENIES A HIGHER HONOR. THIS ALLOWS PARTNER TO COUNT DECLARER'S TRICKS IN THAT SUIT.

Furthermore, if West has a chance to make an early discard and he elects to discard a spade, he discards the queen to show partner his original holding. Notice that these seemingly flashy discards never cost a trick. By simply discarding the highest card in the remaining sequence you give partner helpful information.

In the last example, if West simply follows with the three the second time the suit is played (assuming declarer plays the king), East might play West for A9873. From the previous examples we see how the opening leader can help his partner. Third hand can return the favor.

```
                     North
                     S. 763

West                                     East
S. J1094                                 S. 852

                     South
                     S. AKQ
```

West leads the jack of spades and East knows immediately that declarer has three tricks in the suit. East plays the DEUCE to deny an honor. Now West knows that South has three top spades. Some players stubbornly play the five (second highest) in this situation, giving West cause to believe that East has, perhaps, Q52 or K52.

In the chapter "Signalling vs. No Trump Contracts", it was mentioned that when the opening lead is a <u>small</u> <u>card</u> and dummy wins the trick with the <u>queen</u> or <u>less</u> the partner of the opening leader (who obviously does not have the higher honor or else he would have played it) gives the count signal. This enables the opening leader to gauge the distribution of the suit plus the number of tricks declarer has available.

<u>North</u>
S. KJ10

<u>West</u>
S. A983

<u>East</u>
S. 762

<u>South</u>
S. Q54

West leads the three, dummy plays the ten, and East the deuce, showing an odd number of cards. West knows immediately that the suit is divided 4-3-3-3 and that there is a chance to develop his long spade.

Contrast the previous diagram with this one:

```
                        North
                        S. KJ10

West                                              East
S. A983                                           S. 72

                        South
                        S. Q654
```

Again West leads the three and dummy plays the ten, but this time East should play the seven. Since the seven can be read as East's highest spot card, West knows that East has a doubleton and that declarer started with four to the queen.

III. THE DUMMY.

Turning your neck a quarter turn to the left or right enables you to take a peek at the dummy. Looking at dummy a bit more closely gives you a reasonable idea of your expectations of defeating the contract.

For example, if dummy raises one no trump to three with: S. Q543 H. AQ5 D. Q65 C. J65, defensive chances do not look bright. Declarer is probably playing this hand with a total point count of 27 or 28. However, if you are sitting in back of dummy holding: S. KJ9x H. KJx D. xx C. xxxx you have a good chance of defeating the contract since both major suit queens in dummy are dead because of your holding in those suits. In other words, it's as if the dummy has 7 points instead of 11.

Conversely, some 7 point dummies play like 11 because finesses are all working. The point is you must understand how to think by considering your hand in relation to the dummy. Tricks are also counted in this fashion.

We have already seen how to count tricks in the suit partner has led. Now try to count tricks in side suits:

a.   <u>North</u> (Dummy)
                          C. AQJ10xx

                                        <u>East</u> (You)
                                        C. xxx

When dummy has a long suit it is important that the defenders know as quickly as possible how many tricks declarer can take in that suit. In this case, unless South has a singleton or void, (which you may have been able to determine by the bidding), count declarer for six club tricks.

b.   <u>North</u> (Dummy)
                          C. AQ1054

                                        <u>East</u> (You)
                                        C. KJ92

Here it will be difficult for declarer to realize more than one club trick, perhaps two if he has sufficient dummy entries and time to set up the suit. The point is, East knows that dummy's long suit will yield little or nothing - but what about West?

Strangely enough, East's defense tells him! If East adopts a passive line of defense and doesn't panic by attacking new suits, West will get the message that there is nothing to worry about in the club department. On the other hand, if East has three small clubs and sees the same club holding in dummy, he counts declarer for five club tricks and his defense takes a more aggressive turn, thus alerting partner that he fears the club length.

c.
                              North (Dummy)
                              C. KQJ10x

                                        East (You)
                                        C. xxx

When either defender sees a strong suit in dummy, missing the ace, he cannot always be sure who has the ace. However, as the play develops it becomes obvious. If the declarer, for example, shuns the suit, he must have the ace. If he did not, he would surely attack the suit as quickly as possible. So East counts the declarer for either four or five club tricks, depending upon whether or not he attacks the suit. The same reasoning holds true when a long suit missing the king hits the table.

Dummy
C. AQJ10x

West (You)
C. xxx

At first West cannot be sure who has the king. If declarer attacks the suit immediately East almost surely has the king. If declarer leaves the suit alone then it is declarer who probably has the king. (See Chapter on "Inferences".)

Difficult problems arise in estimating declarer's tricks when dummy has a shorter suit.

Dummy
C. AQ2

East (You)
C. J65

Depending upon the bidding, declarer can have anywhere from two to seven club tricks.

Dummy
C. KQ5

East (You)
C. J10762

This one is a bit easier. Declarer has either two or three club tricks depending upon who has the ace.

Most difficult of all is to count tricks in a suit in which dummy has a few small cards.

                            Dummy
                            C. 654

                                                    East (You)
                                                    C. 3

Assuming declarer has bid clubs, it is difficult to
judge the club position. However, it is better to
have shortness, which means partner has length (and
hopefully strength) in back of declarer, than to have,
for example, Qxx in front of the bidder.

IV. PARTNER'S SIGNALS AND DISCARDS.

Trick counting can be facilitated by watching partner's
cards closely.

East-West vul.   North
Dealer North   S. J43
                            H. AJ8
                            D. 76
                            C. AKJ108

        West   East
        S. 108752   S. AKQ
        H. 4   H. 32
        D. Q8532   D. A94
        C. Q6   C. 97432

                            South
                            S. 96
                            H. KQ109765
                            D. KJ10
                            C. 5

        North   East   South   West
        1C   Pass   1H   Pass
        2H   Pass   4H   All pass

Opening lead: Five of spades

East wins the first two spades, noticing partner's deuce on the second. A high-low indicates either two or five cards, and the partner of the opening leader is supposed to work out which it is from the bidding.

In this case, West must have five spades or else, if the lead were a doubleton, South would have started with five spades, which would be inconsistent with the bidding.

If East is a real player he shifts to a low diamond at trick three. South is apt to finesse the jack (South has seen East's high spade honors so he will probably place the ace of diamonds in the West hand), resulting in a one trick set after West wins the queen and returns the suit to partner's ace.

The key to the defense was East's knowing that only two spade tricks were cashable. Had West played a higher spade at trick two, East would simply have cashed three spades and a diamond knowing that West started with only three or four spades and therefore that declarer held at least three.

Another problem that has plagued defenders over the years is the following:

Both sides vul.   North
Dealer North   S. 75
                         H. AKQ
                         D. 94
                         C. QJ10964

     West   East
     S. K1082   S. AJ63
     H. 52   H. 10987
     D. Q8753   D. J62
     C. K2   C. 75

                         South
                         S. Q94
                         H. J643
                         D. AK10
                         C. A83

     North   East   South   West
     1C   Pass   2NT   Pass
     3NT   All pass

Opening lead: Five of diamonds

South wins the first diamond with the king. (At no trump it is far more deceptive for declarer, when holding the ace-king of a suit, to win with the king, particularly when he has a tenuous stopper in another suit. If declarer wins the ace it arouses suspicions, since he would probably hold up if his only stopper were the ace.)

At trick two South crosses to a high heart and takes a losing club finesse. From West's point of view, declarer has at least ten tricks ready to run outside of the spade suit. (He knows the diamond position from partner's play of the jack; he can see three heart tricks and five club tricks.)

Obviously West must shift to a spade and hope for four tricks in that suit. So West shifts to the deuce of spades, East wins and returns ... a diamond ... West's first suit!! Declarer takes eleven tricks.

What went wrong? You say East made a terrible mistake? But what if West had started with A10xxx of diamonds and no king of spades? Then East must return a diamond to defeat the contract.

The point is: How does East know whether to return partner's original suit or his second suit? Relax, there is a rule to cover this teaser.

WHEN PARTNER SHIFTS TO A <u>LOW</u> CARD IN A NEW SUIT (LOW FROM AN HONOR) HE WANTS THE SECOND SUIT RETURNED; WHEN PARTNER SHIFTS TO A <u>HIGH</u> CARD IN THE SECOND SUIT (TOP OF NOTHING) HE WANTS THE FIRST SUIT RETURNED.

Had West started with something like A10xxx of diamonds and Q7xx or 107xx of spades he would shift to the seven of spades, announcing no interest in that suit. The theory behind this rule is similar to the one discussed in the chapter "Leads vs. No Trump Contracts". It was mentioned that holding something like: S. AQJ9   H. 10873   D. 953   C. 76 and leading against the bidding 1NT - 3NT the proper lead is the eight of hearts. This tells partner that you are weak in the suit you are leading and have a stronger suit (usually a four card suit) that you were reluctant to lead originally for fear of giving up an unnecessary trick.

It should be noted here that it is much easier to count declarer's tricks at no trump than it is to count his tricks at a suit contract -- because of the ruffing possibilities.

None the less, it has to be done. Here are some tips about counting tricks at a suit contract -- tricks concerning the trump suit itself:

```
                    Dummy
                    S. 432

   West                              East
   S. 106                            S. J75

                    South
                    S. AKQ98
```

South is entitled to five spade tricks if he draws trumps. If the defenders make him ruff in the long hand (South hand) he gains nothing because he would have made his small trumps anyway. However, if South can manage to ruff anything in the short hand (dummy) before drawing trumps he makes extra tricks. THEREFORE, DEFENDERS ARE CONCERNED WITH PREVENTING DECLARER FROM RUFFING IN THE SHORT HAND. MAKING DECLARER RUFF IN THE LONG HAND IS USUALLY A GOOD DEFENSIVE PLAY, PARTICULARLY WHEN ONE DEFENDER HAS FOUR TRUMPS.

Trump leads are very effective if the defenders are trying to stop ruffs in the short hand. Trump leads are also very effective when declarer is planning a crossruff.

```
                    Dummy
                    S. AQ109

West                                    East
S. 65                                   S. 432

                    South
                    S. KJ87
```

If declarer has a short suit in his hand and one in dummy he can conceivably take eight trump tricks if he can trump four times in one hand. The moment the defenders lead a trump they cut down declarer's trick potential to seven. Two trump leads bring it down to six, three trump leads to five.

Also, when declarer plans to establish a long suit in dummy and the only entry is in the trump suit he cannot both ruff in dummy and establish dummy's long suit. Observe.

East-West vul.
Dealer North

```
                    North
                    S. A105
                    H. AK765
                    D. J4
                    C. 632

    West                                East
    S. 762                              S. 43
    H. 984                              H. QJ10
    D. KQ3                              D. 109876
    C. A987                             C. QJ10

                    South
                    S. KQJ98
                    H. 32
                    D. A52
                    C. K54
```

North	East	South	West
1H	Pass	1S	Pass
2S	Pass	4S	All pass

Opening lead: King of diamonds

Assuming the opening lead is ducked and West continues with the queen, South wins the ace but loses the hand if he ruffs a diamond in dummy!

Once a diamond is ruffed, declarer kisses the heart suit goodbye. To make the hand he must instead play ace, king and ruff a heart. Once that suit breaks he plays three rounds of trumps ending in dummy, using the hearts for club discards.

Defenders who are aware of the dummy-forcing principle would defeat the following hand, but you could count them on the thumbs of your left foot.

```
East-West vul.          North
Dealer South            S. 63
                        H. 72
                        D. AK8543
                        C. A104

        West                            East
        S. AKQ72                        S. 1098
        H. KQ10                         H. J98543
        D. Q9                           D. J102
        C. 765                          C. 3

                        South
                        S. J54
                        H. A6
                        D. 76
                        C. KQJ982

        South       West        North       East
        1C          1S          2D          Pass
        3C          Pass        5C          All pass
```

Opening lead: King of spades

Most defenders, if the truth were to be known, would cash two spades and shift to the king of hearts. Declarer wins, plays one high trump, the ace, king of diamonds and ruffs a diamond high, and then two more trumps ending in dummy. The good diamonds provide a parking place for the losing heart and spade and on to the next hand. Whoa Nellie!

This hand can be defeated if West plays three rounds of spades. Dummy must ruff and there goes the later entry to the diamonds. Declarer ends up losing a heart.

Knowing how declarer uses dummy's length is important to the defenders for two obvious reasons: (1) If they

can remove dummy's entry prematurely, e.g. force
declarer to ruff in dummy, they nullify the force
of the long suit. (2) If either defender has more
trumps than dummy it is obvious that declarer cannot
draw trumps ending in dummy. In such cases trump
leads are safe. (Providing the long suit needs ruffing establishment and is not already good.)

Another example of counting tricks and how it can save
your life!

Both sides vul.   North
Dealer North   S. A32
                                H. A1094
                                D. AQJ106
                                C. 10

        West   East
        S. J54   S. KQ97
        H. 632   H. 87
        D. 875   D. 932
        C. Q972   C. A653

                                South
                                S. 1086
                                H. KQJ5
                                D. K4
                                C. KJ84

        North   East   South   West
        1D   Pass   1H   Pass
        3H   Pass   4D   Pass
        4S   Dbl.   Pass   Pass
        6H   All pass

Opening lead: Four of spades

Dummy wins the ace and three rounds of trumps are
drawn. At this point East knows that South cannot

take more than five trump tricks (the three he has already taken plus one on each side). Now come five diamond tricks, South discarding two spades and a club. Finally the singleton club is led from dummy. East must play low!

He knows declarer has ten red suit tricks plus the ace of spades. If declarer has the king of clubs there is no hope, unless he holds the jack as well and misguesses. On the actual hand, if South misguesses and ducks the ten of clubs the hand is beaten. But if East panics and wins the ace (never right) the hand is made. Counting tricks is the answer.

I. East-West vul.   North
    Dealer North   S. 653
                                  H. AKQ92
                                  D. QJ10
                                  C. 76

        West   East
        S. K42   S. AQ97
        H. J10   H. 876
        D. A64   D. 975
        C. J9432   C. 1085

                                  South
                                  S. J108
                                  H. 543
                                  D. K832
                                  C. AKQ

        North   East   South   West
        1H   Pass   2NT   Pass
        3NT   All pass

    Opening lead: Three of clubs

II. Neither side vul.   North
    Dealer North   S. Q3
                                  H. 65
                                  D. AQ4
                                  C. AKQ1086

        West   East
        S. 76   S. AJ1092
        H. KJ94   H. A73
        D. 109762   D. 85
        C. J4   C. 732

                                  South
                                  S. K854
                                  H. Q1082
                                  D. KJ3
                                  C. 95

        North   East   South   West
        1C   1S   1NT   Pass
        3NT   All pass

    Opening lead: Seven of spades

III. Both sides vul.
    Dealer North

North
S. 76
H. 432
D. KQJ98
C. AK10

West
S. J10983
H. AQ98
D. 32
C. 76

East
S. Q52
H. J106
D. A10
C. 98532

South
S. AK4
H. K75
D. 7654
C. QJ4

North	East	South	West
1D	Pass	2NT	Pass
3NT	All pass		

Opening lead: Jack of spades

IV. Both sides vul.
    Dealer South

North
S. 764
H. 43
D. KQJ98
C. AQ10

West
S. J10983
H. A975
D. 7
C. 652

East
S. Q52
H. J106
D. A1065
C. 987

South
S. AK
H. KQ82
D. 432
C. KJ43

South	West	North	East
1NT	Pass	3NT	All pass

Opening lead: Jack of spades

I. South wins the first club with the king (with three
    equals it is most deceptive to win with the middle)
    and leads a low diamond, trying to steal a ninth
    trick early.

    West can see five heart tricks staring him in the
    face because of his unfortunate holding, knows of
    three club tricks from partner's play of the ten,
    so he realizes that the hand cannot be defeated
    unless partner has good spades. West wins the
    FIRST diamond play and shifts to a low spade (or
    the king). If a low spade is led East must trust
    West to have a high honor in spades and must con-
    tinue spades rather than revert back to clubs. Had
    West led a middle spade then East would win and re-
    turn a club.

II. East must win the first spade (dummy should play
    low to induce East to also play low) and shift to
    a low heart. East can see six clubs, at least two
    diamonds, and a spade, ready to go, so he must
    shift to a heart at once. The defenders take four
    hearts and a spade.

III. South wins the first spade with the king and drives out the ace of diamonds. East can count nine quick tricks for declarer outside of hearts: four diamonds, two spades and at least three clubs with the AK10 in dummy. East shifts to the jack of hearts and the defense reels off four hearts and a diamond to sink the contract.

IV. This time East has the diamond suit under control and declarer can take only two quick diamonds, two spades, and hopefully no more than four clubs. In this case East returns a spade hoping partner has the ace of hearts. The spade return is right for two reasons: the diamonds are not yet established, and it is impossible for partner to hold the AQ of hearts. East has 7 high card points, dummy 12, and declarer at least 15 or 16, giving partner at the absolute maximum 6 high card points. Since he has already produced the jack of spades, he cannot possibly have six points in hearts. As expected the spade return (the queen to unblock) defeats the contract one trick. (You play so beautifully.)

(In all these problems it is assumed that the lead of a jack denies a higher honor and that the lead of a 9 or a 10 shows zero or two higher honors.)

I. East-West vul.
    Dealer South

    North
    S. 32
    H. 432
    D. AQ1076
    C. Q64

    East (You)
    S. A76
    H. J76
    D. 984
    C. 7532

South	West	North	East
1C	Pass	1D	Pass
2NT	Pass	3NT	All pass

Opening lead: Jack of spades

Plan your defense.

II. Both sides vul.
     Dealer South

    North
    S. 763
    H. QJ
    D. K843
    C. AQJ9

    East (You)
    S. Q84
    H. 1095
    D. AJ102
    C. 743

South	West	North	East
1NT	Pass	3NT	All pass

Opening lead: Eight of hearts

Dummy's jack wins, declarer playing the deuce, and a low diamond is led from dummy. Plan your defense.

III. Both sides vul.   North
      Dealer West   S. 65
                              H. AK10
                              D. 84
                              C. KQJ987

                                                East (You)
                                                S. 1087
                                                H. 874
                                                D. A103
                                                C. 5432

      West   North   East   South
      1S   2C   Pass   2NT
      Pass   3NT   All pass

Opening lead: Three of spades

Your ten loses to declarer's queen. A low club is

led at trick two to partner's ace.

   1. Partner shifts to the deuce of diamonds

       at trick three. Plan your defense.

   2. Partner shifts to the nine of diamonds

       at trick three. Plan your defense.

IV. East-West vul.   North
     Dealer South   S. J5
                             H. Q7
                             D. QJ10963
                             C. A109

      West (You)
      S. Q10872
      H. KJ94
      D. A4
      C. 82

      South   West   North   East
      1NT   Pass   3NT   All pass

Opening lead: Seven of spades

Dummy's jack wins, partner playing the three and declarer the six. At trick two declarer leads the three of diamonds to his king, partner playing the deuce. Plan your defense.

V. Both sides vul.
    Dealer North

North
S. A62
H. Q7
D. KQJ10
C. QJ103

West (You)
S. J10987
H. A65
D. 842
C. K6

North	East	South	West
1D	Pass	2NT	Pass
3NT	All pass		

Opening lead: Jack of spades

Dummy wins the ace, partner plays the three, and declarer the five. At trick two the queen of clubs is led, partner producing the five and declarer the eight. Plan your defense.

VI. Both sides vul.
    Dealer North

North
S. AJ9
H. 54
D. 76
C. AQ10652

East (You)
S. 762
H. AJ3
D. J1098
C. 987

North	East	South	West
1C	Pass	2NT	Pass
3NT	All pass		

1. How do you defend if your partner leads the nine of hearts?

2. How do you defend if your partner leads the ten of hearts?

VII. North-South vul.
Dealer North

North
S. AK652
H. 95
D. 765
C. K62

West (You)
S. J7
H. K43
D. KJ8
C. QJ1093

North	East	South	West
Pass	Pass	1H	2C
2S	Pass	4H	All pass

Opening lead: Queen of clubs

Dummy's king wins, partner playing the five and declarer the four. At trick two the nine of hearts is played, partner producing the deuce and declarer the seven. Plan your defense.

VIII. Both sides vul.   North
       Dealer South   S. 9876
                                H. 54
                                D. AKJ76
                                C. Q9

                                                East (You)
                                                S. QJ102
                                                H. A93
                                                D. 10985
                                                C. 43

       South   West   North   East
       1C   Pass   1D   Pass
       3NT*   All pass

       *Long solid or semi-solid minor, 15-17 high card points.

       Opening lead: Queen of hearts

       Plan your defense.

IX.   Both sides vul.   North
       Dealer South   S. AKQ2
                                H. 974
                                D. 986
                                C. QJ5

       West (You)
       S. J7
       H. AJ63
       D. Q10732
       C. K9

       South   West   North   East
       1C   Pass   1S   Pass
       1NT   Pass   3NT   All pass

       Opening lead: Three of diamonds

       Partner's jack fetches declarer's king. At trick

       two the five of spades is led to dummy's queen,

       partner playing the three, and the queen of clubs

       is led from the table.

1. If partner plays the deuce and declarer the three, how do you defend?

2. If partner plays the seven and declarer the three, how do you defend?

I.

	North	
	S. 32	
	H. 432	
	D. AQ1076	
	C. Q64	

West
S. J10984
H. AQ108
D. J52
C. 10

East
S. A76
H. J76
D. 984
C. 7532

South
S. KQ5
H. K95
D. K3
C. AKJ98

The imposing diamond suit in dummy plus the queen of clubs to fit declarer's suit makes it necessary to give up on the spade suit, a suit in which declarer is known to have two stoppers. East should win the ace of spades at trick one and shift to the jack of hearts. The only hope is in the heart suit, and it is necessary to play the jack to prevent declarer from ducking the lead into partner's hand. This is one of the rare occasions when a defender leads the jack without holding the ten. Four tricks are needed and East must play West for the AQ10x. (A clever declarer might drop the queen of spades at trick one under the ace to encourage a spade continuation, perhaps avoiding the embarrassment of a heart switch.)

II.

```
                        North
                        S. 763
                        H. QJ
                        D. K843
                        C. AQJ9
        West                            East
        S. AJ109                        S. Q84
        H. 8763                         H. 1095
        D. 76                           D. AJ102
        C. 865                          C. 743
                        South
                        S. K52
                        H. AK42
                        D. Q95
                        C. K102
```

This is somewhat similar to the first problem. The lead marks declarer with the ace-king of hearts and there is a strong likelihood that declarer has four hearts. Those four tricks, along with the four club tricks that can be seen in dummy, give declarer eight. The diamond lead is an obvious attempt at snatching a ninth trick early, before we settle down. East should rise with the ace of diamonds and return the queen of spades, because four spade tricks are needed immediately.

Notice how important it is for West to lead the eight of hearts (showing no interest in the suit) as opposed to a fourth best heart, which would cause unnecessary defensive confusion.

III.

                              North
                              S. 65
                              H. AK10
                              D. 84
                              C. KQJ987

West   East
S. KJ932   S. 1087
H. 963   H. 874
D. KJ92   D. A103
C. A   C. 5432

                              South
                              S. AQ4
                              H. QJ52
                              D. Q765
                              C. 106

1. Partner's shift to a LOW diamond asks for a
    return in that suit. Win the ace of diamonds
    and return the TEN.

2. If partner shifts to a HIGH diamond at trick
    three, win the ace and return the eight of
    spades. His return of a high diamond shows
    no interest in that suit and a desire for his
    original suit to be returned. For his return
    of the nine, partner might have had this hand
    originally: S. AJ932   H. 963   D. Q952   C. A

IV.

North
S. J5
H. Q7
D. QJ10963
C. A109

West
S. Q10872
H. KJ94
D. A4
C. 82

East
S. 943
H. A32
D. 872
C. 7643

South
S. AK6
H. 10865
D. K5
C. KQJ5

Declarer is marked with nine certain tricks outside of hearts: three spades, five diamonds, and a club. Clearly the only hope of defeating the hand is to get four heart tricks.

The best play is the king of hearts! This caters to partner holding three hearts to the ace and declarer four to the ten. If you return a low heart you have just held your side to only three quick heart tricks. Shame, shame.

V.

                              North
                              S. A62
                              H. Q7
                              D. KQJ10
                              C. QJ103

        West   East
        S. J10987   S. 43
        H. A65   H. KJ109
        D. 842   D. 963
        C. K6   C. 7542

                              South
                              S. KQ5
                              H. 8432
                              D. A75
                              C. A98

Judging from partner's play at trick one, declarer
has three spade tricks. After the club finesse loses
declarer will have established three club tricks. If
declarer has the ace of diamonds that is ten quick
tricks. If partner has the ace of diamonds and declarer the king of hearts there is no way to defeat
the contract unless partner has six hearts and declarer
Kx. In any event a heart shift at this point is mandatory. It matters little whether the ace or a low one
is played, just as long as a heart is out there on the
table at trick three.

VI.   North
                             S. AJ9
                             H. 54
                             D. 76
                             C. AQ10652

West   East
S. Q108   S. 762
H. K10987   H. AJ3
D. K432   D. J1098
C. J   C. 987

                             South
                             S. K543
                             H. Q62
                             D. AQ5
                             C. K43

1. With the lead of the nine of hearts East cannot
    be 100% sure whether the lead is from K109, Q109,
    or top of nothing, but the simplest defense usu-
    ally proves best. Win the ace and return the
    jack, hoping for K109xx in partner's hand.

2. If the ten of hearts is led East KNOWS South has
    both the king and queen; and looking at that dum-
    my a heart return is the height of futility. Win
    the ace of hearts and return the jack of diamonds,
    hoping partner has:

            S. Q108   H. 109876   D. AQ32   C. J

VII.
                              North
                              S. AK652
                              H. 95
                              D. 765
                              C. K62

West   East
S. J7   S. 10984
H. K43   H. 62
D. KJ8   D. A432
C. QJ1093   C. 875

                              South
                              S. Q3
                              H. AQJ1087
                              D. Q109
                              C. A4

Declarer's bidding indicates at least a six card
heart suit, so that means five trump tricks after
you take the king. You know declarer has the ace-
king of both black suits, for a total of nine tricks,
so the hand cannot be defeated if declarer has the
ace of diamonds. You must assume partner has that
card and shift to the eight of diamonds. If partner is on the ball he wins the ace and returns the
suit to defeat the contract one trick.

If you fail to shift to a diamond, declarer discards
one diamond on a spade to make the contract.

VIII.

North
S. 9876
H. 54
D. AKJ76
C. Q9

West
S. A43
H. QJ1087
D. 432
C. 76

East
S. QJ102
H. A93
D. 10985
C. 43

South
S. K5
H. K62
D. Q
C. AKJ10852

The bidding has told you that declarer has at least seven club tricks ready to go, you know he has the king of hearts, and you can see the diamond suit, so it must be spades to attack.

Knowing which suit to play is not always enough! A defender must ask himself how many tricks he needs in the suit. In this case the answer is four. Therefore partner must have the ace, but even that is not enough. If the queen is led, declarer covers and dummy's spots become a fourth round stopper. Needing four tricks in spades, East must conceive of declarer holding Kx and he must lead a low spade! Few declarers are clairvoyant enough to play low in a spot like this, and if declarer makes the normal play of the king you have your four spade tricks.

IX.

                          North
                          S. AKQ2
                          H. 974
                          D. 986
                          C. QJ5

West   East
S. J7   S. 109643
H. AJ63   H. K85
D. Q10732   D. J4
C. K9   C. 632

                          South
                          S. 85
                          H. Q102
                          D. AK5
                          C. A10874

The count signal becomes very important on this hand.

1. Partner's play of the three of spades (his
    lowest) indicates an odd number, obviously
    five, limiting declarer to three spade
    tricks. Partner's play of the deuce of
    clubs (also his lowest) shows an odd number
    of clubs, presumably three, and from your
    point of view gives declarer four club
    tricks after the king is taken. This,
    along with two known diamond tricks, means
    that declarer has nine tricks ready to go,
    so the only chance is to shift to a low
    heart and hope partner has the king. (Re-
    member your shift to a LOW heart asks for
    a heart rather than a diamond return.)

2. If partner plays the seven of clubs at trick
   three you have a bona fide problem. If the
   seven is from 1087 you must defend as before,
   trying to defeat the hand with four heart
   tricks, as once again declarer has a five
   card club suit. But if the seven is from
   8743 then declarer has a four card club suit
   (three club tricks) and you need not shift
   to a heart at all. Simply win the club and
   punch back a high diamond, establishing your
   suit, knowing that declarer cannot come up
   with nine tricks. Partner's count signals
   have told you that declarer has only eight.

XIII. RECOGNIZING DUMMY TYPES

In this chapter we will restrict our discussion to hands which have dummys that contain trump support -- because the majority of hands, or anyway those played by non-masochists, have at least an eight card trump fit.

The first order of business is to keep in mind the basic ways declarer has of obtaining extra tricks at a trump contract:

1. Setting up a long suit for discards.

2. Ruffing in the short hand (the hand that started with fewer trumps, almost always the dummy).

3. Endplays, dummy reversals, crossruffing, etc.

From experience we know that the first two methods dominate suit play, so the defenders must know how to counteract each one.

Obviously, if declarer is going to set up a long suit for discards we must either kill the entries to the hand which has the long suit or take our tricks quickly in the other suits before the long suit can be established.

If declarer is planning to either ruff in the short hand or crossruff, then trump leads are best. However, one thought must remain at all times: IF THE DECLARER CANNOT THROW AWAY HIS LOSERS ON A LONG SUIT OR RUFF THEM IN DUMMY HE EVENTUALLY WILL HAVE TO PLAY THE SUIT OR SUITS IN WHICH HE HAS LOSERS.

Keeping this in mind, you will realize that the best defense against hands on which there is no long usable side suit in dummy is passive. In other words, there is no need to break new suits -- let the declarer do the work himself. Meanwhile, back at the ranch, declarer is going to try to force you to break new suits for him -- thus the never ending struggle.

Now let's isolate dummy types:

Type I: The Balanced Hand

When the dummy hits with a balanced hand, a hand that does not even have a four card side suit (or if it does, it is obvious from the bidding that at least one of the defenders has four equally good cards in the suit, making it impossible to establish), the defenders go into their shells and play the passive game.

What exactly is the passive game? The passive game is leading a suit or suits that are unlikely to cost tricks. For example, if dummy has four small in a suit and declarer turns up with a singleton, making declarer trump can't cost.

Trump leads, hopefully when partner does not have the queen, are also passive.

```
East-West vul.              North (Dummy)
Dealer South               S. A965
                           H. A64
                           D. J72
                           C. 1054

        West (You)
        S. 73
        H. KQ105
        D. A854
        C. Q72

        South        West          North         East
        1S           Pass          2S            All pass
```

Opening lead: King of hearts

You lead the king of hearts which holds, partner playing the deuce. In this situation partner's play of the deuce denies the jack, so it is extremely dangerous to continue hearts.

You immediately see that this is a TYPE I dummy, balanced. So you are looking to play the passive game. Here a trump switch looks safe, so you lead the three of spades. (Remember high-low in trumps shows three.)

Now take a look at the whole hand:

                         North
                         S. A965
                         H. A64
                         D. J72
                         C. 1054

West   East
S. 73   S. K10
H. KQ105   H. 982
D. A854   D. Q1093
C. Q72   C. K986

                         South
                         S. QJ842
                         H. J73
                         D. K6
                         C. AJ3

First, familiarize yourself with the card combinations
in the side suits.

Notice South's semi-automatic duck of the opening lead,
and notice in particular how important it is that neither
defender attack either minor suit!

If declarer attacks diamonds he is entitled to zero diamond tricks; if declarer attacks clubs he is entitled to
one club trick.

However, if either defender attacks diamonds declarer
must make one trick in the suit; and declarer comes to
two tricks in clubs if either East or West starts the
suit.

If there ever was a hand that called for passive defense
this is it! But declarer can force the defenders to

break at least one minor suit. Assume the spade is ducked and East returns a heart. Dummy wins, the remaining trumps are removed, and West is thrown in with a heart. Now West must either concede a ruff-sluff or break a minor suit. In either case South makes the contract.

TYPE II: The Dummy That Has Ruffing Power But

Little Else

East-West vul.
Dealer South

North
S. A54
H. 82
D. 6543
C. K765

West (You)
S. 3
H. KJ95
D. QJ109
C. Q1082

East
S. K62
H. AQ107
D. 872
C. J43

South
S. QJ10987
H. 643
D. AK
C. A9

South	West	North	East
1S	Pass	2S	Pass
4S	All pass		

You lead the queen of diamonds, partner plays the deuce and declarer the ace. At trick two declarer leads the three of hearts, you win the nine, partner playing the seven. Now what?

Apparently declarer is trying to make tricks by ruffing
in the short hand. He can't use dummy's length because
you have both suits bottled up. Your best shot is to
shift to a trump and hope you can knock out dummy's
trumps before declarer can ruff hearts in dummy. Your
genius at analyzing declarer's motives pays off.

Twist or squirm as he will, declarer must lose three
hearts and a spade after a trump switch, and trump con-
tinuations by East.

Type III: The Dummy That Has A Long Side Suit

This is probably the most common type of dummy in a suit
contract. Sometimes it is obvious to both players that
the side suit is solid -- either because you are staring
at a solid suit or because the declarer has supported
the suit. Nevertheless, this type must be subdivided as
follows:

    a. A long, usable side suit.

    b. A long, unusable side suit.

The strategy of the defense varies with the usability
of dummy's side suit. If the suit is solid or will be
shortly, the defenders must hurry to take their tricks.

On the other hand, if the side suit is not usable the defenders can fall back and defend as if it were either a Type I or Type II dummy. In other words, either play passively or lead trumps to cut down dummy's ruffing power.

Remember, any time dummy has a long suit with trump support there will be a corresponding short suit. If declarer cannot use the long suit he must fall back on ruffing in the short hand. Your best defense now may be to lead trumps.

Shift around to the East seat and look at a Type III dummy:

Both sides vul.
Dealer South

North
S. Q7
H. 74
D. 8632
C. AKJ94

East (1)
S. 1093
H. A85
D. J105
C. 8763

East (2)
S. 1093
H. A85
D. J105
C. Q1083

South	West	North	East
1S	Pass	2C	Pass
2S	Pass	3S	Pass
4S	All pass		

Assume your partner leads the three of hearts and you win the ace, declarer dropping the six. With each East hand what do you play at trick two?

With (1) shift to the jack of diamonds immediately; the club suit is so menacing that you must take side suit tricks as quickly as possible. With (2) shift to a trump! You know that declarer cannot set up clubs, and by leading a trump you are telling your partner (and declarer if he is shrewd) the same thing. In fact, a trump switch by you guarantees that the club suit is under control!

In (1) declarer's hand may well be:
S. AKJxxx   H. Q10x   D. Kx   C. 10x   and a diamond shift at trick two defeats the contract.

In (2): S. AJxxxx   H. Q10x   D. AK   C. xx   a trump shift at trick two defeats the contract because declarer can no longer engineer a heart ruff.

Expert defenders can occasionally turn a Type III dummy into a Type I dummy by killing a discard.

Neither side vul.   North
Dealer North   S. A107
                  H. AK3
                  D. Q10872
                  C. 65

West   East
S. 62   S. 43
H. Q104   H. J976
D. AKJ96   D. 3
C. 1092   C. KQ8743

                  South
                  S. KQJ985
                  H. 852
                  D. 54
                  C. AJ

North	East	South	West
1D	Pass	1S	Pass
2S	Pass	4S	All pass

Opening lead: King of diamonds

When East plays the three of diamonds West recognizes
it as a singleton, for East is obliged to give a high-
low with a doubleton when the queen is in dummy and
partner leads the king.

If West shifts to either a heart or a club at trick two
declarer draws trumps and leads up to the queen of diamonds for his tenth trick. However, if West plays a low
diamond at trick two, allowing East to ruff, South is
unable to use the queen of diamonds as a later trick,
and must go down one.

Type IV: The Hidden Two-Suiter

Whenever declarer plays a trump contract with a <u>concealed</u> second suit he has an incredible advantage. That is the reason experts disdain showing a two suiter once they have found a major suit fit unless they are interested in making either a game or slam try.

Consider this hand:

```
                       North
                       S. Q32
                       H. A765
                       D. 765
                       C. 654

West                                      East
S. J109654                                S. AK7
H. 832                                    H. 9
D. 8                                      D. 10943
C. AQ7                                    C. J10983

                       South
                       S. 8
                       H. KQJ104
                       D. AKQJ2
                       C. K2
```

For the sake of argument, say that South is playing five hearts after East-West have bid to four spades, and West leads the jack of spades.

Well, if there ever was a Type I dummy this is it. But it's not! If the defenders play spade and spade, South ruffs, draws trumps and discards two of dummy's clubs on his fourth and fifth diamonds. As you can

see, the only defense is for East to win the first
spade (whether or not dummy plays the queen) and
shift to the jack of clubs. How can East know to
make this play?

To answer this we must go back to the bidding which
was not given. If South has shown a strong red two
suiter, then East should be alive to this. If South
has somehow concealed that diamond suit the defense
is going to have trouble defeating five hearts.

Notice that for there to be anything to fear from a
two suiter in the declarer's hand at least one trump
must remain in dummy after trumps are drawn for the
declarer to gain an extra trick. For example, if
this dummy had three trumps and, say, four spades,
declarer could not draw trumps and still leave one
in dummy for a club ruff.

In fact, when dummy has three trumps, declarer a
known two suiter, and one defender four trumps,
the best defense is almost always the forcing game.
(Make declarer trump.)

Both sides vul.
Dealer South

```
                      North
                      S. J43
                      H. K742
                      D. 765
                      C. Q109

      West                                East
      S. Q862                             S. 9
      H. J1098                            H. A65
      D. J4                               D. 983
      C. A76                              C. KJ8432

                      South
                      S. AK1075
                      H. Q3
                      D. AKQ102
                      C. 5
```

South	West	North	East
1S	Pass	1NT	Pass
3D	Pass	3S	Pass
4D	Pass	4S	All pass

Opening lead: Jack of hearts

East wins the ace (South might have the bare queen), and when no queen falls he knows declarer has at most one club. East also knows that West has four trumps, from the bidding, and shifts to the four of clubs.

West wins the ace and returns a club, forcing South to ruff. Twist and squirm as he may there is no way for South to make this hand once the defenders have forced him to trump. If he gives up a spade, another club forces him to ruff again and now West has more trumps than South. If South plays the ace-king of spades and then diamonds, West ruffs.

Another oddball situation which is sometimes difficult
to diagnose is when the dummy has more trumps than the
declarer. In that case you have to look at the dummy
as if it were the master hand and ask yourself what is
declarer (the short hand) going to do with his losers.

Neither side vul.
Dealer East

North
S. AK
H. 8
D. QJ986
C. 109832

West
S. J109432
H. 7
D. A32
C. K76

East
S. Q86
H. AKQ104
D. 5
C. QJ54

South
S. 75
H. J96532
D. K1074
C. A

East	South	West	North
1H	Pass	1S	2NT
3S	5D	Dbl.	All pass

Opening lead: Seven of hearts

After winning the first trick what should East play?
East should consider dummy the master hand, and should
realize that the only losers outside of the trump suit
are in clubs. What is South going to do with North's
clubs? Trump them, that's what. If East switches to
a trump at trick two and West continues with a second
trump the hand is defeated one trick. Any other defense and goodbye Charlie.

Another defensive concept is that of "killing the dummy".

```
Both sides vul.        North
Dealer South           S. J642
                       H. AQJ3
                       D. 65
                       C. 1052

    West                                    East (You)
    S. Q7                                   S. K853
    H. 109872                               H. 54
    D. 92                                   D. A7
    C. AJ93                                 C. Q8764

                       South
                       S. A109
                       H. K6
                       D. KQJ10843
                       C. K

    South       West        North       East
    1D          Pass        1H          Pass
    3D          Pass        3S          Pass
    4NT         Pass        5D          All pass
```

Opening lead: Ace of clubs

South drops the king and West shifts to the ten of hearts to South's king. South plays the king of diamonds. How should East defend?

First, declarer's distribution. He obviously has one club and is unlikely to have three hearts on the bidding. He can't have one heart or else he would have taken immediate spade discards. So declarer must have precisely two hearts to go with seven diamonds and three spades. If this is the case a heart return, forcing declarer to take his discards while you still have a trump, must be best.

Strangely enough, if you had one more heart and one less black card a heart return is still the only defense to break the contract. (Declarer gets only one spade discard before you ruff.) Of course if West had shifted to a spade at trick two there would have been one less hand for this chapter.

Every example and each discussion in this chapter has started with the defender making his lead and then looking at the dummy to see what type it is. Expert defenders try to visualize what the dummy will look like even _before_ they see it, so they can start planning their defense. They are not always right, but it pays to think in these terms:

I.   If no long suit figures to appear in dummy the passive game is usually best, but the opening leader must be pretty sure of himself before making this assumption.

II. If dummy figures to have a long usable side suit, then an active attacking defense is surely best.

III. If dummy figures to have ruffing power or the defenders seem to have the majority of the high cards, then trump leads are usually best.

IV. If declarer is known to have a two suiter the forcing game is best, particularly when one defender has four trumps.

I. North-South vul.
    Dealer East

North
S. 102
H. 6
D. AQ8753
C. J543

West
S. Q74
H. KQJ109
D. 102
C. Q109

East
S. 85
H. A753
D. KJ94
C. 876

South
S. AKJ963
H. 842
D. 6
C. AK2

East	South	West	North
Pass	1S	2H	Pass
3H	3S	Pass	4S
All pass			

Opening lead: King of hearts

II. Neither side vul.
     Dealer West

North
S. 108
H. 105
D. 5432
C. 87632

West
S. A65
H. 76
D. QJ976
C. Q54

East
S. 432
H. QJ98
D. A108
C. J109

South
S. KQJ97
H. AK432
D. K
C. AK

West	North	East	South
Pass	Pass	Pass	2C
Pass	2D	Pass	2S
Pass	2NT	Pass	3H
Pass	3S	Pass	4H
Pass	4S	All pass	

Opening lead: Queen of diamonds

III. East-West vul.   North
Dealer South   S. 643
                                    H. K106
                                    D. AJ10
                                    C. J632

        West   East
        S. AK102   S. J75
        H. 983   H. J5
        D. 975   D. Q862
        C. K74   C. A1098

                                    South
                                    S. Q98
                                    H. AQ742
                                    D. K43
                                    C. Q5

        South   West   North   East
        1H   Pass   2H   All pass

    Opening lead: King of spades

IV. Both sides vul.   North
Dealer South   S. KJ5
                                    H. J7
                                    D. KQ9762
                                    C. A2

        West   East
        S. 3   S. 42
        H. Q1064   H. A953
        D. 1084   D. A53
        C. QJ985   C. K1076

                                    South
                                    S. AQ109876
                                    H. K82
                                    D. J
                                    C. 43

        South   West   North   East
        3S   Pass   4S   All pass

    Opening lead: Queen of clubs

I. East, who can see that dummy's diamonds are worthless, overtakes the opening lead to return a trump. Declarer can no longer ruff two hearts in dummy and winds up losing two hearts, a club and a trump. (West cannot safely lead trumps from his side.)

II. West, who might have lead a trump on the go, elected to lead a diamond. East wins the ace and shifts to a trump. Obviously dummy's only use to declarer will be for heart ruffs. The trump switch and continuation defeats the hand, as declarer must lose two hearts, a diamond and a trump.

III. East plays the five of spades at trick one, denying either the queen or a doubleton. Looking at a balanced dummy West shifts to a trump. If the defenders play properly they can eventually force South to guess the diamond situation. If South plays properly he will play every other suit hoping for a diamond switch. Eventually he will see West turn up with 10 high card points and should on percentages play East for the queen of diamonds. (West might have bid with 12 high card points.)

IV. Dummy wins the lead and declarer tries to sneak a low
diamond at trick two. East wins the ace (no point in
ducking), cashes a club, and shifts to a <u>low</u> heart.
East sees that the defense needs two heart tricks.
If partner has the king it doesn't matter which heart
East plays first, but if partner has the <u>queen</u> it is
necessary to shift to a low heart to put declarer to
the guess.

I. North-South vul.   North (Dummy)
    Dealer South   S. KQJ98
                            H. 1095
                            D. 862
                            C. K8

        West (You)
        S. 107
        H. K2
        D. K1074
        C. QJ1074

South	West	North	East
1H	Pass	1S	Pass
3H	Pass	4H	All pass

Opening lead: Queen of clubs

Dummy's king wins, partner playing the deuce and

declarer the three. At trick two the ten of hearts

rides around to your king. Now what?

II. Neither side vul.   North (Dummy)
    Dealer South   S. AK103
                            H. Q76
                            D. 53
                            C. AKQJ

                                            East (You)
                                            S. 84
                                            H. A1032
                                            D. A76
                                            C. 10653

South	West	North	East
Pass	Pass	1C	Pass
1S	Pass	4S	All pass

Opening lead: Queen of diamonds

Plan your defense.

III.   Both sides vul.   North (Dummy)
       Dealer North   S. Q95
                                H. A107532
                                D. 32
                                C. 32

          West (You)
          S. A43
          H. 4
          D. Q1084
          C. K9654

          North   East   South   West
          Pass   Pass   1S   Pass
          2S   Dbl.   4S
          All pass

Opening lead: Four of hearts

Dummy's ace, partner's nine and declarer's queen

constitute the first trick. At trick two declarer

leads a low diamond to the nine and ten, partner

furnishing the five. What is your next play?

IV.   Neither side vul.   North (Dummy)
      Dealer North   S. K32
                                H. QJ53
                                D. K102
                                C. J82

          West (You)
          S. QJ98
          H. K6
          D. 8765
          C. K106

          North   East   South   West
          Pass   Pass   1H   Pass
          3H   All pass

Opening lead: Queen of spades

Dummy's king wins, partner playing the four and de-

clarer the five. The queen of hearts loses to your

king at trick two. What is your next play?

V. Both sides vul.   North (Dummy)
    Dealer North   S. KQ2
                         H. 654
                         D. 76
                         C. AKJ109

                                          East (You)
                                          S. 54
                                          H. A1032
                                          D. AJ109
                                          C. 765

        North   East   South   West
        1C   Pass   1S   Pass
        2S   Pass   4S   All pass

Opening lead: Three of diamonds

You win the ace, declarer playing the five. What

is your next play?

VI. East-West vul.   North (Dummy)
     Dealer East   S. 10
                         H. Q863
                         D. QJ1092
                         C. AQ8

                                          East (You)
                                          S. A98742
                                          H. 52
                                          D. AK
                                          C. KJ10

        East   South   West   North
        1S   2H   Pass   4H
        All pass

Opening lead: Three of spades

You win the first trick, declarer playing the jack.

What is your next play?

I.
                              North
                              S. KQJ98
                              H. 1095
                              D. 862
                              C. K8

West   East
S. 107   S. A543
H. K2   H. 63
D. K1074   D. Q53
C. QJ1074   C. 9652

                              South
                              S. 62
                              H. AQJ874
                              D. AJ9
                              C. A3

You should shift to a low diamond. If declarer has

the ace of spades you must collect your diamond tricks

before declarer discards his diamond losers on the

spades. If partner has the ace of spades you must

develop two diamond tricks before the ace of spades

is dislodged.

II.
                              North
                              S. AK103
                              H. Q76
                              D. 53
                              C. AKQJ

West   East
S. 62   S. 84
H. KJ4   H. A1032
D. QJ1098   D. A76
C. 987   C. 10653

                              South
                              S. QJ975
                              H. 985
                              D. K42
                              C. 42

You should win the ace of diamonds and shift to a low heart. Declarer has ten easy tricks without the king of hearts so there is no hope unless partner has that card. He needs the jack as well, but perhaps this is your lucky day.

III.

```
                        North
                        S. Q95
                        H. A107532
                        D. 32
                        C. 32

    West                                    East
    S. A43                                  S. 2
    H. 4                                    H. KJ986
    D. Q1084                                D. K75
    C. K9654                                C. QJ108

                        South
                        S. KJ10876
                        H. Q
                        D. AJ96
                        C. A7
```

The big danger here is that South is going to ruff diamonds in dummy. The heart suit is no menace, which West knows both from the bidding and the play to the first trick. West must swing the ace and a spade to defeat this contract, giving up on any non-existent heart ruff he may be dreaming about.

IV.

```
                          North
                          S. K32
                          H. QJ53
                          D. K102
                          C. J82

   West                                      East
   S. QJ98                                   S. 764
   H. K6                                     H. 102
   D. 8765                                   D. AJ43
   C. K106                                   C. Q754

                          South
                          S. A105
                          H. A9874
                          D. Q9
                          C. A93
```

You should return your remaining heart. Partner's
play to the first trick has denied the ten of spades
(he signals with a higher spade if he has the ten)
and the looks of the dummy makes it fairly clear that
the defenders should avoid breaking any new suits.

Declarer might actually go down on this hand if left
to his own devices. For example, he might win the
heart return in dummy (retaining the four of hearts)
and lead a diamond to the queen and a diamond to the
ten and jack. If East returns a spade, South must
win, enter dummy with the five of hearts and ruff a
diamond. Now South exits with the ten of spades
forcing West to lead a club. (If West leads the king
of clubs, South might play him for the queen and lead
low to the jack after winning the ace, for a one trick
set.)

In any event, it would take an expert South to counteract the passive defense of a trump return.

V.

```
                        North
                        S. KQ2
                        H. 654
                        D. 76
                        C. AKJ109

West                                        East
S. 63                                       S. 54
H. Q97                                      H. A1032
D. K8432                                    D. AJ109
C. 432                                      C. 765

                        South
                        S. AJ10987
                        H. KJ8
                        D. Q5
                        C. Q8
```

This dummy is definitely one to fear. From East's point of view four red tricks must be taken. As it is impossible to take more than two diamond tricks even if partner has the king (and you can't be sure he has) you must try for two or three heart tricks. Your play is a low heart at trick two, forcing declarer to guess the position if he happens to have the king-jack. If you woodenly return a diamond, partner wins the king but must lead a heart from his side, making life easy for declarer.

VI.

```
                    North
                    S. 10
                    H. Q863
                    D. QJ1092
                    C. AQ8
        West                            East
        S. K653                         S. A98742
        H. 7                            H. 52
        D. 8765                         D. AK
        C. 9543                         C. KJ10
                    South
                    S. QJ
                    H. AKJ1094
                    D. 43
                    C. 762
```

Something has gone wrong here. East-West can make five spades but are defending four hearts, and are very apt to let them make this contract unless East leads a club into the ace, queen!

East can see two diamond tricks, along with a spade. He must try to build up a club trick before his diamond entries are removed. Constant club plays by East will defeat this contract one trick.

Notice also that West, with a worthless hand, one that does not figure to be on lead again, should break the rules and lead the king of spades! This will enable him to lead through dummy's strength if necessary. East plays low on the king asking for a shift, and the club switch at trick two is not too terribly difficult.

Leading a low spade forces East to make a brilliant return. Did you come through for your bumbling partner?

XIV. DEVELOPING EXTRA TRICKS IN THE TRUMP SUIT

Defenders have many techniques for establishing extra trump tricks. The most obvious, of course, is to ruff away either declarer's or dummy's good tricks.

GETTING A RUFF

Obviously the best way to get a ruff is to lead your short suit. These leads work particularly well when holding trump control and when partner has an entry.

```
North-South vul.              North
Dealer West                   S. 2
                              H. K965
                              D. AQ103
                              C. A876

        West                                      East
        S. KQ108643                               S. AJ97
        H. A3                                     H. 42
        D. 7                                      D. 864
        C. 1032                                   C. Q954

                              South
                              S. 5
                              H. QJ1087
                              D. KJ952
                              C. KJ
```

West	North	East	South
3S	Dbl.	4S	5H
All pass			

West, with trump çontrol, leads his singleton diamond rather than from his spade sequence. South wins and makes the deceptive play of the jack of hearts, feigning a finesse, to avoid a ruff. West steps up smartly and leads a spade to partner's ace (preferably the queen or a low one to make sure

-445-

partner overtakes), and the ensuing diamond return defeats the contract one trick.

The point to note is that if West leads a spade and then shifts to a diamond he is unable to put East in for the diamond ruff.

When the opening leader is obviously leading a singleton (perhaps both opponents have bid the suit, or perhaps you and partner have bid and supported one suit yet he leads another) third hand should signal where his outside strength lies, rather than what he holds in the suit led. That way the opening leader will know how to put his partner in for a ruff.

North-South vul.
Dealer South

North
S. KQ76
H. J1054
D. Q73
C. 72

West
S. 2
H. A3
D. K842
C. KJ10543

East
S. J53
H. 2
D. AJ1065
C. Q986

South
S. A10984
H. KQ9876
D. 9
C. A

South	West	North	East
1H	2C	2H	5C
5H	Dbl.	All pass	

Opening lead: Deuce of spades

West makes a speculative double on the assumption that he will get a spade ruff. When West leads a spade rather than a club, particularly after doubling, East smells a rat.

-446-

Assuming dummy wins the trick, East plays the jack to tell partner where his entry is -- in this case, the higher ranking suit,
diamonds. When West wins the ace of hearts he leads a diamond,
not a club, to get his spade ruff.

If East had three small spades and the ace of clubs, he would
play his smallest spade at trick one no matter which spade is
played from dummy.

Sometimes third hand must take charge of the defense in order
to get a ruff.

```
Both sides vul.          North
Dealer North             S. J4
                         H. AJ32
                         D. AKQ108
                         C. 65

        West                             East
        S. 5                             S. A976
        H. 1086                          H. Q75
        D. 97654                         D. J
        C. J1082                         C. AKQ93

                         South
                         S. KQ10832
                         H. K94
                         D. 32
                         C. 74
```

North	East	South	West
1D	Dbl.	2S	Pass
3S	Pass	4S	All pass

Opening lead: Jack of clubs

East must overtake the opening lead and shift to the jack of
diamonds. The best declarer can do is try to draw trumps.
East wins the ace and underleads his club honors to partner's

probable ten (he did lead the jack) and again the ensuing diamond ruff defeats the contract.

Notice that East has the ace of trumps to insure regaining the lead. Trump control is very important when trying for a ruff in a long suit the opponents have completely under control.

GIVING A RUFF

Sometimes a defender does not have a short suit of his own but can tell from the bidding that partner must be short. For example, if the opponents bid and raise diamonds and eventually play hearts, and you are on lead with four or five small diamonds, you can anticipate a singleton or void in partner's hand. A diamond lead becomes particularly attractive if you happen to have the ace or king of trumps as well.

Other times a defender can tell from the looks of the dummy plus the bidding that partner is very short in a side suit, perhaps even void!

East-West vul.   North
Dealer South   S. 853
          H. 874
          D. AJ10
          C. Q943

West   East
S. 96   S. A42
H. QJ932   H. A1065
D. 876543   D. 9
C. none   C. J8762

     South
     S. KQJ107
     H. K
     D. KQ2
     C. AK105

South	West	North	East
1S	Pass	1NT	Pass
3C	Pass	3S	Pass
4S	All pass		

Opening lead: Queen of hearts

East wins the lead and is reasonably sure after gazing at dummy's four clubs that partner is void. East also knows from the bidding that partner has only two trumps. (It is important to know how many trumps partner has when considering ruffs.) In other words, East can give West only one club ruff. (When East wins the ace of trumps, West will not have any more trumps.)

East has a chance to make an expert play because he knows he can always give West that club ruff upon gaining the lead with the ace of trumps. East must switch to his own singleton before giving partner the obvious club ruff. Notice the effect of this play.

Dummy wins the diamond return and leads a trump. East wins the ace, gives his partner a club ruff and in return ruffs a diamond to defeat the contract. East has gained a trick by not giving partner a premature ruff! Instead he has set up a situation whereby he can also trump something after partner gets his ruff.

One more example of this type of play:

```
Both sides vul.              North
Dealer East                  S. AJ76
                             H. K5
                             D. KJ108
                             C. K72

        West                                       East
        S. 98542                                   S. 10
        H. AJ98                                     H. Q10763
        D. 93                                       D. AQ62
        C. 64                                       C. A53

                             South
                             S. KQ3
                             H. 42
                             D. 754
                             C. QJ1098
```

East	South	West	North
1H	Pass	2H	Dbl.
Pass	3C	All pass	

Opening lead: Nine of diamonds

West, with a weak looking defensive hand, tries for ruffs by leading the nine of diamonds. Dummy covers and East wins the queen. The average player at this point plays ace and a diamond and is elated when partner ruffs. West cashes his ace of hearts and later East makes the ace of trumps to defeat the contract, and East-West rejoice, thinking they know what they are doing.

Watch what happens if East, holding the trump ace, shifts to the ten of spades at trick two. Declarer wins and leads a trump. East wins and plays ace and a diamond. West ruffs, gives East a spade ruff, and East puts West in with the ace of hearts to ruff another spade. Down three. Now East-West really have something to be happy about.

When holding the ace of trumps and being in a position to give partner a ruff, also consider switching to a doubleton before giving the ruff, with the same thought in mind -- being able to get a ruff after giving a ruff.

Neither side vul.
Dealer East

```
                       North
                       S. Q82
                       H. J104
                       D. KQJ
                       C. 8765
         West                              East
         S. KJ1065                         S. 73
         H. 65                             H. A32
         D. 2                              D. A108653
         C. 109432                         C. QJ
                       South
                       S. A94
                       H. KQ987
                       D. 974
                       C. AK
```

East	South	West	North
1D	1H	1S	2H
Pass	3H	All pass	

Opening lead: Deuce of diamonds

Something went wrong in the bidding because North-South can make three no trump, but that is not the defenders' problem. They have to figure out some way to defeat three hearts. Can you see how?

East must win the opening lead and shift to the seven of spades. South does best to duck, so West wins and returns the suit. Now East grabs the first round of hearts, gives his partner a diamond ruff, and in turn gets a spade ruff. Had East given West an immediate diamond ruff he never would have gotten his spade ruff.

Still another consideration before giving partner a ruff in dummy's long suit is the possibility of developing a side suit trick first and giving him the ruff later.

```
Both sides vul.              North
Dealer South                 S. 1098
                             H. 1098
                             D. KQ10987
                             C. Q
            West                                    East
            S. 62                                   S. A43
            H. K432                                 H. 765
            D. 2                                    D. A65
            C. J65432                               C. K987
                             South
                             S. KQJ75
                             H. AQJ
                             D. J43
                             C. A10

            South       West        North       East
            1S          Pass        2S          Pass
            4S          All pass
```

Opening lead: Deuce of diamonds

Again East has the ace of trumps, a suit partner can possibly ruff, and the knowledge that partner has no more than two trumps. (If East had, for example, Ax of trumps he would suspect three trumps in his partner's hand and could plan to give West TWO diamond ruffs, one at trick two and one when in with the ace of trumps.)

East must accept the fact that he can give West only one diamond ruff and that the suit will then be established for possible heart discards. The better defense by East is to win the ace of diamonds and shift to a heart, building up a trick in that suit. Now East can still give West his diamond ruff but the established trick in hearts defeats the contract. If East gives West an immediate ruff, West cannot attack hearts and the hand is made.

As always, when giving partner a ruff you must tell him by the size of the card you return which suit you want back. (We saw this play in the chapter "Signalling vs. Suit Contracts".)

```
North-South vul.              North
Dealer West                   S. 74
                              H. 9753
                              D. K762
                              C. KJ3

        West                                        East
        S. Q92                                      S. 6
        H. AQJ62                                    H. K108
        D. 10843                                    D. J9
        C. 2                                        C. A1097654

                              South
                              S. AKJ10853
                              H. 4
                              D. AQ5
                              C. Q8


        West        North       East        South
        Pass        Pass        3C          4S
        All pass
```

Opening lead: Deuce of clubs

East wins the ace of clubs and returns the ten for partner to ruff. Returning a high spot card asks partner to return the higher ranking of the two remaining side suits after ruffing.

If West is a trusting soul, he will return a low heart (if East had a singleton heart he would have shifted to a heart at trick two to set up a defensive crossruff) to East's king. A third club by East promotes the queen of spades in the West hand for the setting trick.

Another problem when giving partner a ruff is deciding whether partner's lead is a singleton or a doubleton. This dilemma often comes up when you hold the ace of the suit partner has led with NO outside entry.

```
Both sides vul.          North
Dealer North             S. KQJ
                         H. Q109
                         D. KQJ32
                         C. 54

         West                             East
         S. 93                            S. A8642
         H. K54                           H. 32
         D. A965                          D. 1087
         C. Q763                          C. J98

                         South
                         S. 1075
                         H. AJ876
                         D. 4
                         C. AK102

         North       East        South       West
         1D          Pass        1H          Pass
         2H          Pass        4H          All pass
```

Opening lead: Nine of spades

The fate of this contract depends upon East's play to the first trick. If East wins the ace and returns a spade (the winning play if West is leading a singleton) the hand can no longer be defeated, for West can then never ruff a spade.

On the other hand, if East plays West to have a doubleton spade and encourages with the eight, then when West gains the lead in either hearts or diamonds he can return the three of spades and get his beloved ruff.

How can East tell? Many times with no outside entry East must take an educated guess using the bidding to guide him. But, if East has an outside entry he does not have to guess!

Assume East has the ace of diamonds instead of West and the lead is the same. East wins the ace and returns the eight of spades, showing an entry in the higher ranking side suit. If the lead is, in fact, a singleton West ruffs, returns a diamond and gets a second spade ruff.

If the lead is a doubleton, when West gets in with the king of hearts he returns a diamond and gets his spade ruff.

Conclusion: When partner leads an obvious short suit and you have the ace plus an outside entry, win the ace and give partner a suit preference return. If you have no outside entry try to use the bidding to guide you. If you think the lead is a singleton win your ace and return the suit; if you think it

is a doubleton encourage your partner with a high spot card.
If you don't think anything, you're playing the wrong game!

THE OVERRUFF

Another common method of promoting extra tricks in the trump
suit is to put partner in a position where he can overruff
either declarer or dummy.

```
East-West vul.                  North
Dealer West                     S. 1095
                                H. 1094
                                D. KJ9
                                C. AQ108

            West                                    East
            S. J43                                  S. 62
            H. KQ6                                  H. AJ832
            D. 743                                  D. AQ106
            C. K432                                 C. 75

                                South
                                S. AKQ87
                                H. 75
                                D. 852
                                C. J96

            West        North       East        South
            Pass        Pass        1H          1S
            2H          2S          All pass
```

Opening lead: King of hearts

East plays the <u>deuce</u> of hearts at trick one to discourage a
heart continuation. West shifts to a top diamond and dummy's
nine fetches East's ten. East returns a low heart to West's
queen and subsequently cashes two more diamond tricks after
West returns the suit. At this point, East plays a fourth
diamond promoting West's jack of spades for the setting trick.

In this particular instance nobody at the table had diamonds when East played a fourth round. More often than not though, dummy will have the suit that is being led but both declarer and the defender playing after declarer will be void; this allows the defender an opportunity to overruff declarer... which brings about another idea on defense; namely, <u>refusing to overruff</u>.

Both sides vul.
Dealer West

North
S. 54
H. 10973
D. KJ53
C. KJ2

West
S. Q962
H. 86
D. 10987
C. 1065

East
S. 3
H. AKQJ2
D. 64
C. Q9873

South
S. AKJ1087
H. 54
D. AQ2
C. A4

West	North	East	South
Pass	Pass	1H	Dbl.
Pass	2D	Pass	3S
Pass	4S	All pass	

Opening lead: Eight of hearts

East wins the first two hearts and plays a third, South ruffing with the jack of spades. If West overtrumps, South takes the balance easily. If West discards, his Q962 now become worth two trump tricks.

There are any number of similar situations whereby a defender who has the opportunity to overtrump must refuse to do so in order to promote additional trump tricks for himself.

The position is most easily recognizable when declarer is known to have long trumps and the defender who has a chance to overtrump has three or four cards to an honor along with a ten, nine or eight in the trump suit. It is surprising how often the lower cards become additional tricks if the defender does not overtrump.

```
                         North (Dummy)
                         S. 2

West                                         East
S. J843                                      S. Q

                         South
                         S. AK109765
```

Imagine East playing a suit that neither South nor West has. South trumps with the ten. If West overtrumps, East-West take no more trump tricks. If West discards he later takes two tricks with his jack-eight.

The same principle applies when given the opportunity to overtrump dummy. Consider here how many tricks you make if you overtrump and how many you make if you refuse.

```
Both sides vul.               North (Dummy)
Dealer South                  S. K109
                              H. J3
                              D. AK765
                              C. K32

        West                                      East
        S. none                                   S. QJ75
        H. AKQ1065                                H. 84
        D. 10942                                  D. 83
        C. 954                                    C. QJ876

                              South
                              S. A86432
                              H. 972
                              D. QJ
                              C. A10

        South       West          North         East
        1S          2H            3D            Pass
        3S          Pass          4S            All pass
```

Opening lead: King of hearts

West plays three rounds of hearts, dummy trumping the third with
the nine. Most East players would overtrump without giving the
matter a second thought. But then again most East players have
not read this chapter. East should see that if he discards a
diamond instead of overtrumping he must make two trump tricks,
but if he overtrumps he makes only one. That seven of spades
is a pretty big card on this hand.

THE UPPERCUT

Once the principle of refusing to overtrump in order to promote
additional trump tricks is understood, then the principle behind
the uppercut, another trump promoting play, can easily be assim-
ilated.

The uppercut is equivalent to refusing to overruff. How's that
again? Let's see.

                         North
                         S. 2

     West   East
     S. J843   S. Q

                         South
                         S. AK109765

It was noted that if East led a side suit and South ruffed with
the ten West would be better advised not to overtrump. The
same effect can be achieved if West leads a side suit and East
trumps with the queen. Now when South overtrumps West makes
two trump tricks although he seemingly is entitled to but one.

                         North
                         S. 32

        West   East
        S. A94   S. 105

                         South
                         S. KQJ876

Again, when East leads a side suit and South trumps high, if
West refuses to overtrump he must come to two tricks.

Analogously -- if West leads a side suit and East trumps with
the ten, South must lose two trump tricks whether or not he
overruffs.

North-South vul.   North
Dealer North   S. Q95
                    H. A63
                    D. K86
                    C. AJ104

West		East
S. AK8643		S. 107
H. 1084		H. Q7
D. 94		D. QJ10732
C. 82		C. K95

                  South
                  S. J2
                  H. KJ952
                  D. A5
                  C. Q763

North	East	South	West
1C	2D*	2H	2S
2NT	Pass	3C	Pass
3H	Pass	4H	All pass

*Weak Jump Overcall

Opening lead: King of spades

West begins with three rounds of spades forcing East to ruff.
If East ruffs with the seven South overtrumps, loses no trump
tricks and one more club trick, to make his game. If East
trumps with the queen, <u>uppercutting</u> South, South overtrumps
and must lose a trump trick to West's ten in addition to the
king of clubs, thus suffering a one trick setback.

In the previous example third hand uppercut declarer's trump
holding. It is also possible to uppercut dummy's trump holding.

```
Both sides vul.              North
Dealer South                 S. QJ107
                             H. KQ109
                             D. QJ
                             C. 954

        West                                       East
        S. 84                                      S. K95
        H. 8632                                    H. 75
        D. 76542                                   D. 1098
        C. 106                                     C. AKQ87

                             South
                             S. A632
                             H. AJ4
                             D. AK3
                             C. J32

        South       West        North       East
        1NT         Pass        2C          Dbl.
        2S          Pass        4S          All pass
```

Opening lead: Ten of clubs

East cashes three clubs and West discards the diamond deuce. East can tell by adding his points to dummy's that partner cannot have more than a jack, but there is no law against his having the eight of spades. East plays a fourth club, West uppercuts dummy with the eight, dummy overtrumps, but East has a natural trump trick coming, once an honor from dummy has been removed.

THE FORCING GAME

Earlier we saw how a ruffing defense can be planned when holding the ace of trumps. There is also an art to knowing when to win the ace of trumps when playing the forcing game.

Neither side vul.
Dealer South

North
S. J7
H. Q65
D. AK1086
C. 843

West
S. 43
H. 10872
D. 952
C. KQ105

East
S. A652
H. 93
D. J74
C. AJ96

South
S. KQ1098
H. AKJ4
D. Q3
C. 72

South	West	North	East
1S	Pass	2D	Pass
2H	Pass	2S	Pass
4S	All pass		

Opening lead: King of clubs

South ruffs the third club and plays the king of spades. East should know from the bidding that at this point he very likely holds the same number of trumps as South - four. If East can force South to trump a club he will have gained control of the hand since he will then hold more trumps than declarer.

Obviously, if he wins the first spade and plays a fourth club, South will not trump in his own hand, shortening himself, but rather in dummy, and will still have his remaining three trumps to draw East's remaining three. Which is the point of the whole hand: WHEN TRYING TO FORCE THE LONGER TRUMP HAND TO RUFF A SUIT IN WHICH BOTH DECLARER AND DUMMY ARE VOID YOU MUST WIN THE TRUMP THAT EXHAUSTS THE DUMMY, in this case the second round. If East

wins the second round of trumps and plays a fourth club the hand
is defeated.

After studying that hand, this one should be easily comprehensible:

```
Both sides vul.            North
Dealer South               S. Q1083
                           H. 82
                           D. Q102
                           C. KQ72

          West                              East
          S. A642                           S. 5
          H. Q974                           H. AKJ10
          D. 75                             D. 9843
          C. 963                            C. J1085

                           South
                           S. KJ97
                           H. 653
                           D. AKJ6
                           C. A4
```

South	West	North	East
1NT	Pass	2C	Pass
2S	Pass	4S	All pass

Opening lead: Four of hearts

West, holding four trumps, leads from his longest suit, usually
the best strategy. If East is with it he will win his two top
hearts and play a third, forcing dummy to ruff. (East knows
from his own trump holding that West has four trumps.) Declarer
begins to draw trumps. West knows that he must force South to
ruff another heart but that he cannot do so until dummy's trumps
are removed. If West ducks the first two trump leads and wins
the third he can play a fourth heart forcing South to ruff with

his last trump; this promotes West's six of trumps to the setting trick.

If declarer refrains from playing a third trump and plays minor suits, West will ruff the third diamond with the blessed six of spades and again the hand is defeated.

Notice that these ducking plays with the ace (or king) of trumps are not necessary if dummy is not void in the "forcing" suit. In that case declarer has no choice but to ruff in his own hand. It is only when both declarer and dummy are void that the defender must win his trump trick at the proper moment.

THE RUFF-SLUFF

The ruff-sluff, as every beginner knows, is a terrible defensive play. It allows declarer to sluff a loser in one hand while ruffing in the other. Indeed, ruff-sluffs can be very costly when declarer has a loser to discard. However, there are any number of hands on which eagle-eyed defenders can see that declarer cannot possibly have any side suit losers, and that by leading a suit in which both declarer and dummy are void an additional trump trick can be promoted for the defense.

Neither side vul.　　　　　North
Dealer North　　　　　　　S. AKQ
　　　　　　　　　　　　　H. 1087
　　　　　　　　　　　　　D. AKJ53
　　　　　　　　　　　　　C. A10

West　　　　　　　　　　　　　　　　　　East
S. 63　　　　　　　　　　　　　　　　　S. J42
H. AKQJ5　　　　　　　　　　　　　　　H. 93
D. Q94　　　　　　　　　　　　　　　　D. 1082
C. J98　　　　　　　　　　　　　　　　C. 76532

　　　　　　　　　　　　　South
　　　　　　　　　　　　　S. 109875
　　　　　　　　　　　　　H. 642
　　　　　　　　　　　　　D. 76
　　　　　　　　　　　　　C. KQ4

North	East	South	West
2NT	Pass	3S	Pass
4D*	Pass	4S	All pass

*Slam try with spade support

Opening lead:　King of hearts

West cashes the first three hearts, East discarding the club deuce.　Obviously, East has no interest in clubs, the diamond finesse works if declarer needs it, so what's left?

The best chance lies in the trump suit.　Partner may have the jack of spades.　West plays a fourth heart and East must make his jack of spades to defeat the contract.

Strangely enough, even if West had Jxx of spades he should lead a fourth heart.　Partner may have the ten of spades; or declarer may have six spades and ruff high in dummy, fearing that East has a doubleton jack.

In this case a ruff-sluff allowed a defender to overruff dummy. The more common situation is a ruff-sluff allowing partner to overruff declarer.

```
Neither side vul.              North
Dealer East                    S. 10642
                               H. Q5
                               D. AKQJ
                               C. AQ10

        West                                       East
        S. J73                                     S. A
        H. J92                                     H. AK10743
        D. 1092                                    D. 865
        C. 8765                                    C. 942

                               South
                               S. KQ985
                               H. 86
                               D. 743
                               C. KJ3

        East        South       West        North
        1H          1S          Pass        4S
        All pass
```

Opening lead: Deuce of hearts

East cashes two hearts and sees that there are no tricks coming in the side suits. So he turns his attention to the trump suit. He hopes that by playing a third heart, ridding his partner of the jack, he will be able to play a fourth heart when on lead with the ace of spades; then if partner has Jxx or Qx of spades this will be the only defense to break the contract. Sure enough it is!

For an uppercut to be an effective defensive play one partner must ruff with his highest trump, forcing either dummy or de-clarer to overtrump. This in turn, hopefully, promotes partner's

trump holding. Many times a ruff-sluff is necessary for an uppercut to succeed.

```
Neither side vul.                North
Dealer South                     S. KQ
                                 H. Q4
                                 D. AKQ76
                                 C. K842

            West                                    East
            S. 8                                     S. 976542
            H. AKJ10876                              H. 53
            D. 102                                   D. 9853
            C. J96                                   C. 10

                                 South
                                 S. AJ103
                                 H. 92
                                 D. J4
                                 C. AQ753

            South      West        North       East
            1C         3H          4D          Pass
            4S         Pass        5C          All pass
```

Opening lead: King of hearts

The average player cashes two rounds of hearts and shifts to his

singleton spade, blissfully thinking in terms of ruffing a spade.

Of course, declarer has no trouble against this defense.

The more advanced player sees that the only chance for defeating

this hand is to hope partner has the ten of clubs. (Obviously

he doesn't have the ace of spades, South opened the bidding.)

So he plays a third heart. East ruffs with the ten and West has

promoted a trump trick for his J96.

Ruff-sluffs have a way of destroying declarers who are playing a

4-3 trump fit, particularly when one defender has four trumps.

Neither side vul.   North
Dealer North   S. A32
                                     H. AKQ74
                                     D. AK
                                     C. 1076

        West   East
        S. 64   S. Q987
        H. J5   H. 10862
        D. 98543   D. 106
        C. KQJ9   C. A82

                            South
                            S. KJ105
                            H. 93
                            D. QJ72
                            C. 543

        North   East   South   West
        1H   Pass   1S   Pass
        3D   Pass   4D   Pass
        4S   All pass

Opening lead: King of clubs

Three no trump, of course, is cold, but four spades is more fun

to defend.

West leads the king of clubs, East signalling with the eight.

IF WEST WANTS TO HOLD THE SECOND CLUB TRICK HE CONTINUES WITH

THE QUEEN; IF HE WANTS HIS PARTNER TO OVERTAKE HE CONTINUES

WITH THE JACK.

In this particular instance a far-sighted West would continue

with the jack of clubs forcing partner to overtake. East re-

turns a third club and West is now in a position to play a

fourth. Whichever side declarer takes the ruff, East discard-

ing a diamond, he will be unable to avoid the loss of a trump

trick. Had the defenders shifted to a red card at trick four, declarer simply takes the percentage play in spades (ace and low to the jack), cashes two high diamonds, repeats the finesse and claims the balance.

Even some cozy 4-4 trump fits can be attacked by a ruff-sluff to advantage, particularly when one defender has four trumps.

```
Both sides vul.              North
Dealer South                 S. KJ98
                             H. AKJ10
                             D. Q4
                             C. J52

         West                                    East
         S. A632                                 S. 4
         H. 752                                  H. 986
         D. AK1098                               D. 7532
         C. 8                                    C. 97643

                             South
                             S. Q1075
                             H. Q43
                             D. J6
                             C. AKQ10

         South       West        North       East
         1C          1D          1H          Pass
         1S          Pass        4S          All pass
```

Opening lead: King of diamonds

West wins the first two diamond tricks and doesn't even care if declarer has any side suit losers. He <u>knows</u> he can develop two trump tricks for himself by playing a third diamond. How does he know?

Well, either North or South must ruff the third diamond; then West, who has been reading this chapter, knows enough to win the <u>third</u> round of trumps with the ace and play a fourth diamond, forcing either declarer or dummy to use his last trump. This defense actually defeats the hand two tricks.

A wise declarer will give up on playing a third round of trumps and simply try to cash club tricks (having presumably discarded a club and ruffed in his hand on the first ruff-sluff) after playing the ace-king of hearts.

This results in West ruffing the second club and defeating the hand one trick. (Notice that if West were 2-2 in the off suits declarer could still overcome his diabolical defense by adopting the recommended line of play: Two hearts and then clubs after only _two_ rounds of trumps.)

I. East-West vul.   North
    Dealer South   S. 643
                                      H. J102
                                      D. AK98
                                      C. J103

        West   East
        S. QJ5   S. AK1097
        H. 6   H. A543
        D. 1065432   D. Q7
        C. 752   C. 96

                                      South
                                      S. 82
                                      H. KQ987
                                      D. J
                                      C. AKQ84

        South   West   North   East
        1H   Pass   2H   2S
        3C   Pass   4H   All pass

    Opening lead: Queen of spades

II. Neither side vul.   North
     Dealer South   S. 4
                                      H. 1083
                                      D. KJ9
                                      C. AKQ965

        West   East
        S. K102   S. 93
        H. AKQ764   H. 92
        D. 83   D. 76542
        C. 43   C. J1087

                                      South
                                      S. AQJ8765
                                      H. J5
                                      D. AQ10
                                      C. 2

        South   West   North   East
        1S   2H   3C   Pass
        4S   All pass

     Opening lead: King of hearts

III. North-South vul.   North
      Dealer South   S. Q985
                                  H. 643
                                  D. AKQJ4
                                  C. 7

West   East
S. 76   S. A4
H. 2   H. AJ10987
D. 108765   D. 3
C. Q6543   C. J1092

                                  South
                                  S. KJ1032
                                  H. KQ5
                                  D. 92
                                  C. AK8

South   West   North   East
1S   Pass   2D   2H
2NT   Pass   4S   All pass

Opening lead: Deuce of hearts

IV. Both sides vul.   North
     Dealer South   S. 73
                                  H. 852
                                  D. 9643
                                  C. KQJ10

West   East
S. Q865   S. 92
H. 764   H. 1093
D. 85   D. AKQJ10
C. 9873   C. 652

                                  South
                                  S. AKJ104
                                  H. AKQJ
                                  D. 72
                                  C. A4

South   West   North   East
2C*   Pass   2D**   Dbl.
2S   Pass   3C   Pass
3H   Pass   3S   Pass
4S   All pass

     *Strong and artificial
    **Negative response

Opening lead: Eight of diamonds

KEY PLAYS

I. South ruffs the third spade and tries to drive out the ace of hearts. East must win the <u>third</u> round of hearts in order to force South to ruff a second spade. If South does not play a third trump (best) East ruffs the third round of clubs.

II. West cashes two high hearts and then plays a <u>low</u> heart at trick three, forcing partner to ruff. A good East will ruff with the nine rather than the three, promoting an additional trump trick for West when South overtrumps with an honor.

III. East wins the heart lead and shifts to his singleton diamond at trick two. East then wins the first trump lead, gives partner a heart ruff and in turn receives a diamond ruff to defeat the contract.

IV. East plays three rounds of diamonds and South ruffs with the jack (or ten). West must not overtrump with the queen. If West refuses to overtrump he later makes two tricks with the Q8.

I. Neither side vul.   North (Dummy)
    Dealer West   S. AKQ5
                               H. AK87
                               D. J4
                               C. 943

        West (You)
        S. 432
        H. 109
        D. KQ10732
        C. A10

        West   North   East   South
        2D*   Dbl.   3D   4C
        All pass

        *Weak Two Bid

Opening lead: King of diamonds

You cash your king-queen of diamonds, everyone follow-

ing. What is your next play?

II. North-South vul.   North (Dummy)
     Dealer East   S. KJ106
                               H. KQJ5
                               D. K4
                               C. 984

                                               East (You)
                                               S. Q94
                                               H. 1063
                                               D. J32
                                               C. AKQJ

        East   South   West   North
        1C   Dbl.   Pass   2C
        Pass   2S   Pass   4S
        All pass

Opening lead: Deuce of clubs

You cash three rounds of clubs, all following. What

is your next play?

III. Both sides vul.   North (Dummy)
                               S. K984
                               H. 1032
                               D. K1075
                               C. Q5

        West (You)
        S. 1032
        H. 75
        D. 962
        C. J10987

        South   West   North   East
        3NT*   Pass   4C**   Pass
        4S   Pass   6S   All pass

         *25-26 balanced
        **Stayman

Opening lead: Jack of clubs

Dummy plays the queen, partner the king, and declarer
wins. Now three rounds of trumps, partner discarding
the club deuce on the third. Three top hearts follow,
you discarding a club and partner playing up the line.

Declarer now leads the three of clubs which you are
forced to win as partner follows. What is your next
play?

IV. North-South vul.   North (Dummy)
     Dealer North   S. 9864
                               H. J
                               D. KJ7
                               C. KQ1092

                                             East (You)
                                             S. 72
                                             H. 9732
                                             D. A1086
                                             C. J85

          North   East   South   West
          Pass   Pass   1S   Pass
          4S   All pass

     Opening lead: Nine of diamonds

     Dummy plays the king. Plan your defense.

V.   Neither side vul.   North (Dummy)
     Dealer North   S. AQJ
                               H. J765
                               D. KQ84
                               C. 42

                                             East (You)
                                             S. 5
                                             H. A2
                                             D. A109763
                                             C. J986

          North   East   South   West
          1D   Pass   1H   Pass
          2H   Pass   4H   All pass

     Opening lead: Deuce of diamonds

     Dummy plays low. Plan your defense.

VI. North-South vul.   North (Dummy)
     Dealer North   S. 93
                             H. J106
                             D. AQ4
                             C. KQJ109

          West (You)
          S. K862
          H. AKQ75
          D. 32
          C. 52

          North   East   South   West
          1C   Pass   1S   2H
          Pass   Pass   3H   Pass
          4C   Pass   4S   All pass

Opening lead: King of hearts

You play three rounds of hearts, declarer ruffing the
third with the four of spades. Declarer leads the
seven of diamonds to the ace, partner playing the
five, and leads a low spade from dummy. Partner plays
the five and declarer the queen. Plan your defense.

VII. Both sides vul.   North (Dummy)
  Dealer South   S. QJ10
           H. Q963
           D. AK98
           C. 75

                  East (You)
                  S. A8652
                  H. 84
                  D. 1043
                  C. AJ6

South	West	North	East
1NT	Pass	2C	Pass
2H*	Pass	4H	All pass

*North-South bid their <u>stronger</u> major if they
 happen to have both.

Opening lead: Nine of spades

Plan your defense.

VIII. Neither side vul. North (Dummy)
   Dealer North   S. KQ7
           H. J754
           D. AJ10
           C. A94

                  East (You)
                  S. A108542
                  H. none
                  D. K73
                  C. Q652

North	East	South	West
1NT	2S	4H	All pass

Opening lead: Three of spades

Dummy plays the queen. Plan your defense.

IX.

North
S. none
H. QJ4
D. AK10742
C. A952

West
S. A93
H. AK8762
D. 93
C. 43

East
S. 872
H. 93
D. QJ865
C. 876

South
S. KQJ10654
H. 105
D. none
C. KQJ10

Can you see any legitimate way for East-West to defeat a contract of four spades with West on lead?

I.

North
S. AKQ5
H. AK87
D. J4
C. 943

West
S. 432
H. 109
D. KQ10732
C. A10

East
S. J1076
H. QJ65
D. A96
C. J2

South
S. 98
H. 432
D. 85
C. KQ8765

Because there is no possible chance for a major suit trick, West should try to promote his ten of clubs. The first step is to play a third diamond to rid partner of the ace. Now West wins the first club and plays a fourth diamond, allowing East to upper-cut declarer with the jack and promoting the ten for the setting trick.

II.

North
S. KJ106
H. KQJ5
D. K4
C. 984

West
S. 83
H. 984
D. 109875
C. 532

East
S. Q94
H. 1063
D. J32
C. AKQJ

South
S. A752
H. A72
D. AQ6
C. 1076

A fourth club. Your queen of spades is hardly a secret because the strength of the dummy marks all the missing high cards in your hand. Therefore, your best play is a fourth club hoping partner has the eight of spades. If he does, he can uppercut dummy and insure a trump trick for you.

III.

```
                          North
                          S. K984
                          H. 1032
                          D. K1075
                          C. Q5

West                                         East
S. 1032                                      S. 75
H. 75                                        H. J9864
D. 962                                       D. Q8
C. J10987                                    C. K642

                          South
                          S. AQJ6
                          H. AKQ
                          D. AJ43
                          C. A3
```

A club. The fall of the cards, as well as partner's discard of the deuce of clubs to show four, have given you a complete count on declarer's hand. As long as declarer is known to have four diamonds, a club play, which is a ruff-sluff, cannot help him. He will still have to seek that elusive queen of diamonds. If you play a diamond for him the show's over. Another situation where a ruff-sluff may save the day.

IV.

North
S. 9864
H. J
D. KJ7
C. KQ1092

West
S. K53
H. K1064
D. 92
C. A643

East
S. 72
H. 9732
D. A1086
C. J85

South
S. AQJ10
H. AQ85
D. Q543
C. 7

It is more likely, but not certain, that partner's lead is a doubleton rather than a singleton. (If the lead is a singleton, declarer has five diamonds and at least five spades; this gives partner a minimum of ten cards in clubs and hearts, in which case he might have made some sounds at this vulnerability.)

Once you decide it is a doubleton signal with the ten, hoping partner has a trump entry. Then he can return his remaining diamond to your ace and get his ruff. Had you a certain outside entry you could afford to win the first diamond and return the suit.

V.   North
                                         S. AQJ
                                         H. J765
                                         D. KQ84
                                         C. 42

          West   East
          S. K98762   S. 5
          H. 43   H. A2
          D. 2   D. A109763
          C. Q1053   C. J986

                                         South
                                         S. 1043
                                         H. KQ1098
                                         D. J5
                                         C. AK7

Win the diamond lead (an obvious singleton) and return your singleton spade. Win the first heart,
give your partner a diamond ruff by playing the ten,
and ruff a spade in return. If partner doesn't give
you a spade ruff, turn him in for a newer model.

VI.   North
                                         S. 93
                                         H. J106
                                         D. AQ4
                                         C. KQJ109

          West   East
          S. K862   S. 75
          H. AKQ75   H. 432
          D. 32   D. J9865
          C. 52   C. 876

                                         South
                                         S. AQJ104
                                         H. 98
                                         D. K107
                                         C. A43

Duck this trick! Your plan is to force declarer one
more time in hearts. You cannot do this as long as

dummy has another spade. If declarer repeats the
finesse you win and play a heart, defeating the
hand two tricks. If declarer smells out your plan
and plays the ace of spades and then runs minor
suit winners you ruff and defeat the hand one trick.
If you win the spade prematurely there is no way to
take another trick.

VII.

North
S. QJ10
H. Q963
D. AK98
C. 75

West
S. 9
H. 1075
D. J76
C. Q98432

East
S. A8652
H. 84
D. 1043
C. AJ6

South
S. K743
H. AKJ2
D. Q52
C. K10

This time you don't care if the lead is a singleton
or a doubleton since you have a certain outside entry, the ace of clubs. Win the ace of spades and
return the deuce, showing where your entry is. If
partner has a singleton spade the hand is immediately defeated; if partner has a doubleton there is
still a chance for him to get his ruff if he has a
quick trump trick (ace or king).

VIII.

North
S. KQ7
H. J754
D. AJ10
C. A94

West
S. 3
H. A82
D. Q9642
C. 10873

East
S. A108542
H. none
D. K73
C. Q652

South
S. J96
H. KQ10963
D. 85
C. KJ

Win the ace of spades and return the ten to show
where your outside strength is. Best chance to
defeat the contract is to hope that partner has
led a singleton rather than from a three card
holding.

On the actual hand partner ruffs and returns a
diamond. Declarer has to lose a trick in each
of the red suits along with the first two tricks
already conceded.

If West returns anything but a diamond at trick
three, declarer makes the hand by finessing the
jack of clubs, establishing the ace for a diamond
discard. The immediate diamond attack destroys
declarer's opportunity to make this play for lack
of dummy entries.

IX.

North
S. none
H. QJ4
D. AK10742
C. A952

West
S. A93
H. AK8762
D. 93
C. 43

East
S. 872
H. 93
D. QJ865
C. 876

South
S. KQJ10654
H. 105
D. none
C. KQJ10

West plays three rounds of hearts and East ruffs with the seven, driving out an honor from the South hand. West wins the <u>first</u> spade with the ace (assuming an honor is led) and plays a fourth heart. East ruffs with his now lone eight of spades, forcing another honor from the South hand, and eventually the nine of spades becomes the setting trick. <u>A</u> <u>double</u> <u>uppercut</u>.

XV.   CARD COMBINATIONS

The aim of this chapter is to familiarize you with some basic
card combinations. The more combinations one recognizes the
easier it is for him to defend.

I.   SURROUNDING PLAYS

After the opening lead is made, dummy comes down,
and declarer starts to play the hand, it may become apparent to either one or both defenders that
a certain suit must be attacked.

Frequently, very frequently, it is important to
attack that suit with the proper card. Keep in
mind that standard leads such as top of a sequence,
low from an honor, and fourth highest apply before
dummy comes down.

Once the dummy is visible the attacking card often
varies. This is a constant source of frustration
to a player not familiar with card combinations.

East-West vul.   North
Dealer East   S. AQ108
                  H. Q
                  D. 1075
                  C. AKJ104

West   East
S. J9   S. 42
H. 863   H. AJ109752
D. A862   D. KJ9
C. 7653   C. 2

                  South
                  S. K7653
                  H. K4
                  D. Q43
                  C. Q98

East	South	West	North
3H	Pass	Pass	Dbl.
Pass	4S	All pass	

Opening lead: Three of hearts

East wins the ace of hearts and sees at a glance that
diamonds must be attacked immediately because of the
danger of club discards after trumps are drawn.

On opening lead one normally leads low from KJx. However, now that dummy is in full view and the ten is
visible East must attack with the _jack_.

This is called a "surrounding play" because East has
the ten surrounded with the J9 plus a higher honor.
Notice that if East attacks diamonds with any other
card declarer can always take one diamond trick, but
the jack leaves declarer defenseless.

How does East know to play the jack? He knows his
partner needs the ace for there to be any chance
(he knows he needs three diamond tricks), and he
is familiar with the card combination. East would
play the same card if he held AJ9.

Now we can study other "surrounding plays" using
diagrams rather than entire deals. For simplicity,
assume North is dummy, East is attacking, and the
suit is a girl's best friend.

                        North (Dummy)
                        D. 1043

        West   East
        D. A95   D. KJ82

                        South
                        S. Q76

This time East does not have a perfect surrounding
combination (either KJ9 or AJ9), which means that
he must find more in his partner's hand. Nevertheless, the best card for East to lead (most of the
time) is the jack.

That "most of the time" is written for self-protection.
There are times when the jack can lead to disaster:

                        North (Dummy)
                        D. 1043

West   East
D. A765   D. KJ82

                        South
                        D. Q9

In this case leading the jack eventually establishes
the ten and makes South wonder why he hasn't played
against East more often.

When the dummy has the nine and no other honors East
frequently attacks with the ten if he has Q108, K108
or A108, with or without added small cards.

                        North (Dummy)
                        D. 943

West   East
D. K75   D. Q1086

                        South
                        D. AJ2

If East wants to restrict South to one diamond trick
he had better lead the ten. Interchange the queen
and king and the ten has exactly the same effect.
If East leads the six, South plays low and later
makes two tricks.

                    North (Dummy)
                    D. 943

West   East
D. Q2   D. A1087

                    South
                    D. KJ65

Again East does best to attack with the ten. This

should restrict any South player not using mirrors

to one diamond trick. If East attacks with the more

conventional seven South might well duck, forcing

West to win the queen; South will then score two

tricks.

This next one is a bit far out, but partner will

think you are a genius if it ever comes up:

                    North (Dummy)
                    D. A84

West   East
D. J32   D. Q976

                    South
                    D. K105

This is one of the few times a defender can surround

an eight spot! East starts with the nine, limiting

South to two tricks. If East leads the six South

does best to duck, capturing West's jack with the

ace and retaining a finesse position with the king-

ten over East's queen.

The preceding combination leads us to:

```
                    North (Dummy)
                    D. A84

West                                      East
D. 932                                    D. QJ76

                    South
                    D. K105
```

Here East does best to attack with a <u>low</u> diamond.
South normally plays low hoping an honor will appear from the West hand. In this case the nine
appears and declarer makes only two tricks. If
East instead leads an honor, South comes to three
tricks.

East makes the same play from QJxx even if the
eight is not in dummy. Perhaps declarer has K108
and dummy A54. The principle is the same and declarer's normal play with this combination is the
eight spot.

All these plays are identical when the suit is
started from the West position.

Back to our original surrounding combination, only
this time we give <u>West</u> the KJ9 and <u>dummy</u> the Q43.

                    North (Dummy)
                    D. Q43

West   East
D. KJ9   D. A862

                    South
                    D. 1075

Assume West decides it is necessary to attack dia-

monds. This time he sees the queen to his left,

not, as East in our first hand, the ten to his

right. He must "visualize" the ten before making

the proper play of the jack.

                    North (Dummy)
                    D. AJ2

West   East
D. Q1086   D. K75

                    South
                    D. 943

Later in the hand West decides to attack diamonds.

He knows that if declarer has the king there is no

hope, but if partner has the king the defenders are

in business ... provided West leads the ten, visu-

alizing the nine in declarer's hand. (If partner

has both the king and the nine nothing has been

lost.)

A few other combinations to store away. Back to East attacking:

North (Dummy)
D. 943

West
D. 1086

East
D. KQ75

South
D. AJ2

If East is looking for more than one diamond trick he leads low. (That nine in the dummy is a very important card.) South normally ducks, hoping East has led from honor-ten, and consequently is held to one trick. (Of course the play is the same if the hand is turned around and the AJ2 are in the dummy and West is leading from KQ75.)

And now a swindle play:

North (Dummy)
D. 1064

West
D. J83

East
D. AQ92

South
D. K75

East leads the queen. South thinks that East might have QJ9, in which case his proper play is to duck, making it impossible for East to continue the suit without giving up a trick. So South ducks. Now East leads the deuce. If South retains his original impression he ducks again, assuming the ace is going

to be forced to win. When the jack takes the trick
he knows he's been had.

A very similar combination is the following:

                    North (Dummy)
                    S. 1065

West   East
D. AJ98   D. Q43

                    South
                    D. K72

East needs four diamond tricks to defeat the contract
so he must assume partner has either AK or AJ. If
partner has AK there is no problem; but if partner
has AJ that ten in dummy is going to cause trouble
because South can simply duck any low card around to
the ten. So East leads the queen!

Now, looking at the entire diagram it is easy to see
that if South covers he establishes a trick with dummy's ten. But South is afraid that East is leading
from something like QJ93 and West has A84. If that
is the case and South covers he loses four tricks,
but if he ducks he retains control of the suit. South
must guess. If South guesses wrong the defenders have
their four tricks. (East plays the same when holding
Jxx.)

Another common swindle:

                    North (Dummy)
                    D. 654

West   East
D. J92   D. AK73

                    South
                    D. Q108

As long as East knows that South has more than two
diamonds it is safe for him to lead low. South
will usually finesse the ten and the defenders take
three tricks against a suit contract and four against
no trump.

Again, all of these plays are the same when West is
leading and the North-South cards are reversed. After
these diagrams it should be easier to understand the
following hand.

II. LEADING UNPROTECTED HONORS

```
Both sides vul.            North
Dealer South               S. AJ3
                           H. 9
                           D. 7632
                           C. AKQ95

        West                                       East
        S. 76                                      S. 5
        H. KQ872                                   H. AJ653
        D. AJ10                                    D. Q84
        C. 1062                                    C. J843

                           South
                           S. KQ109842
                           H. 104
                           D. K95
                           C. 7

        South       West            North          East
        3S          Pass            4S             All pass
```

Opening lead: King of hearts

East must appreciate the dummy. South is marked with
seven spades and dummy's spades certainly solidify the
suit. This means seven spade tricks. Dummy has three
top clubs, for ten, plus a long club can certainly be
established by ruffing a club in the closed hand. Furthermore, South can make an additional trick by ruffing
a heart in dummy. Obviously South has more than enough
tricks if left to his own devices. Clearly the defense
must attack diamonds - now!

As is frequently the case, only one defender can profit-
ably attack a suit because certain honors in either dummy or declarer's hand must be led through.

In this case East sees that three diamond tricks are needed. He knows his partner does not have the ace-king or else he would have led the suit. He needs West to hold AJ10 to get three diamond tricks so he overtakes the king of hearts and leads the <u>queen</u> of diamonds at trick two. Fortunately partner has the desired holding and the hand is defeated. Had East ducked the opening lead or switched to a small diamond at trick two the hand would have been made.

The key, of course, to this defensive play as well as most, is the number of tricks needed. For example, if the contract were five spades (perhaps North bid too much) East thinks in terms of <u>two</u> diamond tricks.

Again he needs the ace in partner's hand, but now partner needs less. For example, the AJ without the ten will do, or even the ace alone if declarer has the KJ and misguesses. So defending five spades, East overtakes and switches to a <u>low</u> diamond.

III. AVOIDING AN END PLAY

Basically, defenders have two techniques at their disposal to combat an end play. Card combinations enter into each.

Neither side vul.   North
Dealer South   S. J864
                           H. 632
                           D. 62
                           C. K842

        West   East
        S. 32   S. 5
        H. QJ9   H. 10754
        D. KJ873   D. 10954
        C. J75   C. Q1096

                           South
                           S. AKQ1097
                           H. AK8
                           D. AQ
                           C. A3

        South   West   North   East
        2C*   Pass   2D**   Pass
        2S   Pass   3S   Pass
        4C   Pass   5C   Pass
        5D   Pass   5S   Pass
        6H   Pass   6S   All pass

        *Strong and artificial
        **Negative response

Opening lead: Queen of hearts

Poor South made three cue bids trying for seven and

couldn't even make six!

South won the opening lead, East signalling with the

seven to show an equal honor. South now proceeded

to play: one high trump, the ace, king and ruff a

club, back to dummy with a trump and ruff dummy's

last club. Now he plunked down his other high heart.

If West woodenly plays low, he is thrown in with the

jack of hearts and must lead a diamond into declarer's

AQ. However, if he unblocks the jack, East wins the

third heart and can lead a diamond through declarer.

(A clever declarer would have cashed his second heart
sooner, masking his end play intentions, but West has
East's signal to fall back on and should unblock anyway.)

Sometimes it is impossible to avoid being thrown in
and forced to either play a suit declarer wants you
to play or give him a ruff-sluff. In situations such
as these it definitely pays to know your combinations.

Neither side vul.   North
Dealer South   S. 1065
                    H. K1092
                    D. K3
                    C. KQ87

West   East
S. KQJ8   S. 9742
H. Q74   H. J83
D. J984   D. 10765
C. 63   C. 52

                    South
                    S. A3
                    H. A65
                    D. AQ2
                    C. AJ1094

South	West	North	East
1C	Pass	1H	Pass
2NT	Pass	3C	Pass
3H	Pass	3NT	Pass
6C	All pass		

Opening lead: King of spades

There is only one way to play this hand. Win the lead,
draw trumps, play three diamonds, discarding a <u>spade</u>
from dummy, and lead a spade. At this point West has
the lead and the count. He knows that South has three

hearts headed by at least the ace. If South has the
AJ there is no hope for the defense. A ruff-sluff
can't be right because declarer will ruff in dummy
and discard a losing heart. So hearts must be led.
But which one?

West must play East for the jack and lead the <u>queen</u>
to give South a guess. If West leads low, South has
no option but to play for split honors. He inserts
the ten from dummy, wins the jack with the ace and
later finesses the nine. But if West leads the queen
South must decide whether the honors are split (in
which case he must win the king and run the ten through
East) or whether West has both the queen and jack (in
which case he must win the ace and finesse the ten).

IV. PLAYING CARDS YOU ARE KNOWN TO HOLD

Defenders must keep in mind that while they are counting
the declarer's hand and watching his high card points
fall the declarer is doing the same with the defenders'
hands. Maddening isn't it?

Defenders, therefore, have to keep a few secrets. The
best way to do this is to tell declarer, whenever possible, something he already knows. We all know the bore
who tells the same story over and over: well on defense
this strategy works.

For example, take this very common position:

                    North (Dummy)
                    S. QJ10

West (You)   East
S. AK8765   S. 92

                    South
                    S. 43

Assume hearts are trumps and you, West, lead the
king, ace and a third spade, partner ruffing and
declarer overruffing. At the point your partner
ruffs the third spade, declarer knows you started
with six spades. Therefore, when discarding, discard spades ... giving declarer no information he
doesn't already have.

                    North (Dummy)
                    S. 654

West (You)   East
S. K972   S. AQ1083

                    South
                    S. J

Hearts are trumps and you and partner have been bidding spades. You lead the deuce to partner's ace
(declarer now knows you have the king), and partner
returns a spade, which declarer ruffs. You needn't
play your king this time (because declarer knows you
have more than two), but the next time a spade is
played you should. If you keep your king it is just
one more card declarer knows about in your hand.

                    North (Dummy)
                    S. 654

West (You)   East
S. QJ93   S. AK102

                    South
                    S. 87

Hearts are trumps and you lead the queen followed by
a low spade to partner's king. When he plays the ace
and declarer ruffs you must play the jack, a card you
are known to hold, if you do not want to be branded
a beginner for the rest of your days.

The same principle applies when sitting East.

                    North (Dummy)
                    S. 1074

West   East (You)
S. KJ5   S. AQ632

                    South
                    S. 98

Spades are an unbid suit and West leads the five. You
win the ace. (At this point declarer suspects partner
has the king and you the queen. Presumably you would
win the trick with the king holding ace-king, and
partner would lead the king holding king-queen.) You
return the three of spades. Partner wins the jack and
plays the king. You know declarer is going to ruff
and you know declarer knows you have the queen. So
play it!

Notice that none of these plays can either cost a trick or fool partner, but all of them make it harder for declarer to count your hand. Next we come to this:

                          North (Dummy)
                          S. AJ2

West (You)   East
S. Q106   S. 843

                          South
                          S. K975

South is playing a no trump contract and early in the hand leads a small spade to the jack, which holds. You know that South has the king and South knows you have the queen. The ace of spades is played from dummy. Your queen and ten are equals because the jack has been played, so you must drop the queen. You must. If you play the ten (hopeless) declarer, knowing you have the queen, simply leads a spade to the king ... dropping your queen and establishing his nine. If, however, you drop the queen, declarer is apt to finesse the nine, allowing you to take a trick with the ten.

                    North (Dummy)
                    S. AQ65

West (You)   East
S. K1043   S. J987

                    South
                    S. 2

South is playing a heart contract and early in the
hand leads a spade to the queen, which holds. South
now knows you have the king. He plays the ace of
spades, on which he discards. You must drop the
king! If you play low it will be easy for South
to ruff a spade with a low trump knowing you still
have the king. However, if you drop the king declarer will always entertain doubts about ruffing
a spade low.

The Rule: DEFENDERS PLAY EVERY CARD THEY ARE KNOWN
TO HOLD IF THE PLAY WILL NOT COST A TRICK. IN OTHER
WORDS, IF PARTNER HAS A CARD EQUAL TO THE ONE THAT
IS KNOWN TO BE HELD THE KNOWN CARD SHOULD BE PLAYED
AS SOON AS POSSIBLE.

                    North (Dummy)
                    S. AQ32

West (You)   East
S. K76   S. 1098

                    South
                    S. J54

South leads a spade to the queen and then plays the ace of spades. Even though you are known to hold the king you must not throw it under the ace because you have no way of knowing who has the jack. Had declarer discarded something on the ace of spades you would naturally throw the king.

Now contrast the above position to this:

                    North (Dummy)
                    S. AQ32

West (You)   East
S. K65   S. J987

                    South
                    S. 104

Defending a suit contract, South leads a spade to the queen and then plays the ace of spades, dropping the ten. Can you, West, afford to play the king, a card you are known to hold? Yes. Because this time you see declarer's ten and you know (infer) that if declarer had the jack he would not have played the suit as he did. He would have led the jack or ten and let it ride. Therefore partner must have the jack and it is safe to play the king.

When declarer is ruffing losers in dummy defenders must apply maximum pressure.

```
                    North (Dummy)
                    S. 102

West                                         East (You)
S. 653                                       S. KJ98

                    South
                    S. AQ74
```

Hearts are trumps and early in the hand declarer leads
a spade from dummy, finessing the queen. Next comes
the ace of spades. If you play low declarer will be
able to ruff a spade low in dummy knowing you still
have the king. If you play the king under that ace
declarer will think twice about ruffing low.

Keep in mind that experts are all familiar with this
concept of "playing every card you are known to hold",
but John Q. Average seldom makes such plays. Therefore, when defending against a non-expert you will
scare the daylights out of him nine times out of ten
with these falsecards. Besides, for all declarer
knows, expert or not, you might be making an honest
play.

And now three somewhat different positions in which
declarer knows the situation so you must inform
partner.

1.   North (Dummy)
                            S. 1098432

West   East
S. Q   S. AKJ5

                            South
                            S. 76

West leads his singleton queen of spades,

which is allowed to hold. Later in the

hand you get the lead and decide to con-

tinue spades. Which spade should you play?

You should play the jack so that West can

plan his discards easier. If you play the

ace or king West will think that South has

the jack and might misjudge the defense.

Notice that you are simply playing a card

you are known to hold (when West shows out,

South will know everyone's exact spade

holding), at the same time telling partner

something declarer already knows.

2.   North (Dummy)
                            S. K7

West   East (You)
S. A10   S. QJ8642

                            South
                            S. 953

You have bid spades and hearts are trumps. West
leads the ace and a spade to dummy's king. Later
in the hand South ruffs his nine of spades as
West discards. When South sees West discard he
knows the original distribution of the spade suit,
but West does not know whether or not South has
another spade. In situations like this -- when
declarer is ruffing his last remaining card in a
suit -- you can let partner know what's going on
by playing your highest card in the suit, in this
case the queen.

3.
                        North (Dummy)
                        S. 654

West   East (You)
S. A10   S. J9832

                        South
                        S. KQ7

You have bid spades and hearts are trumps. West
leads the ace and a spade to South's king. At
this point you know South has the queen, but
West may not know. If you get a chance you
should discard the jack of spades (discards of
honors show lower equals but deny the honor
directly above) in order to let West in on the
secret.

V. MANDATORY FALSE CARDS

In order to understand the principle behind mandatory false cards you have to put yourself in declarer's chair for a while.

```
                        North (Dummy)
                        S. AJ32

        West                              East (You)
        S. K4                             S. 1095

                        South
                        S. Q876
```

Spades are trumps and South leads the six of spades to dummy's jack. Assuming both defenders play low, South has <u>no option</u> but to lay down the ace and hope for the king to fall to his left.

But, if East plays the <u>nine</u> under the jack, South has an option: He can either play the ace and hope the king falls, or reenter his hand and play the queen hoping to blot out a possible 10-9 doubleton in the East hand. By playing the nine under the jack East gives South two ways to play the suit, one of which fails. By playing the five East gives South no choice but to make the right play. Of course, to make these defensive false cards you have to be familiar with some new combinations. Combinations with the ten-nine offer promise:

                    North (Dummy)
                    S. AK32

West   East (You)
S. Q4   S. 1095

                    South
                    S. J876

When the ace of spades is played from dummy East must
play the nine. Now South has to decide whether to
reenter his hand to play the jack or to simply play
the king. (The play of the king loses if the nine
is either a singleton or from 10-9 doubleton.) If
East plays the five South has no choice but to play
the king.

                    North (Dummy)
                    S. 2

West (You)   East
S. J106   S. A5

                    South
                    S. KQ98743

Spades are trumps and South leads the deuce from dummy
to the king in his hand. If West plays the six, South
has no choice but to lead low from his hand hoping the
ace is doubleton. However, if West plays the ten or
jack South has an extra option. He can try to blot out
a possible J10 doubleton by playing the queen.

                    North (Dummy)
                    S. Q832

West   East (You)
S. 4   S. J965

                    South
                    S. AK107

Spades are trumps and South leads the ace. If East,

who has seen West follow, and who knows declarer's

exact spade holding, plays low declarer has no option

but to lead low to the queen, playing East to have

J9xx. (If West has that holding the suit cannot be

picked up.) However, if East plays the nine declarer

has an additional option. If the nine is singleton

then West can be finessed out of Jxxx and declarer's

winning play after cashing the ace would be to play

the king.

I. Neither side vul.
    Dealer South

North
S. J32
H. 2
D. KJ92
C. AK432

West
S. 1095
H. AJ10
D. 876
C. J1065

East
S. K4
H. 76543
D. 543
C. 987

South
S. AQ876
H. KQ98
D. AQ10
C. Q

South	West	North	East
1S	Pass	2C	Pass
2H	Pass	3S	Pass
4NT	Pass	5D	Pass
6S	All pass		

Opening lead: Eight of diamonds

II. Both sides vul.
     Dealer East

North
S. KJ2
H. QJ10
D. K763
C. 975

West
S. 975
H. 98753
D. 54
C. K32

East
S. 108643
H. A2
D. A8
C. Q1086

South
S. AQ
H. K64
D. QJ1092
C. AJ4

East	South	West	North
Pass	1NT	Pass	3NT
All pass			

Opening lead: Nine of hearts

III. East-West vul.   North
    Dealer South   S. A106
                          H. AQ5
                          D. 764
                          C. AQJ9

West   East
S. KQ8753   S. J94
H. 6   H. 93
D. AQ10   D. J852
C. 752   C. K843

                        South
                        S. 2
                        H. KJ108742
                        D. K93
                        C. 106

South	West	North	East
3H	3S	4H	All pass

Opening lead: King of spades

IV. North-South vul.   North
    Dealer South   S. 1084
                            H. AJ2
                          D. KQJ10
                          C. 543

West   East
S. AJ6   S. Q953
H. 73   H. 54
D. 842   D. A9763
C. J10987   C. 62

                        South
                        S. K72
                        H. KQ10986
                        D. 5
                        C. AKQ

South	West	North	East
1H	Pass	2D	Pass
3H	Pass	4H	All pass

Opening lead: Jack of clubs

I.   Dummy wins the diamond lead, and when a spade is led to the queen West must play the nine! This gives South an option in the play of the trump suit. If he believes the play is from ten-nine doubleton he will return to dummy with a club and lead the jack of spades. This will result in a one trick set. If West plays the five under the queen South has no choice but to lay down the ace and catch the king. (West must make the same play defending six no trump, an alternate contract.)

II. East wins the opening lead and sees no future in that suit. So he decides to shift to a club before his ace of diamonds is removed. However, he must shift to the ten of clubs to defeat the contract.

III. Declarer wins the opening lead, draws trumps, and takes a losing club finesse into East. East must return the jack of diamonds. He knows his side needs three diamond tricks (his partner probably has six spades for his vulnerable three level overcall, missing the AJ10), so East must play West for the AQ10 of diamonds. And guess what?

IV. This time East must win the first diamond and go all out for three spade tricks. His only play is the queen! If South ducks, assuming East has QJ9, the hand is immediately defeated. If South covers, West must win and return a <u>low</u> spade, putting it to South one more time.

CARD COMBINATIONS   PROBLEMS

I. East-West vul.   North (Dummy)
    Dealer South   S. Q76
                                H. 843
                                D. 65
                                C. KQJ103

                                                East (You)
                                                S. 82
                                                H. AK6
                                                D. 8432
                                                C. A765

        South   West   North   East
        1S   Pass   2S   Pass
        4S   All pass

Opening lead: Queen of diamonds

Declarer wins the ace, plays the ace-king of spades,

West following with the three and jack, and then plays

the eight of clubs. Partner plays the nine and dummy

the ten. Plan your defense.

II. Both sides vul.   North (Dummy)
    Dealer North   S. 8
                                H. A63
                                D. KQ10865
                                C. K102

                                                East (You)
                                                S. A1073
                                                H. J1097
                                                D. A974
                                                C. 9

        North   East   South   West
        1D   Pass   1S   Pass
        2D   Pass   2NT   Pass
        3NT   All pass

Opening lead: Seven of clubs

Dummy's ten wins, declarer playing the five. A low
diamond is led to the jack and a low diamond back to
dummy's king, West discarding the queen of clubs.
Plan your defense.

III. Both sides vul.   North (Dummy)
      Dealer West   S. J104
                               H. AJ103
                               D. 1043
                               C. Q53

                                              East (You)
                                              S. 8732
                                              H. 7654
                                              D. KJ95
                                              C. A

West	North	East	South
Pass	Pass	Pass	1C
Pass	1H	Pass	2NT
Pass	3NT	All pass	

Opening lead: Jack of clubs

Dummy plays low; you win the ace, declarer playing the
deuce. Plan your defense.

IV. Neither side vul.   North (Dummy)
     Dealer East   S. K754
                               H. QJ98
                               D. 1092
                               C. AK

      West (You)
      S. Q63
      H. 76
      D. 873
      C. 109876

East	South	West	North
1D	1H	Pass	4H
All pass			

Opening lead: Three of diamonds

Dummy plays the nine, partner the jack, and declarer the ace. Next comes the ace of hearts and a low heart to dummy's queen, partner playing the five and ten. The top clubs are cashed from dummy, partner playing the three and deuce. Now a low diamond is led to partner's queen and he cashes the king of diamonds, all following. At trick eight partner switches to the deuce of spades and declarer plays the jack. Do you cover? Why or why not?

V. Both sides vul.   North (Dummy)
    Dealer South   S. 943
                             H. 72
                             D. AQJ1043
                             C. K4

                                                East (You)
                                                S. K1086
                                                H. AJ5
                                                D. 762
                                                C. 1098

        South   West   North   East
        1NT   Pass   3NT   All pass

Opening lead: Ten of hearts

Plan your defense.

VI.   North
                             S. J32

        West   East
        S. 1095   S. Q4

                             South
                             S. AK876

Spades are trumps and South leads. Can you see any way East-West might get a spade trick?

VII.
North
S. none

West
S. J105

East
S. K4

South
S. AQ987632

Spades are trumps and South leads. Can you see any
way the defenders might get two spade tricks?

VIII.
North (Dummy)
S. J92

West
S. 543

East
S. Q10

South
S. AK876

Spades are trumps and dummy leads. Can you see any
way East-West might get a spade trick?

IX.
North
S. J92

West
S. 543

East
S. K10

South
S. AQ876

Spades are trumps and dummy leads. Can you see any
way East-West might get a spade trick?

I.

                          North
                          S. Q76
                          H. 843
                          D. 65
                          C. KQJ103

West   East
S. J3   S. 82
H. J975   H. AK6
D. QJ1097   D. 8432
C. 92   C. A765

                          South
                          S. AK10954
                          H. Q102
                          D. AK
                          C. 84

You can win the second club if you like and shift to a <u>low</u> heart. You need three heart tricks to defeat this contract. If partner has the queen it doesn't matter which heart you play, but if partner has the jack you must lead low.

If partner shows out on the second club (unlikely because he probably would have led a singleton), simply cash the ace-king of hearts. Declarer cannot possibly have more than two hearts once he turns up with three clubs. (Six spades and two diamonds you know about.)

II.

```
                         North
                         S.  8
                         H.  A63
                         D.  KQ10865
                         C.  K102

         West                             East
         S.  KJ62                         S.  A1073
         H.  Q85                          H.  J1097
         D.  2                            D.  A974
         C.  QJ874                        C.  9

                         South
                         S.  Q954
                         H.  K42
                         D.  J3
                         C.  A653
```

Partner's discard of the queen of clubs promises
the <u>lower</u> missing club spots but none of the higher.
Therefore, declarer has the ace of clubs. Once you
know that, you know that declarer has nine sure
tricks outside of spades (five diamonds, three clubs,
and one heart). So you must attack spades for four
tricks. Your only play is the <u>ten</u>. If you play any
other spade and declarer has Q9xx (the only critical
holding) you will no longer be able to take four
tricks.

III.   North
                                  S. J104
                                  H. AJ103
                                  D. 1043
                                  C. Q53

            West   East
            S. 96   S. 8732
            H. 982   H. 7654
            D. A82   D. KJ95
            C. J10987   C. A

                                  South
                                  S. AKQ5
                                  H. KQ
                                  D. Q76
                                  C. K642

A diamond shift is called for and certainly a player

of your caliber will shift to the jack rather than a

small one. This will surround the ten in dummy and

earn you four tricks every time partner has three or

four to the ace and declarer the queen. Leading the

jack also saves a trick if declarer has AQx, as he

can no longer duck to his ten spot.

IV.

North
S. K754
H. QJ98
D. 1092
C. AK

West
S. Q63
H. 76
D. 873
C. 109876

East
S. A92
H. 105
D. KQJ4
C. QJ32

South
S. J108
H. AK432
D. A65
C. 54

You should duck. You need two spade tricks to defeat
this contract. If partner has the A10 remaining it
won't matter whether you cover. If declarer started
with J109 it also won't matter whether you cover.
But if partner remains specifically with A9, the only
holding that does matter, you must duck. If you cover,
declarer wins the king and leads back towards the ten,
losing only one spade trick. If you duck and later
cover the ten if it is led, you must come to two spade
tricks. Notice that declarer could have made the hand
by playing the _eight_ when partner shifted to the deuce
of spades. An interesting card combination.

V.

```
                        North
                        S. 943
                        H. 72
                        D. AQJ1043
                        C. K4

West                                            East
S. A752                                         S. K1086
H. 109863                                       H. AJ5
D. 5                                            D. 762
C. Q76                                          C. 1098

                        South
                        S. QJ
                        H. KQ4
                        D. K98
                        C. AJ532
```

This was inserted to teach you some humility! You

probably thought that you should shift to the ten

of spades at trick two. Wrong! Although it is right

to shift to a spade (declarer is marked with the king-

queen of hearts from the lead), you must shift to a

low one! Why? Because you need four spade tricks,

not three. (Partner can have no more than seven high

card points, which means that declarer has one black

ace -- for a total of nine tricks if allowed to get

the lead.) Needing four spade tricks, you must play

partner for either Axxx or AJx, and in either case a

switch to a low spade is correct. (If you got this

one right you are tough.)

VI.   North
                             S. J32

     West   East
     S. 1095   S. Q4

                             South
                             S. AK876

When South leads the ace or king, West must play the
nine or ten. This may induce South to think that West
has the ten-nine doubleton, in which case he will cross
to dummy to lead the jack!

VII.   North
                             S. none

     West   East
     S. J105   S. K4

                             South
                             S. AQ987632

When South leads the ace West must play an honor. If
he does not South has no option but to lead a low spade
and hope the king is doubleton. If, however, West plays
an honor, South might try to blot out a possible jack-
ten doubleton by playing the queen. In any case, the
play can't cost a trick but might gain one.

VIII.   North
                               S. J92

          West   East
          S. 543   S. Q10

                               South
                               S. AK876

When dummy leads low East plays the <u>queen</u>. If South
believes this play he will win and finesse dummy's
nine on the way back, the correct play if East did,
in fact, start with a singleton queen.

IX.   North
                               S. J92

          West   East
          S. 543   S. K10

                               South
                               S. AQ876

When dummy leads low East plays the <u>king</u>. Again, if
South believes this play he will win the ace and finesse
the nine ... and then you can chortle.

Bridge Conventions

A Guide to Understanding Techniques of Modern Bidding

Edwin B. Kantar

CONTENTS

144 Pages ... $12.00 postpaid

This book can be obtained from your book dealer or directly from:
Melvin Powers, 12015 Sherman Road, No. Hollywood, CA 91605

A TO Z INDEX